PRAISE FOR *PURE GOLD*

'A time capsule of treasures from one of our most gifted interviewers.'

John Connolly

'Eamon Carr has been blessed with sublime powers of observation, understanding and articulation. Through this collection of encounters, he offers us real insight, not only into the minds of the remarkable cast of real-life characters he has assembled, but into ourselves, our time and the way we were. A wonderful read.'

John Creedon

'The art of conversation is showcased in this insightful, quirky and eclectic collection. Eamon Carr's backlist confirms him as an intuitive interviewer who reaches for genuine engagement with his subject.'

Martina Devlin

Writer, musician and art historian **Eamon Carr** is a widely published commentator on culture, arts and sport. A member of Horslips, he co-wrote and recorded a series of innovative best-selling albums. His published work includes *The Origami Crow*, *Deirdre Unforgiven*, *Foundation Song* and *Showbusiness with Blood*. His dramas include *DUSK* and *CúChulainn Awakes*.

to my lovely Linenhall Library —

Eamon Carr

PURE GOLD

MEMORABLE CONVERSATIONS WITH REMARKABLE PEOPLE

Eamon Carr

MERRION PRESS

First published in 2025 by
Merrion Press
10 George's Street
Newbridge
Co. Kildare
Ireland
www.merrionpress.ie

© Eamon Carr, 2025

978 1 78537 556 9 (Paper)
978 1 78537 557 6 (eBook)

A CIP catalogue record for this book is
available from the British Library.

All rights reserved. No part of this publication may be reproduced, stored in a retrieval system, or transmitted, in any form or by any means (electronic, mechanical, photocopying, recording or otherwise), without the prior written permission of both the copyright owner and the publisher of this book.

Typeset in Minion Pro 12/18 pt and Gotham

Cover design by Fiachra McCarthy

Merrion Press is a member of Publishing Ireland.

For Cynthia Lowe

CONTENTS

	Introduction	1
1.	In at the Deep End	7
	Jack Charlton	13
	Eartha Kitt	33
2.	Spinning a Yarn	45
	Malcolm McLaren	52
	John Mortimer	63
3.	In the Moment	75
	Brenda Fricker	80
	Rudolf Nureyev	98
4.	A Balancing Act	107
	J.P. Donleavy	113
5.	Leaning in Gently	136
	Shane MacGowan	144
	Brian Behan	157
6.	Into the Lion's Den	163
	Ralph Steadman	169
	'Mad' Frankie Fraser	180
7.	Striking a Chord	192
	Josephine Hart	196
	Sheila Mooney	213
8.	Through the Mill	221
	Willy Russell	224
	Tony Warren	244
	Epilogue	255
	Acknowledgements	259

Introduction

I WAS IN A BROOM closet with an older man. I could feel his breath on my face. Surrounded by mops, buckets and containers full of cleaning chemicals, there was barely the width of the small tape recorder I was holding between us in this confined space. So I was looking straight into his unflinching eyes.

They were eyes which, for almost four decades, peered into the souls of men and women from all walks of life – celebrities, Hollywood A-listers, award-winning authors, rock stars, politicians, Church leaders, sporting champions, many of the most famous people of the twentieth century – and consistently asked pertinent questions.

The man I was with was Gay Byrne, host of *The Late Late Show*, Ireland's flagship television chat show, which had been running since 1962. Gay was an institution. While at Granada in Manchester in the early 1960s, he chatted with The Beatles on their first TV appearance. On his mid-morning radio show, as well as on television, he had steered decades of debates on all the major issues in Ireland. Having appeared on the TV show a few times, I could vouch for Gay's ability to slip in a zinger of a question when least expected. He was a master of his craft. The consummate interviewer.

But that night I was the one expected to ask the questions.

You see, sometime in the 1990s, there was a big soirée in a fancy restaurant to honour Gay. The newspaper's 'Social Diarist' was on holiday so, asked by my editor to report on the event, I mingled and observed. It was a glitzy affair – a room full of what society columns refer to as movers and shakers.

Thinking I should grab a quick quote from the man himself, I waited until Gay was alongside me. As we spoke, well-wishers continued to glad-hand the main man. Unflustered, Gay glanced around and, ever the professional, opened the nearest door. It was the broom closet.

Bemused, Gay looked at me and said, 'Will this do?'

'Of course,' I replied. Having expected a simple one-line response in answer to my opening remark, I realised I was being granted an interview with the king of interviewers.

This was completely unexpected. There really was no need for the guest of honour to take a break away from the celebrations. A quick soundbite would have sufficed. By then I'd been conducting regular high-profile in-depth interviews in the *Evening Herald* for a while, and Gay was generously acknowledging this fact by affording me his undivided attention. Although unprepared for a formal interview, I needed to think on my feet. Somehow, I managed not to disgrace myself.

Gay Byrne was in superb form. He anticipated questions, and his replies were concise, colourful and insightful. I left with more information than my newspaper report could accommodate.

As we closed the door behind us, a Talking Heads song rang in my head: 'And you may ask yourself, "Well, how did I get here?"'

So how did I?

***

Let me take you back to a time when, early in my career as a journalist, in a state some might know as purgatory, I listened time and again to the same stream of stock responses to my questions.

'This is our best album yet.'

'We wrote sixty songs before we went into the studio.'

'The record label really believes in the band.'

'We make music for ourselves. If other people like it, that's a bonus.'

What transgressions in a past life warranted such cruel punishment as this?

While I enjoyed writing a weekly music column for Dublin's *Evening Herald*, every earnest indie band I interviewed was prone to repeating the same thing. Week in, week out. Their quotes were homogeneous, interchangeable.

Is it any wonder my heart sank the day editor Michael Denieffe said he would like me to front a new double-page weekly interview feature? His plan was for a series of in-depth exchanges with people in the public eye. 'Face to Face' would be a major flagship attraction in a newspaper that was locked in a circulation battle with its rival from the other side of the Liffey. There was one slight problem. I didn't believe I was cut out for the task.

For starters, I felt I didn't have the requisite amount of natural curiosity. An enquiring mind, common-or-garden nosiness, is key to being a good interviewer, I reasoned. And I had scant interest in prying into people's lives. I wasn't big on gossip. Believing people are entitled to privacy, I tended to mind my own business and ignore matters that didn't concern me. As Hank Williams sang, 'If you mind your business, then you won't be mindin' mine.'

Having spent fifteen frantic years as an international touring musician with Horslips, when being interviewed was part of the promotional routine, I dreamt of becoming a recluse, writing haiku and watching a bit of sport. Although I read voraciously, it never once occurred to me to deconstruct the interview process. I had zero interest. Besides, in the demimonde of what passed for social life in Dublin, I'd learned it was prudent not to ask difficult questions. Questions could get you into trouble. If the Ireland of the 1980s had a defining catchphrase, surely it was the title of soon-to-be Nobel laureate Seamus Heaney's hair-raising poem, 'Whatever You Say, Say Nothing'.

However, the latest in a long line of notable swashbuckling editors, Denieffe knew the ropes. His enthusiasm and encouragement were infectious. 'This will be in a question-and-answer format with a brief introduction,' he explained. 'You'll need to ask plenty of questions and coax interesting answers. Given your background, I reckon you're the person for the job.'

The background he referred to wasn't just a brief stint writing copy in Dublin advertising agencies, where early in my career I'd picked up a few awards piggy-backing on the work of more illustrious creative talent. Nor was it editing and publishing small-press poetry magazines, whose place on an international arts grid had guaranteed some stellar names alongside nascent local talent. Michael was aware that, as a member of Horslips, I had been around the world and had appeared on many prestigious stages and chat shows, consorting with the famous and the infamous. Like a keen-eyed football manager, he reckoned he could spot a potentially half-decent utility player when he saw one.

By now I was thinking of the Q&A features I'd enjoyed reading in *Interview*, the snazzy magazine set up by Andy Warhol over a decade earlier. I recalled a Warhol aphorism. Not the obvious 'famous for fifteen minutes' one. What sprang to mind was the rackety, 'Being the right thing in the wrong place and the wrong thing in the right place is worth it, because something interesting always happens.' I buried my misgivings. You could say it was Andy who swung it.

'Right,' said I, 'I'll give it a shot.'

Knowing he was dealing with a novice, and having a refined critical overview, the editor flagged two crucial imperatives. One was to avoid politicians. Too dull. I would later discover that many experienced interviewers also declare actors *verboten*, arguing that film stars, theatre actors and stage school thespians rarely go further than putting the love in 'luvvie'.

'It won't be easy to arrange an interview every week,' Denieffe cautioned. Here was something I hadn't considered; the pressure of meeting a deadline every seven days. But the die was cast. Despite my apprehension, there could be no backing out now.

Ignorant of the steep learning curve ahead, I left his office unsure of just what I'd let myself in for.

***

In the end, I discovered I loved the buzz of interviewing subjects from whom I never knew what I would get. I would spend over thirty years as a journalist conducting hundreds of press or radio interviews with famous people and aspiring stars. However, long after the event, random exchanges with interviewees would, from time to time, pop into my mind unbidden. Recently, I came across a large box marked 'Tadhg's Tapes' and made a startling discovery. Nestled among a friend's gift of collectable mixtapes was a cache of my old interview tapes. I instantly began a process of exploration.

It quickly became apparent that in many cases there was much more preserved on tape than had originally appeared in print.

Much of what I was hearing had never been in the public domain. This seemed like an important discovery, and so I shared a few snippets of the transcripts with a colleague. The response was the excited colloquialism, 'This is pure gold!' I took this to mean that, in an age of practiced TV chat show performances and the churn of social media soundbites, these honest, considered, free-flowing and sometimes introspective responses to testing enquiries were both heartfelt and rare.

It occurred to me that I might not be the only one who would find these discussions fascinating. And so was born the idea of this book, which contains many of the conversations I couldn't shrug off. It wasn't just the thoughts and beliefs of famous people that interested me. Context seemed equally important. These interviews took place in a different era, a different Ireland and it felt important to present them with relevant background detail, not just with regard to the occasion or the setting of the interview itself, but against a wider social and cultural backdrop where possible. I also wanted to explain my process of interviewing; the values I tried to apply when approaching each subject.

For my part, I'm forever appreciative of people's willingness to engage with my line of questioning, no matter how intrusive, and, from a time when one day's newspaper feature page became the next day's chip-shop wrapper, I am privileged to enable these entertaining and insightful voices to shine again.

Chapter One

In at the Deep End

HAVING ACCEPTED MY UNEXPECTED JOURNALISTIC assignment and agreed to deliver an extensive in-depth newspaper interview with a high-profile person every week, I needed to figure things out. And fast.

Despite writing a music column, contributing theatre and book reviews and writing occasional feature columns, I didn't consider myself a real journalist. You know, one of those intrepid newshounds who always seemed to know more angles than Pythagoras. Me? I'd have still thought that 'to doorstep' meant to wipe one's feet.

At school, when my classmates said they planned careers in accountancy, the civil service or medicine, I'd mutter something about journalism. I'd had ideas, of course, and had even gone so far as to send unsolicited handwritten articles to the editors of magazines on spec – it would infuriate me when they'd eventually appear in print, shoddily rewritten under a different byline.

I later discovered I was not the only one whose school ambitions would become reality. When I interviewed Ireland's then Minister for Labour, he revealed how he had won an essay competition when he was thirteen on the subject, 'When I'll be Taoiseach'. He eventually did become Taoiseach, in 1997, for the first of three terms. During his third term, in May 2008, amid concerns over the economy, controversy over his receiving substantial payments from friends and businessmen described as 'dig outs', and a drop in support for Fianna Fáil, he resigned as both Taoiseach and leader of the party. But in 1989 man-of-the-people Bertie Ahern told me, 'I had a huge interest in the Paris Riots of '68 and Che Guevara and the Chilean Revolution, you name it.'

When I left school in the 1960s, the route into journalism in Ireland was difficult, so I went into the glamorous world of advertising instead, got to wear better suits, and then drank with newspaper men, and the occasional newspaper woman, in the evening. But now, in real time, the situation had just escalated. I needed a plan.

Firstly, I would have to persuade famous people to agree to be interviewed. Then it would be necessary to prepare a bespoke questionnaire for each and later spend hours transcribing the responses. This wasn't a drill. There was a lot on the line. Essentially, I needed to figure out how to ensure a double-page spread would be engaging, entertaining and enlightening.

The weeks that followed were a blur. Looking back, I've no idea how I managed it, but among those I engaged with over the first couple of months, were formidable All Blacks captain Wayne 'Buck' Shelford (during his captaincy, his side never lost a game) and celebrated couturier Bruce Oldfield, a charming individual who'd never known his Jamaican father or English mother and had been through the Barnardo's care system. His creations were worn by Charlotte Rampling, Faye Dunaway, Joan Collins and Princess Diana, among countless others.

In at the Deep End

Sometimes interviews came with a unique twist, such as when I met Phil Collins, who was in town promoting the film *Buster*. Already a multimillion album-selling artist, Phil was an astonishing drummer and songwriter. He was also disarmingly unprecocious about his talent. We had a long chat, during which I asked what sort of bloke Prince Charles was. 'I like him a lot,' said Phil. 'You get a feeling that he's real. He's a very sincere person and he actually does care. I've only met Prince Andrew in passing and I don't like him much.'

At one point in the interview, he explained the upsetting behind-the-scenes drama of his appearance with Led Zeppelin at Live Aid in America, when, having played in Wembley, he flew by Concorde for a gig that now had a second drummer added to the line-up. While he told the story, Phil began to show me the rudiments of drumming style. These would have been a helpful drum lesson for a novice, but by then I'd recorded about fifteen albums and had played thousands of gigs. Not wishing to interrupt his story, I simply nodded.

Later, in the hotel lobby his tour manager approached me and, with some excitement, said Phil would be delighted when he met me. I explained that I'd had a wonderful interview and was about to leave. He was dumbstruck. 'Oh, on the flight from London he was saying he couldn't get his Horslips albums on CD in the UK so he would be buying them here. He didn't realise he'd be meeting you.'

I've seldom felt as embarrassed. I remembered how, back in the day, his record label came to a couple of Horslips concerts and had taken us to dinner believing we'd fit well on the roster with Genesis. We didn't sign. But Phil Collins was a fan and bought the vinyl. When the manager suggested we go back to Phil and surprise him, I was mortified. I'd just been asking him difficult questions. I was a journalist. A hack. I couldn't compromise my position. And although I'd have loved to socialise with a talent I respected, I made my excuses and left.

In the 1960s world-renowned mezzo-soprano (and Phil Collins fan) Bernadette Greevy had decided to continue living in Ireland, despite the country's lack of an international music industry infrastructure. 'I wanted to prove a point,' she said. 'The fact that it's a small country, it's more important not to completely fly the coop.'

She had a busy diary scheduled when we met, with upcoming engagements including Britten's *The Rape of Lucretia* in Barcelona, Mahler's Symphony No. 3 with the City of Birmingham Symphony Orchestra, Szymanowski's *Stabat Mater* in the Royal Festival Hall with the BBC Symphony Orchestra and a Belfast Festival concert with the Ulster Orchestra. A CD of her latest album, including recordings of Berlioz's *Les Nuits d'été* and Duparc's *Mélodies*, had just arrived that morning.

When I asked if she had any ideas on how the path for younger singers coming through in Ireland could be smoothed, Bernadette said she'd been working on a proposal that she'd like to keep under wraps until it was finalised. I said, 'No problem, I'll draw a veil.'

Bernadette glanced down and said, 'It's all on tape so ... you rub all that out when you do your work, don't you?'

'Well, oh no, I keep it for ...' I was about to say for reference or queries, but Bernadette was ahead of me.

'Oh, you have an archive of all your recordings. My God, it will come out in the end!'

I hadn't been thinking of it like that. But, yet again, Bernadette was ahead of me. She quickly assessed the situation, smiled one of her more dazzling grins and added, 'There's no problem.'

An archive, eh? Thanks for that, Bernadette.

***

The old rock'n'roll adage still applied: 'You're only as good as your next hit.' I knew enough to know that I should try to launch the new column with a blockbuster, headline-grabbing personality. So the first name on my wish list of potential interviewees was Jack Charlton, the Englishman who'd guided the Ireland national football team to the 1988 European Football Championships. At a time when just eight teams had played in the finals in Germany, this was a very big deal. Ireland had beaten England in their opening match, at which point 'Big Jack' was elevated to the status of national hero in Ireland.

While the public embraced Charlton, some football pundits did not. His often gruff manner and abrasive style of football caused friction. He was both topical and fascinating. I visited the Sports Department, where teams of reporters for three titles – the Sunday, the daily and the evening newspaper – worked. Could anyone give me a contact number for Big Jack?

There was consternation. It was as if I'd stumbled into a medieval guild workshop touting a range of yet-to-be-invented acrylic paints. The sports hacks were aghast. Danger here. Why would the chap who wrote about pop music want the Ireland manager's phone number?

My request was deemed a breach of etiquette. Nobody rushed to be of assistance, but when I announced that I was there on the editor's instructions, a sub-editor reluctantly produced a number.

There were chuckles when, from somewhere else in the room, somebody jibed, 'He'll eat you alive.'

Even if no one recognised it, I had accepted the challenge. Unknown to the sports hacks, their music and arts correspondent probably had more competitive sporting experience than most of them, as he had previously spent five years playing Gaelic football with a demanding squad that included tough Hogan Cup finalists. He'd also been competitive as a sprinter and a basketball player.

I rang the number. The voice on the other end was the unmistakable gruff bark of the Leeds FC legend. 'Bloody hell, have you not got enough fuckin' interviews with me over there?' came the reply when he heard my request.

My heart sank. I realised in horror that maybe I hadn't given this enough thought. But the ball was at my feet. I could see the goal. I needed to get past this resolute defender. 'I'm not interested in your players or your injury list, Jack,' I blurted. 'I just want to have a chat with you about some football heroes of mine: Stan Mortensen, Jackie Milburn, Stanley Matthews, Billy Wright. And players you looked up to as a youth.'

Not one to waste time, Jack didn't miss a beat. 'Right then, come and see me in the hotel on Sunday evening,' he said signing off.

Hotel? Which hotel? Sunday? Someone had just thrown me into the deep end of the pool and we were about to find out if I could swim.

JACK CHARLTON – September 1989

I ring Jack Charlton's hotel late on a Sunday afternoon and realise to my horror that I've just woken him up from a nap.

'Come up to the room,' he says blearily. 'And we'll do the interview.'

'I'm not at the hotel yet,' I reply. 'I'll be with you in thirty minutes.'

It might be difficult for people today to understand the cultural gear changes Ireland would go through as Jack Charlton streamlined the national soccer team. At the time, Gaelic football and hurling were firmly considered Ireland's national sports. A long-standing rule banning Gaelic players from playing or attending 'foreign games' hadn't been abolished until 1971. As a result, soccer was the poor relation, a bit raffish – perhaps not to be trusted.

In the late 1950s, when local lads had formed a soccer club in a small town in County Meath and organised dances in a marquee to help raise funds, sermons were preached from the pulpit forbidding parishioners to attend this 'occasion of sin'.

You can't fight City Hall. The club struggled and young lads in short pants joined their older friends in picking the stones off a local field to create a football pitch.

These lads and other Irish football fans would look on enviously as Northern Ireland competed in the World Cup finals in 1958 and 1982. Maybe one day the Republic of Ireland would get to the finals of a major tournament. But, back then, the nation wasn't holding its breath.

The appointment of Jack Charlton, a former England player, as manager of the Republic of Ireland team had been controversial. Just over 16,000 turned up to watch Ireland play Wales in his first game in charge. Even fewer paid to see the next match against

Uruguay. The FAI lost money. But Jack was already shaping a team to fit his philosophy of football. We didn't know it then, but Ireland were going places.

***

The Irish football team had never qualified for the finals of a major international before the arrival of Charlton. Other managers had come close, but it was 'Big Jack' who delivered and got the team over the line for the European Championship finals in 1988. In doing so, he proved he understood his new environment better than most, although not everyone liked his approach or the style of play his team deployed.

However, my first interview 'in which personalities from all walks of life bare their inner selves', as the blurb puts it, hasn't got off to a good start. And things appear to be getting worse when, at the hotel, the Ireland team's physio miraculously materialises to cut across me and tell the receptionist that the team manager isn't to be disturbed. Just then, over Mick Byrne's shoulder, I spot Jack (54), looking taller than in photographs, arriving in reception.

There's a lot hanging on this interview. In desperation, I barge past Mick to greet the man who had become a national icon following Ireland's heroics in Germany the previous year. It was an epic adventure. The campaign, which saw Jack's team defeat England and draw with Russia, captured the public imagination. The ecstatic homecoming celebrations staged by the people of Ireland were unprecedented and remain unsurpassed.

'Ah, there you are. Pleased to meet you,' says Jack, fresh-faced no doubt from just having had a shower. My first thoughts are that he's more youthful-looking than I'd believed from press and TV.

'I'm just going in for a bit of dinner,' he says. 'Come in and we'll chat.'

'Oh, I wouldn't interrupt a man when he's having his dinner,' I reply. 'I'll have a cup of tea out here and we can have a quick chat when you've finished.'

'Fuckin' 'ell, you'll come in and 'ave your dinner with me,' insists Jack. New to the game, this was starting to look like an obstacle course to me. In the dining room, we join Jack's assistant manager, Maurice Setters. As we sit down, Jack enquires, 'Is Stan in yet?'

'I don't know boss,' says Setters.

'He's in the bar,' I venture, hastily adding, 'drinking mineral water with his parents.'

A brief conversation follows about Steve 'Stan' Staunton, the young Liverpool full-back who'd made his debut for Ireland in a friendly against Tunisia a year earlier. While chatting, I recount a monstrous free-kick Staunton had taken from the Havelock Square corner in the old Lansdowne Road stadium during that match.

'It was Yugoslavia,' corrects Jack testily.

'No, Tunisia,' says I.

'Yugoslavia.'

I haven't even begun the first and most important journalistic interview of my career and already I'm contradicting international football's most notoriously spiky manager. But I'm sure of my ground. I clearly recall both Charlton and Setters conferring in admiration as Staunton's notable piledriver lofted past their dug-out heading for the opposite corner that's closest to the Dart station. At a poorly attended match, I was sitting in prime seats behind them with my mates from The Hill pub. And I'm certain it was Tunisia because the blokes behind us were the staff from our local kebab shop. I play the diplomatic card.

'Sorry Jack. You're the boss. If anyone should know, it's you.'

Charlton turns his attention to Setters. 'Well, who was it?'

'The lad's right, boss.'

'Right,' Jack snorts. 'Have you got a tape recorder? Put it up on the bloody table and we'll start.'

Ninety minutes later my tape runs out with Jack still going strong. I've had the time of my life.

***

After our early set-to, I think it wise to ease into the conversation. So I ask about the senior hurling final he'd attended that afternoon (the 1989 All-Ireland Championship final – Tipperary 4-24, Antrim 3-09). Jack had seen the sport on television before and enjoyed the contest in Croke Park. 'It's very competitive and very skilful on the ball, with great technique. It was a bit one-sided. It might have been a better spectacle if they'd been closer.'

Some people feel that Middlesbrough had taken Manchester United to the cleaners a few weeks earlier when they sold Gary Pallister for a record-breaking £2.3 million. What does Jack think of transfer inflation?

'In this day and age, a million quid is not an outrageous figure. When I was a player, £100,000 was considered ridiculous. But if you're doing well in English League football, playing in front of 30-40,000 every week, the gate receipts are pretty enormous. I've been a manager in the English football league for four years and I remember buying a lad from Yugoslavia for 200,000 quid because I couldn't get anybody of any quality at all in England for under half a million. Four years ago.'

Then he cautions, 'Certainly, a lot of clubs in England have got to be careful that they don't go into debt that they can't recover from because of the amount of money that they're being forced to spend to strengthen their team.'

As we chat about how the game has changed since the 1950s and 1960s, Jack talks freely about his football philosophy.

'It's got too much passion and not enough skill. The technical game has changed a lot.' When he adds, 'There are a lot of clubs who follow the idea that the more times you get the ball in the opposing 18-yard box the more likely you are to score goals,' I venture, 'Are you talking here about Bobby Gould [Wimbledon] and Howard Wilkinson [Leeds United]?'

'Aah, well, some purists write them off as nonsense and say it's not the way to play. When you break it down and look at it sensibly, you say, "Well, what is football about?" The game is not complicated. To make it as easy as possible, the answer is "to score goals". If you knock the ball from the kick-off to the right, knock it wide. Put it into the box and have somebody in there to knock it into the back of the net. That's what the game's about. Scoring goals. How you go about it is simply a matter of opinion.'

He's on a roll now. With me as his class of one, Big Jack takes the opportunity to restate his footballing beliefs and values.

'We've adopted some of that philosophy and it works well for us,' he continues. 'Our philosophy is: play while you've room. But as soon as you haven't got room, knock the ball behind them. It works very well for us. We'll play when we've room to play. When it gets tight, you don't want to play. Because if you move the ball in tight areas, you put a lot of players out of the game.'

Passion and enthusiasm are now in the mix. I'm getting a glimpse of the doggedness of spirit that Jack brings to the training ground and changing room.

'If you've got room to play, then play,' he barks. 'If you haven't room, don't fuckin' try. Get it up. Get it behind them. Make 'em turn and then close 'em down facing their own goal.'

He takes a breath.

'It's worked for us at international level. Because the philosophy of football throughout the world has been that you play from the back. We'd have never won the games that we have had we played from the back. Because people throughout the rest of the world have been doing that and their expertise in doing it would be greater than ours. Their leagues play that way. Our leagues don't. The fans in England would never tolerate you playing square balls across the back for five minutes. So we put the best of what we thought would cause people concern together. And it does cause them concern the way we play.'

I'm listening to a manager publicly revealing his tactics. This seems like folly. Jack may have read something in my expression.

'People have said to me, "Why do you keep telling people how you play?" But it's there to see. Any coach can come and see it immediately. But they've got to upset their style of play to cater for ours and in doing that they spoil the way they play best. Most teams that we've played have had to do this and in doing it they've spoiled the way they play.'

As our chat continues, Jack tucks into his dinner and scans the dining room for players arriving for duty. Mick McCarthy comes in and, as he walks by, teases the manager, 'The new haircut takes years off you, Jack.'

***

While things feel relaxed, it's clear Jack's on duty. The upcoming friendly match on Wednesday in Dublin against West Germany will allow him to fine-tune plans ahead of Ireland's last two World Cup qualifying matches.

The mood is good so I don't feel I'm prodding a lion when I remark that in every public house there are punters who say that if Ireland qualifies for the finals in Italy, then the team will have to change its style of play to allow for the heat.

Jack responds with indignation. 'We said that in the beginning,' he thunders. 'I said that after the games in Germany, when it was obvious to me that our type of game is not suited to playing in the heat. We had to play England in the heat. We had a game against Russia when we didn't play in the heat and we looked a fuckin' good team. We'll play anybody at our type of game if the conditions are right. Then we played Holland, and Holland play a very spread wide game [forcing the opposition to run more], which made our game even harder in the heat. When we came back, we said that if we did qualify for the World Cup, we'd have to change our game a bit.'

In case I think he's capitulating, he adds trenchantly, 'We're not going to change the way we play. What we said was, we'll have to learn to take rests. We're not going to change the way we play, but we'll have to not do it as much as we did. I said to them when we went to play Holland, "You're going to struggle in the heat with the way they play to keep up the pressure and the running, so we're going to have to take rests." So we said to Paul [McGrath], "When Packie's got the ball and we push up front for the kick-out, you run back and have the ball played to the edge of the box and just stand there with it. Just keep it there until one of their players has to come to you and then give it back to Packie."

'That way we gave the lads a bit of a rest every now and then. We did this and the referee was becoming annoyed with us. He kept fuckin' shoutin', "Play. Play." Now, had Paul been knocking it to the full-back, to the centre-back, and from the centre-back to the full-back, had we kept it free and open doing that, the referee would have said nothing. But because he was a player actually standing with the ball, and he's doing nothing wrong, having a rest and giving all our players a rest, the referee didn't understand it.'

Referees aren't the only ones to take issue with Jack's pragmatism. Many pundits and commentators believe he's underselling his players' talent. But Jack isn't for turning.

'We know what we've got to do,' he states. 'We've got to play the type of game where we play in bursts. We've got to slow the game down in certain areas without ever putting the ball at risk. We've got a bit of work to do on that. It's not going to be complicated. It's just that we'll need to take a rest, and the only way you can take a rest is for us to have the ball.'

As we speak, Jack is very much in the moment and becoming more animated as he considers the subject. 'If you say are we going to start building it from the back and doing what some of the pundits over here talk about, the answer's "No. We're not." We've proved that our game causes people fuckin' concern. And I'll tell you what, we've changed the face of European football. You'd be amazed how many of the European teams are now adopting more of our attitude to the game. There's a lot of people now looking at our game and saying there's a lot to be offered in the way we play.'

It's time to steer back to smoother waters. So I head for the safety of Jack's boyhood heroes. Would Jackie Milburn have been one of those?

The manager doesn't appear to notice the abrupt gear change and he rattles off a litany of names: 'Joe Harvey, Frank Brennan, Wilfie Mannion, Len Shackleton, all great north-eastern players.

Stan Matthews, Tom Finney, when he came to play at Newcastle, Sam Bartram. All people who became friends later on. When I sit down at a table with Tom Finney, and I do regularly, or Malcolm Barrass or Stan Mortensen, or if Stan Matthews comes over and says, "Hello, Jack, how are ya?", I go, "Fuckin' 'ell". I mean they're still me heroes to this day. I sit there talking football with the likes of Tom Finney and Stan Matthews and Nat Lofthouse, and they're listenin' to what I'm saying. Fuckin' 'ell, I can't believe it.'

I find it endearing how Jack's voice drops in reverence and he sounds incredulous. 'Your heroes are always your heroes. Now they're all friends. It's terrific.'

At heart, he's a football fan like the rest of us, which begs the question, 'Were there any of your contemporaries that you'd liked to have played with?'

'I'd like to have played with our kid [Bobby Charlton] more. I think our kid was my type of midfield player. He couldn't tackle, but he never knew when he was having a bad game. But if things weren't going for him, he'd just work harder and harder. He'd run more and more. He'd want the ball more and more. He wanted to put it right. I played with most of the people on the England team that I'd like to during my era. Denis Law. I'd like to have played with Denis Law.'

'What about Pelé? Or George Best?'

I sense possible trouble when there's a pause. Jack clears his throat. 'I'd never have tolerated George in my team as a player. I mean ...'

There's another pause. Jack could be about to change the subject, but he doesn't.

'George doesn't like me and I don't know him. I've only met the kid three or four times. And he started to get the idea that I didn't like him. I don't like what he did because I always believed that within football there's got to be a certain discipline as a player and George is totally undisciplined as far as the game is concerned. In the years that he was fartin' about he caused a great deal of embarrassment because the wives and the people that you work with fuckin' all got the impression that we all did the same as what George had done. And we didn't.'

I find the thought that Jack and his teammates were discommoded at the prospect of being brought into disrepute by the antics of George Best highly amusing.

'We did the things that all young lads do,' he admits. 'We'd get pissed on the odd occasion when we shouldn't have done, but we prepared for a game and we knew the disciplines that were self-explanatory in football. The lads here can have a drink tonight [Sunday], but they won't have any tomorrow or Tuesday. And they won't go anywhere. They accept the discipline. They won't take advantage. They know if they break the rules they'll have to suffer. And the rules are the way we were brought up in football.'

***

Jack scans the room, pushes back his chair and goes to chat to some of his players who've just arrived from England. This isn't my first encounter with the Ireland squad. Months before Ireland's trip to Germany for the European Championship finals, I received a call asking me to go to Windmill Lane Studios on a Sunday morning to take part in the recording of a new single by the squad. I immediately phoned a few of my chums who were ardent football fans, and so I arrived with Robbie Foy, George Byrne and Declan Lynch.

The assembled players had to wait until the engineers had prepared rough mixes of the recording in progress and looked ill-at-ease in the unfamiliar setting. That wouldn't be conducive to an upbeat performance when the microphones and cameras were switched on, I thought. So to help break the ice, I suggested they should be allowed to go around the corner to the local pub, The Dockers, while waiting. That's when I discovered to my delight that Paul McGrath had been to see Horslips when we played the National Stadium.

Back in the studio later, the players still looked a bit nervous and uninvolved as the film cameras rolled. To help liven things up, I whispered to my mates that we should moon the players. So, carefully positioned behind the cameras, we dropped our trousers and twerked our pallid backsides at Ireland's heroes. The ice well and truly broken, there was much hilarity in the session and the video cameras caught the team's high spirits. Job done.

I don't mention any of this to Jack, of course. No need to alarm him. But when he comes back to the table I remark on how the morale in the squad is high and clearly was even before they went to the tournament finals in Germany. How did Jack and Maurice create that alchemy?

'We did very little. It just happened. But we've not got any cliques.'

He looks at me inquisitively and adds, 'Well we've got one or two little ones. But they're only with the senior players on the edge who, between you and me and Maury, are worried about whether they mightn't be part of the team.'

He knows the recorder is running. Does he want me to report this or is he testing me? It's hard to know. This will be in print before Ireland's game on Wednesday. Maybe it's a tease. I reach forward and, holding the manager's gaze, make a show of turning off the machine.

Jack eyes me curiously and continues, 'Chippy's got a surprise coming.'

I'm happy. Whatever the surprise might be that awaits Liam Brady ('Chippy'), I don't have it on tape, so I won't need to mention it. But I'm thinking, *This is the sort of hard news that those sports hacks who sniggered when I said I had to interview the manager get paid to discover.* No point in doing their job for them, I reckon. Instead, I nod in acknowledgement. And with a flourish turn the machine back on. Jack doesn't miss a beat.

'When you get that sort of thing happening, you've got to reassure them that they are going to be there. Or you've got to leave them out. But they get a feelin' and when they get this sort of feelin' that they might not be as influential as they have been in the past, they tend to prick up a little bit. And we watch that very carefully.'

This is in-house stuff. I can't believe I'm hearing it and I'm happy to let Jack carry on. 'But we've got a group of players who all like each other. And we never have a row. Mick [McCarthy] kicks shit out of them when we're playing five-a-side and no one falls out with him 'cos he says he can't play any other way. The lads accept it and get on with it. We've no cliques. You can never say who'll be sat next to each other on the bus tomorrow morning. You know that there'll be four on the back seat. And I can tell you who the four will be on the back seat because they're always on the back seat. Paul McGrath will be there. Kevin Moran will be there. Aldo [John Aldridge] will be there. And there's always one or two who will sit alone on the bus.'

Now seems as good a time as any to float the unlikely theory that a regular in The Hill pub insisted to me was hard fact; he'd queried my credentials for demurring. 'Jack, is it true that in your first meeting with the Ireland squad you silenced opposition by producing your 1966 World Cup medal and saying, "When you've one of these you can tell me how to do it"?'

The big man explodes. 'No! Load of crap! Load of fuckin' nonsense. I'd never dream of doin' anything like that. You'd never use that. Last thing in the world.'

He's freestyling now. We're in the deep end as he invokes his seminal years at Leeds United under a manager who'd been a legendary sportsman, a celebrated footballer and cricketer. 'I'd learned years ago with Raich Carter. We called him "the great I am". They [the Irish players] know what we've done. They know that we were good players. We laid down the way that we'd play. We knew most people would accept it. Some, we knew, wouldn't, and would probably try to go their own way. But we made it very fuckin' clear to them that if they didn't change the way they were playing, they wouldn't come.'

He takes a breath. 'If I remember rightly, the basic things we said at the first meeting were, "If you're going to play for Ireland, you come all the time. You don't come when you want to fuckin' come. And you move heaven and earth when you're picked. You don't let managers talk you out of it. You fuckin' well fight to come. And if you don't want to come, tell us and we won't invite you. And you'll play our way, whether you agree with it or not. We dictate the way you play. If it's wrong, we'll get the fuckin' sack. It won't be because of you."'

I turn down the heat by chatting about Jack's pre-season visits to Dublin with Leeds United. And soon he's waxing lyrical about the Dublin Horse Show at the RDS and race meetings at the Phoenix Park. But clearly something's nagging him. He swings back to his arrival as Ireland manager.

'I felt my reception by the press was muted. They didn't know what they were getting. I said, "You might as well work with us because you're stuck with me for three years. So instead of talking about what should have been, it's what has to be. In other words, don't live in the fuckin' past. Let's get on with what's in the future."

'I think the people of Ireland accepted that. The press never did. They fought us for about a year and a half. Lot of hassle. The way we play doesn't please everybody here. But the press will not drive me out of Ireland. The public will. The moment I feel the public have had enough of me, that's the time we'll think about calling it a day.'

'You've said that before,' I remind him.

'You say it wherever you go,' he replies in the manner of St Thomas Aquinas stating an article of faith. 'Funnily enough, that was not the reason I left Newcastle. The reason I left Newcastle was because I didn't like the job. And I didn't like the travelling and I didn't like the press. And I didn't like that the whole system was "you work twenty-four hours a day". If you went away fishing for an afternoon and the press there couldn't get hold of ya, it was in the paper next day: "Jack was unavailable today. He went fishing again." In fact, you might have been travelling down to Birmingham to watch matches. What we've always done, in the first year in the job, you work fuckin' hard. You cover the ground. You see the players and get to know them. You've got to know the standard you're playing in.'

Like myself, Maurice Setters remains silent. Jack is relaxed as he reviews his managerial career. 'When we went to Sheffield Wednesday, me and him, to find out about the Third Division, we went to three matches a week for a solid year. We covered the ground. And we did the same at Newcastle. We were up and down to Birmingham or Manchester or Leeds to see a game. And then I'd got to be back the next morning for 9 o'clock to have a press conference because there were twenty or thirty press lads waiting for you every morning up there. If you didn't come in in the morning, you'd gone fishing again. I'd had enough. I said to Jackie Milburn, who got me to take the job, "I'll do it for a year, Jackie, and then I'll see how I feel." There was only 5,000 at the game and a section of the crowd was unhappy because I hadn't bought a player they thought I should have bought. I turned it down because the deal wasn't a good deal. And Lawrie McMenemy signed the player on the Friday before we played. Eric Gates, it was. They gave me a bit of stick because Sunderland had done what they thought we should have done. Newcastle supporters are not interested in what you do. They're interested in who you buy. And as long as you are buying regularly, they're happy. Whether they can play or whether they can't. They'll make their mind up whether they like them. And if they don't like them, get rid of them.'

I'm getting more than I bargained for here. As Jack runs through his managerial history, other than gathering my belongings and walking out, I'm powerless to stop him.

'We'd done alright,' he continues. 'They'd lost Kevin Keegan and two or three other players. They'd no money. Arthur Cox left because they had no money. We took the job on to keep them in the Third Division, which we did quite comfortably. I sat in the boat by myself in the summer one night and said ...'

His voice tails off, so I'll never know what Jack said to himself in the boat that evening. But it must have been important because that August he handed in his notice and quit his job with Newcastle United.

'If I'd waited until the beginning of September when the balance sheet came out, I'd have had over a million quid to spend. But I left. I could see the writing on the wall with players. I knew that Peter Beardsley would be off as soon as he got the chance. And Chris Waddle left. It was going to be the same at Newcastle forever. You're never going to keep good players at Newcastle. It's too far out in the sticks. Too far away. The call of the big-time is too big. I could see that. I could have built a team at Newcastle second to none if we'd stayed another year and could have kept Chris and Peter. And Gazza [Paul Gascoigne] coming through. But I left. The excuse was that I got a bit of stick from the crowd. That wasn't the reason I left. At Sheffield and Middlesbrough, although they wanted us to stay, it was time to leave. Four or five years in a job is long enough for a manager. You outstay your welcome after that. Whatever you've achieved, you've got to be better every year. And you're not judged on what it was like when you joined. You're judged on what it was like as you are on the day.'

Dessert appears to be out of the question. We've been chatting for quite a while and Jack still has a couple of clubs to add to his list.

'I took Middlesbrough to fifth in the First Division from the top of the Third Division,' he says. 'We just missed out on Europe by a point. And I resigned and left with a lot of money and a lot of good players still there. And Sheffield was the same. We got on the brink of a good team. I sat at a board meeting one day when we got to the quarter-final of the League Cup, the semi-final of the FA Cup and failed to get promotion by a point with thirteen players and we'd played sixty-five games in the year and made a fortune, made money. And one of the directors said, "Well I don't think you've had a good season. We didn't get promotion." So I said, "Well you'd better find somebody who'll give you a better one," and left.'

Maurice Setters provides a coda to Jack's symphony of disappointment. 'We beat Norwich City at home 2-0 and they got promoted.' It was the last game of the 1981-82 season and Norwich finished with seventy-one points. Jack's Sheffield Wednesday had seventy.

Evidently, salt remains in the wound. Yet, Jack hadn't initially been committed to a career in football. 'Before you joined Leeds United, had you ever thought you mightn't become a professional footballer?' Jack brightens. Life, football, they're intertwined.

'Oh yeah. I didn't particularly want to leave home. I was never in great demand as a player as a schoolboy. I played for my school and played for East Northumberland, the area. But I never got to play for Northumberland. A lot of people in Ashington where we lived, everybody, knew at that time that our Bob would be a great player. But not me. I had many other interests apart from football. I went to work in the pits for a while. I didn't like the pits and I applied to be a policeman and I was accepted for an interview. I never went for the interview because Leeds United came along and said would I like to go on trial to Leeds.'

The Ireland manager has come a long way since he received that invitation. Among his achievements as a player are a League medal, an FA Cup medal, a Football League Cup medal, a couple of Inter-Cities Fairs Cup medals and a FIFA World Cup medal. But none of this was guaranteed for the young lad who joined Leeds United.

'When you go away to Leeds it was going away from home and the one thing you don't want to do is be a failure and have to go back because you weren't good enough and then have to look for another job. To be fair, I worked very hard for two years at Leeds to be a player. I played in the first team at seventeen. I'd only been there a year, so I must have made great progress in that year. Then I went in the army for a couple of years. When I came out of the army I pretty well knew I was going to be a good player.'

**

Something that had always tickled me was the controversy that sprang up around the tale that as a player Jack had kept a 'black book' in which he recorded players who'd fouled him. On TV in 1970, mentioning such players, he'd declared, 'If I get a chance to do them, I will.' It was no laughing matter, but I wondered if he regretted the debacle it caused.

Much as he did as a centre-back, Jack meets the challenge head on. 'No. That created an image of me that if you wanted somebody who would speak the truth, ask me. I didn't stir any shit. I didn't name any players. I just said there were certain principles that apply in the professional game. I didn't get punished for that. I got warned as to my conduct by the FA, but that was all.'

I'm not the counsel for the prosecution here, but, nevertheless, Jack outlines the facts in his defence. As he delivers his account of the matter, it's obvious he's taking this opportunity to set the record straight.

'The television programme was only going to be shown in the north-east and there was only one reporter there when they showed it for the press. He put certain quotes from it on the wire to London. The quotes read awful. I explained in the interview everything that I said. When I was tried, I was tried on the television. They'd a rule in the FA at the time that television could not be admitted in evidence.

But it was a television programme. Nobody had seen it. When the FA people looked at the programme, they realised that I'd clarified everything I'd said.

'I'd said I'd kick a fella as far as I could, but within the laws of the game, when the ball was there. There's nothing wrong with that.

'They said, "But do you have a vendetta?"

'Well, yeah, if somebody does you a nasty injury you don't forget it. You remember it. When you play against that fella, you're not going to let it happen again.'

As someone who once played a busy full season in goal for a Gaelic football team, back when goalkeepers received scant protection, Jack had my sympathy. And my admiration. You've got to protect yourself in contact sport, even if that sometimes means getting your retaliation in first.

'Everything I said was explained in the programme. I got warned about my future conduct, but I had to apologise. I refused to apologise for what I said. I sat for two hours deciding on how I would apologise. I remember the words exactly. "I apologise that through me I gave the press the opportunity to knock football." That was the press release. I had that publicity all over the world and from being a nondescript, just a good player, I suddenly became a household name.

'I got offered a fortune from national newspapers to do pieces at that time. I refused. It's nonsensical. It became "Jack Charlton's Little Black Book". In many ways it worked well for me.'

From speaking about perceived criminal behaviour (joke), it's just a short hop to asking about his experience of Irish politicians jumping on the bandwagon.

A few names are mentioned but not in an accusatory way. In essence Jack's response can be readily distilled. 'If they want to be photographed with me, okay. But I was requested a couple of times before the last election and I said no. I did have photos taken with several politicians, but I didn't know at the time that they were politicians. Now, whether they tried to use me or not I don't know.'

We talk about fishing and rod licences and also the safety and security required at football stadia in the aftermath of the Hillsborough disaster, in which ninety-five people died in 1989, and much more besides. I can see that my C-90 cassette tape is almost finished. Thinking of my newspaper's readership, I finish with a soft question. Any advice for youngsters coming into the game?

'You never learn how to play football in a book. You can read about what you're supposed to do in a book. But the only way you improve is through hard work and repetitive practice. My great memories of being a kid is having a brother who loved football and me, and we were close enough, we had two and a half years between us, so we were close enough to be able to play against each other. And we spent hours and hours and hours on one-to-ones, heading games. With a tennis ball. We did nothing else but play. We were never coached. Probably if we'd been coached earlier, we might have been better players.

'Coaches only direct you in a way that shows you how it should be done. The person that puts it right is you. They can't stop a ball for you or make a pass for you. You've got to become better at them yourself. There's no substitute for hard work. The more you do a thing, the better you'll become at it. And it's the same in football as it is in any other sport.'

We wrap things up and I slip away, past sporting legends like Paul McGrath, Packie Bonner, Ronnie Whelan and Frank Stapleton.

Ireland drew 1–1 in the international friendly match against West Germany. On the day, Irish supporters and sports journalists were shocked when, thirty-five minutes into the first half, Charlton called off local hero and football legend Liam Brady and substituted him with Andy Townsend.

EARTHA KITT – August 1990

'Hang on a minute please.'

Hearing the husky voice – part purr, part growl – from the other side of the door, my knees feel weak. I'm about to come face to face with a bona fide cultural icon.

Dubbed 'the most exciting woman on earth' by Orson Welles, Eartha Kitt was a dancer and singer whose sultry performances made her a superstar in the 1950s when she had a number of hit singles.

Kitt once described her life in six words: 'Rejected, ejected, dejected, used, accused and abused.' Born in South Carolina, she'd been called a 'yellow gal' and abandoned by her mother because she was light-skinned. It won't be until eight years after we meet in Dublin, in 1990, that Kitt discovers her actual birth date. When her legal case to access her birth record is eventually successful, she learns that she was born on 17 January 1927 and not 26 January 1926 as was on her passport. However, to her bitter disappointment, the name of her father has been redacted on the document. He's purported to have been a local doctor. Kitt believed her mother, who'd died when Eartha was six, was poisoned.

Looking back, I've no clear recollection of why Ms Kitt was in Dublin that month. It's possible that she was there promoting a single from her album *I'm Still Here*, a deft mix of electronic synth-pop and Kitt's distinctive cabaret stylings.

Although she's still suffering from jetlag and a hay-fever type allergy, Kitt greets me at noon in her penthouse suite. When we sit down, she sounds tired to me and I say, 'You've been very busy. Clearly your schedule is taking a lot out of you.'

'Yes, I'm beginning to feel it now,' she replies. 'Travelling now isn't as much fun as it used to be. Have you been through Checkpoint Charlie, Heathrow, whatever? It's one of the worst experiences I've ever had. I love this part of the world so much and it seems to be having tremendous problems with terrorism stipulations. Why with England so much?'

'England has a problem with the Provisional IRA,' I venture. 'Apart from any potential threats from Libya or so on.'

'Mind you they [the IRA] have never struck at an airline or airport,' Eartha notes. 'They tend to go for government or military personnel. That's a historic problem that looks like it's going to be there for a long time.'

I'm sitting in a plush armchair. Eartha is relaxed on the rug at my feet. I've seen photos of Hollywood stars in similar poses. Her delightful informality creates an intimate atmosphere. I change the subject.

'Was Paris in the 1940s a romantic time?'

'Very. But so were the '50s and '60s. People were banding together because after the Second World War we wanted to get ourselves together again and it seems every time we get ourselves together again something else happens.

'Now look what's happening in Canada. Quebec wants to have her own world. The English want their own world in Canada. It's very confusing. The more you see around you, the more it affects you because you wonder what the hell it's about. Where are we going?

'Our children don't seem to have any real feelings of a future. What are we doing? We're supposed to be a very intelligent people, on all sides of the world. But it seems civilisation is dying because people want to get away from so much bureaucracy. They're tired of being oppressed by bureaucracy, particularly our young people.

'You see that all over the world. So I'm very concerned about the future of my child and the grandchildren. What do you do? It's very confusing.'

Raised by relatives, Kitt was abused as a child. She had to work in the cotton fields to help pay her way.

'Given your espousal of black causes and issues, and your harassment by the CIA and Lyndon B. Johnson in the 1960s, even going back to being blacklisted in the '50s, it seems ironic that you should find yourself picketed by the anti-apartheid movement when you ignored the UN's call for a cultural boycott of South Africa and performed there in the mid-1980s. How do you feel about that in retrospect?'

Kitt is not reticent in her response. 'Well, if you're a thinking person, it's getting more and more difficult to speak your mind. When people try to harass you [and prevent you] from expressing yourself ... We're artists. We're not politicians. We're the ones who keep these doors open to all of the world. And the sports people. Nobody should care about whether the sports people or us want to go to one country or another. Because we are interpreters of everything that's going on. We sing about it. We write about it. We express it. To let people know that this is happening over there and to keep people's minds open.

'I want to be a very alert person. I don't want to go through life saying, "I'm just going to go out and sing my songs and not care about anything." That's not possible for a thinking person. It should be much more free for everybody.

'But if you're going to prevent the sports world and the artists from expressing themselves and sharing our art with other people, then what are we going to do? Where is it going? To prevent people from writing books according to what they feel. Look at [Salman] Rushdie and the book that he's written. It's a book! If you stop people from thinking, this is going to get worse and worse. Because people want to be free. Freedom means that you have freedom of expression. The only way you can have this expression is that you know and see and feel. And you can interpret, rather than just reading a newspaper.

'Naturally, I was sorry that the anti-apartheid people did what they did, because I feel if you want to go to South Africa or anywhere in the world it's a form of expressing your art. You don't go in because you're for or against. You go in because you're an artist.

'But to force you to sign a piece of paper that says if you don't sign this piece of paper you're going to be ridiculed, I think it's very bad to do something like that to another person. It prevents you from thinking and makes you very fearful. But if you get into a position where you don't sign this paper, then they might have thrown a bomb and people would have got hurt.

'So freedom doesn't seem to exist any more. This is what's happening with people who want to be free. Look at Russia. They broke down the wall in Berlin. What took them so long?'

As a teenager, Kitt won a scholarship to the Katherine Dunham School of Cultural Arts, America's first black modern-dance company, and later became a dancer in the company, with which she toured Europe.

In the 1960s she became the first black woman to star on mainstream television, when she was cast as the leather-clad Catwoman in the TV show *Batman*. Racial taboos were broken when Kitt flirted on screen with the main character, played by Adam West. She also became a vocal opponent of the Vietnam War, a stance which effectively ended her career in the US and led to her being discredited and branded 'a sadistic nymphomaniac' in a CIA propaganda campaign.

'You moved away from Hollywood and relocated to Connecticut. Was that to distance yourself from the industry?'

'Well, I had more freedom in Hollywood than other artists because I don't have to depend on Hollywood. I can go anywhere to work. But I think people like us who are so individual they don't know what to do with you ... they don't know what kind of parts ... [phone interruption] ... They're not writing scripts for real people.

'Look what Schwarzenegger is doing. And I adore him. He's a wonderful person. But look at Stallone. Look at this film *Batman* [referring to the 1989 Tim Burton film]. What is that all about?

'When you are what they call "a real artist" in Hollywood, they don't think in terms of you as an artist. They want you to do whatever these scripts are about today. They're writing commercials. I don't think they're writing anything that's benefitting a real artist. It's just kind of an entertainment that doesn't give you anything to think about except to go out and blast your way through.

'And the films that are making big money are films that are really brutal. This is what the children come out with. When we were kids we came out dancing to Fred Astaire and Ginger Rogers.

We were in love. We could sing songs that were meaningful. And now we come out of movies and I think we want to hit somebody, which is not the healthiest thing for the future of our children. The children are not being set the proper kind of examples. Where are your heroes? Real heroes? People who want to say there shouldn't be any hatred anywhere? We're expecting love. Let's hold each other. Let's dance with each other.

'Even the dance musicals, even though I've done some of those records. You'd do the records in the studio and the words that I'm singing with the dance music would be meaningful. But the way they use that in the discos now, it's a lot of noise. I don't know where the devil this is going. Everybody's saying the same thing. Where is the future?

'They called me this morning from Los Angeles about a film they want me to do on Medea. The first thing one of my secretaries said was, "This is not a part that everybody would want to do because of the killing of the children." But it is a very interesting character. And you don't see the killing of the children. It's just spoken about. So we're starting to do that film in January. It's written beautifully and it says a lot about a person who has been rejected in that society and she's rebelling against it. It's going to be a very important film.'

'Who's directing?'

'It's a Greek person and it's Greek and American money. But then you start worrying about what they're going to start thinking about you if you're playing a part where, because of what your husband has done to you, you don't even want him to have the children. You think, should you do the part or not do the part? But if you go through life thinking that I'm not going to do something because somebody out there is going to dislike what you're doing, then you'll never do anything.'

'It sounds like an exciting part to play. That's one of the great archetypes.'

'George Vouros, a Greek gentleman in London, said he had been looking for Medea for a very long time and finally, when he saw me in Los Angeles, he said, "I've found her. You're the only one who can play this part." That's why I got the part. It's such an interesting character. It's a very strong woman.'

'When you were speaking about the system in Hollywood, I couldn't help thinking of your friend James Dean and what you think he might have been doing now had he lived.'

'I think he would be another Sir Laurence Olivier. Maybe even gone beyond that because he was learning so much from people like Sir Laurence Olivier. He was a very thinking person. He felt everything he did to such an extent. He was very annoyed with Hollywood. He used to practically cry to me on the phone because he said that in the last film he did, *Giant*, they put him in with plastic actors and he couldn't grow.

'They were pulling him back to be on the same standards as these other actors and he wanted them to grow with him. He said just because you put grey hair and more make-up on somebody doesn't mean that they are growing with the character. He was very frustrated in Hollywood.

'But I don't think he would have killed himself for it, even though they said he deliberately ... or that he was suicidal. He was a wonderful actor.

'Marlon [Brando] now is also crying over the same thing. So he charges tremendous amounts of money to do what he says are idiotic things now. He too wants to grow, but you have to have things to grow with. You don't have the Tennessee Williams or F. Scott Fitzgeralds any more – people like that, who wrote extremely interesting stories and characters. We don't have anything to utilise as far as the characters are concerned these days in order to show that we've grown with the art history that we feel we have inside us. And with someone like myself whom they felt was such an individual, the agent said to me, "Yes, Eartha, you're a fantastic, beautiful artist, but they don't know what to do with you." They want everyone to be alike so they can easily place you, and you have to have a slot along with how many other people that they have on their rosters.

'If you're an individual, you get lost in the shuffle of the Hollywood kind of thinking. That's one of the reasons why I left. I was over the hill in Hollywood anyway. There was no reason for me to stay there. There was nobody for me to play with. [Laughs] I have very good friends in Hollywood. People like Cicely Tyson. We want to grow and have writing that makes people think. It's not being written any more.'

'Or not getting funded? Funding arts projects is usually problematical.'

'You can't get anybody to fund it. I have a friend who's about my age who's a writer in Hollywood. He was writing things that he hated, like *Dukes of Hazzard* and *Hart to Hart*, which I thought was a very good television show. It was fun, as well as having good people like Robert Wagner, and you never saw anybody getting killed. It was very subtle. It was taken off by the young people coming into the studio. They take off things that are successful and put in their own junk. What's running the business now? Young accountants and young lawyers who are thinking in terms of making a fast dollar.

'This writer told me that for him to get a job as a writer now, he writes the scripts and puts a young person's name on it.' Eartha enjoys a good raucous laugh at this scenario and then picks up the thread. 'I miss my friends in Hollywood, but they weren't in showbusiness. They are teachers and so on.'

'You've had a charmed and marvellous life, apart from those abusive and traumatic childhood years. To have gone from those early years to sharing your life with people like Orson Welles and James Dean ... you're giving to them and they're giving to you.'

'And Orson Welles left Hollywood because ... I would say he was on the verge of genius. They seem to get jealous of people who are capable of doing more than one thing extremely well. Not only could he direct, but he was a fantastic actor and he could do everything extremely well. They tried to accuse him of all sorts of crazy things. That's why he eventually went to Europe. He was trying to do Macbeth. So he did some theatre things, which I've been lucky enough to have been a part of.'

Kitt received rave reviews when she appeared in *Time Runs*, Welles' adaptation of the Faust legend, which mixed Marlowe, Milton, Dante and the music of Duke Ellington.

'I played the part of Helen of Troy. That's when I met Hilton [Edwards] and Micheál MacLiammóir. We were wonderful together. Absolutely marvellous. Because we were stimulating each other. Now you don't find people stimulating each other on the stage. The better the actor is, the better I have to be.

'So I look at what the critics say about Eartha Kitt and it's kind of frightening sometimes. When people like you come to me and say, "They said this about you." It's all very wonderful, but then it's hard to get a job. So you're absolutely lost.'

The hotel phone rings again and interrupts our train of thought. It appears to be a PR person checking on whether or not I've arrived.

The 1980s were a busy time for Kitt who, following a string of hit singles in the 1950s, was back in the charts with 'Where Is My Man', a club favourite. Her success in Stephen Sondheim's *Follies* in London was followed by another club hit, 'Cha Cha Heels' with Bronski Beat, and a successful one-woman show in London's West End.

'There's one other not quite discarded man in your life,' I say in the manner of an investigative journalist. I'm referring to her song 'My Discarded Men'.

Eartha laughs out loud and says, 'That's another joke.'

'Yes, corny I know. But I've said it.'

'There's not even a man around that I can discard. It's a great album title. Did I tell you how I wrote it? I was in my dressing room in London when I was doing *Follies* and doing my one-woman show. Because I love to have animals around me and I couldn't bring my animals with me, my friends from the *Opera* magazine gave me two dogs. So we built a cage in the dressing room. Every time somebody came into the dressing room, they'd say, "Oh, dogs." I'd say, "No. They're not dogs, they're my discarded men." So we wrote a song about it.

'I also wrote a song for one of those dance music ... 'Primitive Man', talking about how government has repressed us. It will never get played on the radio. It's on the last album, *I'm Still Here*. It says I want to get back to a primitive world where people were honest with one another and life was not so complicated, and we pay fools to guide us and then when we ask them where to go they tell us they don't know. I think somewhere along the line somebody is going to pick up on it.'

The doorbell of the suite chimes. We're joined by a PR person I hadn't met until now. He's laid-back and discreet, but his arrival signals it's time for me to leave. I'm on borrowed time.

'You were speaking about James Dean,' I say, hoping that Eartha will become so involved in her subject that her PR person won't wish to interfere and shut down the conversation.

'James Dean was a very sensitive person. Everything around him affected him. We used to go in the middle of the night on his motorcycle up and down Sunset Boulevard. I think he was always in search of knowledge. I've always been in search of knowledge. We were like sponges. Everything we absorbed, we interpreted and put back in the song. But I don't have anybody like James Dean to play with any more.'

'You're soon to become a grandmother. Do you have concerns for the future? For your expected grandchild?'

'My daughter and I hold good conversations. But since we are not holding conversations like we would have done before television and all that, everybody wants to do computers. The children are not using their heads any more. Because business society has said if you cannot use a computer, you're not very intelligent. You don't have to use your head any more. You just use a lot of fingers. If it comes up on the computer, then you're an intelligent person. My head is my computer. My head is getting lost more and more.'

'Yes, it's another language.'

'To me it's another world. When I was writing *Thursday's Child* [her autobiography, published in 1956, the title of which inspired David Bowie to write a song of the same name], I was thinking, *If the gods decided to take me away, instead of having the Last Supper, whom would I have the last conversation with?* And it was Dr [Albert] Einstein.

'So I found him and I went to visit him in Princeton. We had a wonderful conversation. He said if he had known what man was going to do with his participation in the atom bomb, he would have had nothing to do with it. Dr Einstein was thinking in terms of bettering mankind, and it turns out to be the reverse. I don't know what the hell the scientists are doing these days.'

It really is time for me to leave. And I wouldn't wish to impose on the generosity of a woman who's proved to be a sparkling mix of charisma, down-home honesty and fierce, questing intelligence.

Chapter Two

Spinning a Yarn

THE INTERVIEWER'S JOB IS ONE of discovery. The aim is to come away with something engaging or entertaining; to have gleaned some fresh facts, contrary opinions or, better still, some outrageous indiscretion.

I entered this arena against the backdrop of what I considered to be a blight of puff-piece interviews: those anodyne promotional exercises, adored by PR people, that were the main staple of many newspapers and magazines. While I never set out to unearth dirty secrets, I strove to avoid soft-focus wide shots and come away with some revealing close-ups.

Thanks to the editor's outline plan, the Q&A format proved a godsend, in that it cut out the middleman – me – and allowed the interviewee to shape the perception of themselves. I was spared having to make judgements or offer in-depth character assessments. My job, as I saw it, was to cover as many aspects of their life and career as I possibly could in the allotted time, which usually wasn't as lengthy as I'd have liked. The replies to my enquiries would need to do the heavy lifting. And therein lay the rub.

I needed my guests to engage. Monosyllabic responses weren't going to cut it.

I was too inexperienced to know that not every interviewee would prove to be as gregarious as the lanky lad from Ashington, Jack Charlton. That awareness came within a few weeks when, under time pressure, I ignored advice and lined up a politician. He was polite, worthy and deadly dull. His responses seemed to have been preheated by a doughty civil servant. My editor had been right, but I just about got away with it.

I'd never played tennis but, as I filed my interview copy each week, the reality of not knowing who I'd be facing next began to feel like being in an unending Wimbledon tournament. Each interview became a high-stakes contest. How should I serve? Would I have to contend with a vicious backhand or cultured slice? Would this be my last match?

I've heard people say that interviewers only ask questions to which they already know the answers. While that is often true of radio or TV, where researchers do advance groundwork for the interviewer, a lengthy press interview requires the interviewer to venture into unexplored territory. It's a voyage of discovery; an expedition in search of the unknown.

Preparation is important. Today, there are search engines that will access biographical details, archive features and previous interviews. Back then, I often depended on the newspaper's cuttings library to bolster my patchy knowledge of an individual's career.

One day I was mildly disturbed to come across a file on myself, which contained a press story from more than a decade earlier of how I had been arrested in Germany under suspicion of being a member of the Baader-Meinhof gang, and another front-page account of how a gig I'd played in Donegal with Horslips had been raided by machine-gun-toting paramilitaries. I remembered that incident as the night when, during the show, a tour manager placed a briefcase full of money under my drum stool with the instructions 'keep an eye on this' as shots rang out in the foyer. Not for the first time, the drummer felt like a sitting duck.

On occasion, an already published biography of an interviewee would furnish further background detail. Crucially, well-informed friends and drinking companions could be consulted for their views. Quite often their random left-field observations would lead to an unexpected or off-beat line of enquiry.

In these situations, questions are often mere prompts. Listening attentively and deciding whether or not to follow an improbable lead suggested by an aside in the conversation, or even to switch topics completely, can sometimes be the key to a productive encounter. The interviewer needs to be on their game and have their wits about them, because a windy digression by an interviewee could too easily lead into a cul-de-sac and waste valuable time.

Gradually, I discovered how a straightforward question beginning with who, what, why, where, when and how would rarely let me down. Even when an interviewee's response was cursory or curt, a follow-up 'why' or 'what' tended to encourage further reflection.

***

Unused to the routine, undertaking a big interview each week felt somewhat unnatural.

Of course, as a member of Horslips I'd been the interviewee countless times over the years and in all manner of circumstances. Clearly those experiences afforded me important insights, if only on a subliminal level, into the dynamic in play in the process.

As I revisited my archive of recorded 'Face to Face' interviews, originally kept for fear of having to answer queries from disgruntled interviewees or their representatives, one of the first things to strike me was the tenacity and stamina of most of those with whom I engaged. Not all the tapes survived intact. Some were damaged or taped over in parts. But, with the help of contemporaneous notes, I've been able to assemble some notable conversations.

As the interviewer, I'd have been conscious of recent developments in people's careers and would have been duty-bound to enquire into headline incidents or controversies. I wasn't muck-raking and I certainly wasn't interested in rehashing well-reported incidents, but I did need to establish how the interviewee felt about certain events, whether joyous or controversial.

Overall, I was privileged to be afforded a glimpse of people's inner strength and conviction, their resilience and determination, their passion and their courage. Frequently, it proved inspirational.

In 1977 David Norris went to the High Court to challenge the constitutionality of our laws on homosexuality. He was unsuccessful, as was his Supreme Court challenge in 1983. The case then became *Norris v. Ireland* and, in October 1988, the European Court of Human Rights ruled against Ireland's 1861 and 1885 laws. However, when I met Norris, civil rights activist, Trinity College lecturer and member of Seanad Éireann, in February 1990, those laws remained on the Irish statute books.

In answer to the obvious question of why the delay, Norris replied, 'They're nervous of the ruling. We've had a very unfortunate history in these areas. Family Solidarity [an Irish Catholic advocacy group] have been allowed a completely unjustified prominence. Who are they? They're unrepresentative. They're non-elected. They're quite secretive ... They are now gearing up to try and prevent the implementation of the Strasbourg judgment. The government are a little reluctant to get involved for that reason. A substantial majority of young people wish to see the law changed. I would hope the government has the guts and the moral courage to do something decent on behalf of what is probably the most significant minority in the country ... 10 per cent. It's a lot of people.'

Homosexuality was eventually decriminalised in Ireland with the enactment of the Sexual Offences (Amendment) Act 1993, and same-sex marriage was legalised in 2015. In June 2018, the twenty-fifth anniversary of the decriminalisation of homosexuality, an All-Party motion acknowledged the harm done by criminalisation of consensual same-sex relationships and offered an apology to those who were criminalised for their sexuality.

A noted Joycean scholar, David was linked in the public mind to the annual 16 June Bloomsday celebrations. 'The celebration of Bloomsday goes back before my time,' he reminded me, 'to 1955, when John Ryan, Tony Cronin, Paddy Kavanagh and Myles na gCopaleen hired a hansom cab and went off on a skite. In 1982 I ran the centenary celebrations, and we really launched it.'

Concerned I might have linked him to the excesses of the James Joyce souvenir industry, David noted, 'Then Bord Fáilte realised that Bloomsday could become a kind of Mardi Gras. Being dead a hundred years and having the capacity to generate money does an awful lot for your reputation.'

Although not an Irishman like Joyce, Alan Parker, the director of *Bugsy Malone* (1976), *Midnight Express* (1978), *Fame* (1980) and *Mississippi Burning* (1988) told an equally entertaining story about Dublin in *The Commitments* (1991). Widely decorated for his work, I found Parker refreshingly straightforward and direct when we met following the release of the film. Having begun his career as an office boy in a London advertising agency, he remained acutely conscious of the critical elite, acknowledging that 'You do get rather nervous in an industry that is very unforgiving with regards to failure.'

While the initial response to *The Commitments* indicated success was assured, I was interested in Parker's sometimes uncomfortable relationship with the British film industry and wondered if that was perhaps because of his working-class background or an earlier career working on television commercials.

'The whole working-class thing, I try to shrug off now, but, truthfully, it's really hard. I encountered a great deal of snobbery when I started in life. Coming from that background in Britain, which is very class divided in a very odious way, that affects me and how angry I might be about certain things … we were put down because we didn't have the correct credentials … that really pissed me off.'

The variance between public and private persona was always worth discovering. In 1990 actor Mick Lally, who was famous for his portrayal of farmer Miley Byrne in the RTÉ drama series *Glenroe*, revealed a fervent awareness of environmental issues, earnestly urging the preservation of bogland and protesting about the hazards of mining and the creation of what he described as 'parochial airports'.

'We're probably the most self-discussed nation on earth with the amount of people who've access to the airwaves in Ireland,' he argued. 'The dangerous thing about that situation is that by talking so much about it you give the impression that you're doing something about it. Generally speaking, when you talk about it, you wind up doing nothing about it.'

Spinning a Yarn

In 1991 an impending thirty-date concert tour and release of a new album afforded me the opportunity to interview musical theatre star Elaine Paige in London. When I arrived I was conscious that the singer was still making headlines in Britain because of the breakup of her eleven-year romance with lyricist Tim Rice. Ahead of her afternoon rehearsals, Elaine was brisk and business-like. We discussed her stage debut in *Hair* in 1968, and many of her ensuing career successes. Aware that my editor would ask why I hadn't addressed the elephant in the room, I enquired if Elaine found the media coverage of her breakup hurtful or tedious. The way I phrased the question was intended to offer her multiple ways of evading the subject. As it turned out, I got more than I bargained for.

'I'd have to say to you that I really don't want to talk about this,' Elaine replied before launching into a lengthy and detailed analysis of the emotional impact of the reportage. 'I have this conflict going on with myself about it … It's a lot to do with the press in Britain. In America they don't hound you … it's the tone that's unpleasant … Of course it's hurtful … you just have to lump it … I've tried giving interviews and not giving interviews … and you can't win … I'm not going to give any more interviews and that's going to be that.'

If you feel you've been deprived of Elaine's inner thoughts in newsprint ever since, I hold my hands up but plead innocence.

MALCOLM McLAREN – October 1989

I'm surprised when the man from whom I'd bought a Little Richard *Vive le Rock!* T-shirt on the King's Road a couple of years earlier walks into the basement living room of my friend Jane in Belgravia.

It's early evening and the haberdasher is on a mission. Jane creates fifties-style sweaters for Roxy Music, and Malcolm McLaren wants something similar for his shop. The shop has gone through some changes. It was Let It Rock (named after a Chuck Berry song) when I purchased my T-shirt and some odds and ends. It had been Too Fast To Live, Too Young To Die for a while. Now it's called SEX. Malcolm is working with his partner, designer Vivienne Westwood.

This evening he's accompanied by a taciturn shop assistant with a bleach-blonde bouffant, ripped fishnets, impossible high heels and heavily charcoaled eyes. Her name is Jordan, a woman I haven't encountered before. She remains silent throughout as we listen to music by Captain Beefheart. We're joined by an occasional house guest of Jane, who I take to be an undergraduate; a lanky chap with tousled hair who speaks quietly with a slight West Country burr. He likes to travel and appears unexpectedly every few months with exotic combustibles. I wasn't to learn until many years later that my sociable companion was Howard Marks, a personable drug smuggler who became infamous internationally as Mr Nice.

Malcolm and I didn't become personal friends, but we would later find ourselves in similar company drinking in unlikely public houses around Soho. It would be another few months before Malcolm, who spoke in a high nasal tone that reminded me of *Carry On* star Charles Hawtrey, began promoting a bunch of ne'er-do-wells, who hung about his shop, as the Sex Pistols.

Over three tumultuous years, McLaren mentored and guided

a band which revolutionised the popular music industry. Vivienne Westwood's designs, many co-creations with McLaren, changed the face of world fashion, while the Situationist-inspired artwork of ally Jamie Reid and many of the collages worked on by Sophie Richmond, an integral part of McLaren's management company Glitterbest, influenced the grammar of visual art.

McLaren had continued to blaze a trail through popular culture up until the time this interview was conducted, October 1989, even in the aftermath of the Sex Pistols' spectacular implosion in 1978. He had orchestrated further Situationist-style headline-grabbing antics with Adam Ant and Bow Wow Wow, and had been celebrated with an exhibition at the New Museum of Contemporary Art in New York – *Impresario: Malcolm McLaren and the British New Wave*.

He had also reinvented himself as a recording artist in his own right.

***

'One of your parents was Scottish. Am I right?'

'My dad is Scottish from Havana, Cuba. All the McLarens left Scotland in the days of the rebellion when the English went in. They drifted off to the Caribbean. He emigrated back with his father to London. Most of the family are in Havana working for Castro. My mother is Spanish/Portuguese/Jewish.'

'An exotic mix.'

'Yeah, but it didn't last too long. I never knew my father. He left shortly after my birth. I just met him about three months ago. I found him living on the Romney Marsh.'

'Did you find that traumatic?'

'I suppose it was really. He didn't look anything like me. Golden blond hair. A little, short, wiry Scottish-looking guy, very dapper, very elegant. Sitting on the Romney Marsh in green silk shirt and white leather Levis at the age of seventy.'

Malcolm emits a trademark cackle that, at a pinch, could possibly be filed under 'laughter'. I can tell from experience that he's warming up to the task of spinning a few entertaining yarns.

'It was a very strange icon to meet, in the middle of a bunch of goats and a dilapidated Saxon church. My first impressions of him were that he was very much a cad, an obvious adventurer. Having met my father, I don't want to end up like him. I don't want to end up a cad. In some respects, I'm probably looking to construct things now. I'm living in Hollywood, but I've decided to come back here. I've always had no affinity with the English; I could never get on with them. So I've decided to base myself in Paris – not because it's a wonderful place to be creative in, because you're governed by so much historic culture around you it does crush you after a while. But it's still a fantastic railway station. It's a great crossroads, and looking at Europe right now it serves a marvellous purpose to create a base camp.'

The idea of wiry-haired McLaren, who boasts 'it was a delight to cause chaos', on the loose in Hollywood, the belly of the great cultural behemoth, is intriguing.

'Was it the lure of the silver screen that took you to Hollywood in the first place?'

'Purely that. I couldn't fish in the pond any longer in London. The English are incredibly concerned with taking risks. They're not really entrepreneurs. So I thought maybe I should venture to Hollywood and reinvent myself and see if there were opportunities afoot there, and I was absolutely amazed when I went to Hollywood because all the secretaries were major fans. What I found were twenty-eight-year-old high-powered yuppies in these expensive chairs all having doted on the Sex Pistols when they were teenagers. I had already been well and truly categorised, so it was very difficult to reinvent myself. I was caught a little on the hop. I became a sort of *enfant terrible*, flavour-of-the-month, as you can very easily do in Hollywood. But I found certain characters in the movie business, people as illustrious as Steven Spielberg, who befriended my ideas, and I finally struck up certain professional relationships that hopefully will engineer pictures in the near future. The problem was, of course, that everybody in Hollywood only wanted to talk to me about music. Of course, as soon as I designed a music picture, [or presented] a concept, you had to explain what the music was.'

'To explain, "Johann Strauss meets James Brown. Somewhere in the nineteenth century Oscar Wilde discovers rock'n'roll."

'"Yes, well that's all fascinating," they say. "What is it? What would the music sound like?"

'So, "Oh fuck, I've got to go and make a record then, I guess."

'And that's how I came to make this record, *Waltz Darling*, almost as a demo for a musical film that I had sold to Steven Spielberg.'

I nod my assent. 'The record itself is certainly very jolly.'

'Yeah. It's a fun record, which you can't possibly not be with the waltz, of course, because the waltz in itself is such an upbeat thing. You can't get too Gothic. What I liked about it was the optimism in the waltz, and put it to that marching beat of rhythm and blues.'

Aware that he had managed the New York Dolls for a period before the Sex Pistols, and that British guitar legend Jeff Beck and colourful funk disciple Bootsy Collins both worked with McLaren on his most recent recordings, I venture to enquire who he considers to have been the most entertaining musicians he's worked with over the years.

'Oooh, that's a difficult question,' coos Malcolm in his best high-camp accent. 'I had an extraordinary time with these Cuban musicians and the African musicians on the record *Duck Rock* and the World's Famous Supreme Team who I made "Buffalo Gals" with were all joyous and very inspiring experiences.

'Of course I have to say the Sex Pistols, in terms of making a point of view that, to me, was to be a kind of divine comedy, really. It was an attempt to demonstrate that England was never anything in terms of rock'n'roll if it couldn't be thoroughly English. And coming up with titles like "Anarchy in the U.K." and "God Save the Queen" were peculiarly English, even though Johnny Rotten wanted to call it "No Future".

'I said, "My God, no. We've got to hit the nail on the head."

'But it was for that very purpose that I adored Johnny Rotten, because no way an American singer was going to blow his nose over the microphone. There was no way they were ever going to sing out of tune. They're too good. But the English can't sing too well. The great thing about the Sex Pistols was they broke away from all that. You could be Cockney. You could be Irish. And still be rock'n'roll.'

I avoid mentioning the obvious and reminding him that John Rotten (*né* Lydon) had branded him 'the most evil man alive'. Instead, I ask McLaren to evaluate Lydon's contribution to the Sex Pistols.

'Brilliant poet,' rejoins the man they called 'Talcy Malcy', without missing a beat. 'Brilliant ability to pick up on whatever the vibe I would give out and whatever attitude I would have as a brat. I was probably more of a brat than him really at the end of the day.

I would make him feel that he was perfectly able to do anything he bloody wanted to do and have full confidence in doing it. His attitude was enough to carry him. It didn't matter that you can't sing.'

The man's devotion to subversion and causing chaos was impressive. So what motivated his commitment to protest and challenging the establishment and status quo?

'As I said, I was the ultimate spoilt brat at school. At art school. I never really had a job. I lived on my wits and became an entrepreneur on the King's Road as a clothing salesman. But the idea of using my artistry was a way of a … er … sculptor using clay; you use people. And it was a way of creating a scene – that is what I was interested in. I was interested in the exploitation of that shop on the King's Road to create trouble in some shape or form. It was like someone had given me a canvas on the street instead of locking me up in an attic, and … tapping the kind of sensibility of those kids demanding a new look prompted me to exercise opinions and ideas.'

The enormous upheaval and energies created by punk rock weren't meant to be contained. The Sex Pistols spontaneously combusted in a welter of recrimination and lawsuits. Arrested for the second-degree murder of his girlfriend, Nancy Spungen, Sid Vicious went cold turkey in Rikers Island. Preparing for a legal case brought against him by John Lydon, McLaren delegated an assistant to babysit his by then bailed bass player. Tragically, Vicious took heroin and, having detoxed in jail, underestimated its impact. He died of a drug overdose.

'How did you deal with the suggestions that you were responsible, either directly or indirectly, for the death of Sid Vicious?'

'All those things obviously come in your wake because of you being tarnished – rightly so, I don't deny it – of being to some extent irresponsible and not acting as a manager and a Florence Nightingale.

'I was a manager that mismanaged. That was the whole ballgame. Being somewhat naive towards drug-taking, I was not shocked by Sid's addiction to heroin but did many scurrilous things to try and break him from that habit. His death was something that really fell more or less on the responsibility of his mother. I say that sincerely because no matter what I did, Sid's mother undid. She was an addict herself ... Sid having come out on bail accused of murdering his girlfriend and he OD'd. It wasn't my responsibility as much as to say that, at that point, he was no longer in the group. I knew that there was a time bomb, and I knew that the industry itself was absolutely out to get me. There was a paranoia beyond anything I've ever experienced in the industry. I had created such catastrophe they felt that the normal selling of records was no longer possible whilst the Sex Pistols remained.'

Malcolm emits a hollow cackle of laughter. 'All these old groups were retiring.' He laughs again at the absurdity of the situation. 'I suppose Sid's death was a blessing in disguise for the industry because they really felt that whilst we existed The Rolling Stones died. The Who died. Elton John died. We ceased to exist and they could all be reinvented. Jagger got his hair cut and everybody was now revitalised. It was like the Sex Pistols gave a little bit of an injection.

'So it was the perfect moment to point the blame. Who's been responsible for all this madness that we're all now giddy and drunk with? Somebody has to be the scapegoat and naturally it fell in my lap. You live with it, man. Naturally the participation in drug-taking was always across the table. John participated and Steve

Jones did. But Sid got addicted. I think he got addicted through his girlfriend and it ultimately led to his disaster. One's attempts at being the nursemaid didn't work and … after you're eighteen you really are your own boss. I do lay the responsibility for his death at his mother's feet. Because it was his mother that was there – not anybody else. How I can be blamed is only a media response to the fact that I was blamed for punk rock. It was an easy tag.

'The English press are wonderfully pagan. It's one of the nice things about them. They love building up idols and love bashing them down. It's a very pagan, Fleet Street ritual that happens daily.'

Sensing truth in the image he's invoked, McLaren laughs heartily.

Before I shut the door on this era, I ask one final question. 'Is there such a thing as a "punk legacy"?'

'Obviously it's partly responsible for the cultural history of England, whether they like it or not. It was a minor cultural revolution. It was a minor civil war. And it will always have sympathisers because of that. It's read in school.'

He cracks up again, relishing the social upheaval he helped beget. Dressed in a bright, finely tailored, wide-lapelled lightweight suit with striped shirt and floral tie, McLaren could pass as a prosperous hedge fund manager or art dealer.

'Coming back to Britain, having lived in Los Angeles, have you noticed any political changes in England?'

'Major changes. I would say Margaret Thatcher has been incredibly responsible for taking away any sense of culture. The centre of London looks like a shopping precinct on the edge of Amsterdam airport. I don't think there's happiness any more in England. London is going to go into a malaise for a little while because they've slammed the culture to such an extent that people are in a giant sleep. London reminds me of what it must have been like living under Franco.

'In England they're punch drunk. They've been bashed about so much, they don't know who they are any more. It's ridiculous. That's the sadness. And I think the Northern Ireland situation, and the whole thing, are like bitter and dreadful reminders that England is still nasty as a country that refuses to acknowledge that it makes mistakes. They are a horrible, snobby country. They always believe they're right.

'The Italians, as far as the English would say, are the n***ers of Europe. Everyone in Europe is called by derogatory terms because the English believe they are Europe. They're better than anyone. It's bullshit. The English know nothing.

'This hanging on to Northern Ireland is just part of the symptoms, refusing to give in on anything. It's a dreadful cultural snobbery and reactionary, and it doesn't bode well. In England they think they are more important than everyone else, and it's an attitude I think is encouraged through education. It goes right through the culture. It's endemic. The destruction of the arts schools … As I have studied history, I've discovered England has never, never liked artists. They don't like 'em. Full stop. They think they're weird. They're troublemakers. Byron, Keats, Shelley, Wilde … they all had to leave. Same exists today. Everybody has to leave.'

He paints a bleak picture. But how does he see pop culture developing in the near future?

'I think the whole ecology movement is going to have a tremendous impact, ultimately, culturally, because what it's going to do is bring back etiquette and I think the '90s are going to be about rewriting history.

'What's important in the ecology movement is to understand

whether you are interested in the ecologists or whether you're interested in nature. And you have to decide whether you care about human beings or care about nature. There's going to be that division sooner or later.

'It's about manners. Manners seem terribly old-fashioned today, but manners make you think before you speak and I think that manners are something that will definitely be reconsidered again because I do believe the art of conversation, the world bohemian, the world intellectual, will come back simply because the philosophy of the world in the '90s is going to be about living with less rather than more.'

This chat about ecology prompts a final question. 'Would you feel attracted towards political activity on behalf of the Green Party in an effort to get your message across?'

'I've always been concerned with politics. It's an area I've never encroached upon in any way because in *Angleterre*, dear *Angleterre*, I'm beyond reproach.'

At this point, McLaren's laughter becomes almost uncontrollable.

'I'm not going to end up as the court jester on some talk show in England. If I was in power, I would bloody well pass a law instantly that the Royal Family, Prince Edward or Prince Charles or whoever wasn't married would have to marry an African princess. End of story. And I would want to see those little half-castes waving their hands outside Buckingham Palace, and I bet the following morning racism in England would be clearly as big a topic as it is in South Africa and we'd soon see who's black or white. If that doesn't change anything, nothing will.

'It's sympathetic to talk about racism in England. Here you've a Royal Family who've been white forever and ever, as if black people don't exist. And yet you've plundered and scorched the earth. You've turned countries inside out and you're worrying about inter-feudal wars between one tribe and another. But you put the lines across these countries. So if you want to sort it out, you go out there and marry one of those African princesses and have lots of little brown children.'

He's still laughing as I turn off my recording machine.

***

Malcolm died in April 2010. At his burial in Highgate Cemetery, the Sid Vicious recording of 'My Way' played across the graves. Carved on his headstone are the words, 'Better a spectacular failure than a benign success.'

And one final personal note. When I was transitioning from being a musician and record producer to being a full-time journalist in the mid-1980s, some of my early features were written at the home of my friend Sophie Richmond, who allowed me to use her typewriter. Sophie had worked at the centre of Glitterbest as Malcolm's secretary, and her diaries became a vital source for researchers chronicling the punk rock phenomenon. Today, she is an in-demand publishing editor specialising in sociology, cultural anthropology and psychoanalysis.

JOHN MORTIMER – April 1992

I can hear delighted laughter booming from the restaurant as I enter the hotel lobby.

'Mr Mortimer is having lunch with a friend, sir.'

Due to interview John Mortimer, one of the brightest intellects on the British literary scene, I'm dismayed to discover that he is lunching with the vivacious Mariella Frostrup. I'm also mildly apprehensive. Although appealing, an invitation to join the couple for lunch makes my job more difficult and, given the noisy jollifications coming from the corner of the sumptuous dining room, most likely unmanageable.

The chances of engaging the creator of *Rumpole of the Bailey* in a wide-ranging, meaningful conversation are growing remote. I don't relish having to persuade the author of the new novel *Dunster* to focus attention on his book or indeed on anything other than the menu and the wine list.

I opt to wait in the lounge, believing that, entertaining as the encounter would almost certainly be, I'd find it impossible to ask probing questions in such a situation. So I wait. And then wait some more.

Eventually, the boozy hoots became impossible to ignore, and I decide it wise to enter the fray in case the author of *Paradise Postponed* and *Summer's Lease* is suddenly whisked away to other, more pressing engagements. Or, worse still, requires a restorative nap after his leisurely luncheon.

And so, with no little fanfare, I join the welcoming table. It quickly becomes apparent that this engagement will be conducted under the visiting author's rules. Dessert is being polished off and a bottle of Sancerre and a bottle of champagne stand proudly among the debris. It strikes me that I might be about as welcome as a tax inspector. Not wishing to spoil the upbeat mood, I say, 'Yes, of course, a glass of Sancerre, please.'

Mariella and I make a good impromptu tag team, encouraging our sparkling host, who is at his avuncular best, swapping outrageous yarns and hilarious anecdotes, many of which are so ribald as to be unprintable – this before the tape machine is switched on.

When Mariella, an astute professional, has departed, I apologise to our host for being about to pin-ball random topics at him by way of interrogation. But it's nothing he hasn't experienced before. An acclaimed playwright, screenwriter, novelist and eminent barrister, he has also turned his quizzical gaze on the famous and infamous in an acclaimed series of celebrity interviews for *The Sunday Times*, a fact I'm luckily unaware of at the time. Otherwise my unease, engendered by an inferiority complex, would be instantly supersized.

Despite the Conservative Party having just won a United Kingdom general election, when opinion polling had indicated a probable Labour victory, Mortimer (68), an avowed liberal socialist, was in fine fettle and, champagne to hand, proved to be the most agreeable company.

It's with hindsight that I realise in awe how, formidable and kindly, he precisely tailored his responses to suit my tabloid platform. No editing required. And it's with great gratitude that I acknowledge the patience he displayed at some of my lazier lines of enquiry.

***

Two weeks before our meeting, the Conservative Party, with John Major as leader, had won a fourth consecutive British general election. I wonder how, as a long-standing Labour supporter, the author and playwright viewed the result.

'It's such a terrible event for me. I'm still trying to sort it out in my mind. If I can go back to 1945, which is when I first started feeling about politics when I was very young, there was this great Labour landslide after the war and this great [Clement] Attlee government, which produced the health service and the welfare state.

'We thought there'd be a new world and very few Conservatives and social equality and all the things that I care about – which is really the beginning of the book *Paradise Postponed*, which I wrote about all those hopes in England. And those hopes seemed to be alive until the Thatcher government came into power.

'Then I thought the Thatcher years had come to an end when Mrs Thatcher went. It seemed that the tail end of Thatcherism was the Major era, which was nothing very much and we were winning the election campaign. They looked like they wanted to be in opposition. Then suddenly, it seems to me, the British public took fright. When they're frightened, they don't want to change. They want to stick for fear of something worse. The results are absolutely tragic, because it can mean that democracy doesn't mean anything to have one party in power for about twenty years. And for five years after it lost total direction. And also, unless you have a strong opposition, it will have a paralysing effect on the opposition.

'And so I think we're in for a very unhappy period. I can't quite understand how I'm going to react to it. Perhaps I'll just retire to the country and draw up the drawbridge and write a novel and pretend it isn't going on.'

It had been a dramatic election result, with a British tabloid triumphantly claiming, 'It's *The Sun* Wot Won It.' The Conservative

Party had warned against a Labour 'double whammy' of 'tax rises' and 'inflation'. Does John think the Tories set out to deceive the electorate?

'There were a lot of lies told in the election. The Tories certainly told lies about the Labour tax plans. Huge lies. Labour were a bit economical with the truth about the Conservative national health plan. The Liberals? I don't know what they said.

'I wonder whether the terrific, horrendous newspaper campaign of abuse of the Labour Party had a part to play. It must have had some part to play. It would be a terrible thing to think that a democracy is run by tabloid newspapers. But I think the British electorate is quite intelligent and I think they just came to the view that they were frightened about their taxes. And they haven't yet got to the stage where they think that taxes are a price worth paying for living in a decent society where people don't sleep on the streets and where schools are properly equipped.'

Wondering if there'd been a subtle shift in the perception of the Conservative Party, I suggest, 'Unless John Major is simply an extension of your Thatcher analysis that Margaret Thatcher took the Tories from being an aristocratic party to a middle-class party, and John Major is seen as the chap who left school early, maybe the working class could feel happy with him, and his party could be seen as an aspirational party.'

'It's an aspiration in a very narrow field. It's a very selfish, one-dimensional aspiration. And you see, you've got a situation in England now where nobody remembers a real Labour government. Certainly, nobody remembers the 1945 government and nobody even remembers the first Harold Wilson government, which was a good Labour government. They remember the tail end of a bad Callaghan government. We've been brainwashed by Thatcherism, really. We think that the only thing that's important is our own personal wealth. Even myself I can see slightly brainwashed by it. I'm the chairman of the Royal Court Theatre in London and I have accepted these ideas that you have to go out to big business and get money and that the government shouldn't have to [subsidise]. I can understand the young electorate. I'm very old and have never known any different set of values [traditional Labour aspirations of nationalisation, full employment, social security, etc]. It's very sad.'

As John allows himself a wry laugh, I feel it's time to change the subject and move on to more pleasing terrain.

'Do you find in your personal life there's a blurring of the realities between yourself and your character Rumpole? Do people expect you to be Rumpole?'

'They certainly expect me to be Rumpole. I was in the Far East and I went to a restaurant and the woman addressed me as, 'Ah, there you are, Lumpore of the Bayree.' In a way I am Rumpole, because if I say things which I believe, they sound rather trendy and left-wing and objectionable. And if Rumpole says them, they sound rather crusty and conservative and acceptable. So he is useful to me to say things I think. It all goes back to my particular middle-class upbringing. My father and my mother were both English liberals of the old Lloyd George tradition. My mother was a kind of Shavian New Woman.

'Money in those days was a total embarrassment. If anybody talked about money it was deeply embarrassing, not right at all. Rumpole isn't interested in money. He lives a primitive life in a dirty old flat. But he's interested in concepts of justice and right and wrong and so on. It's that terrible money philosophy that's been imposed on England that he finds objectionable.'

I tell my host that many colleagues in the newspaper world have asked me to tell him that they hope he will continue to write Rumpole stories because they are addicted to them. 'The Rumpole plots are always marvellously convoluted. How difficult are they to create?'

'The plots are very difficult for me, but I've found out if you've an hour's television and you've only one plot, it's very thin. If you've two plots, it's a bit better. If you have three plots, it's really thick. So I always have three plots in Rumpole.

'I have the plot of the case, which is the least important one. I have the machinations in chambers, and I have the plot of what is going on at home with She Who Must Be Obeyed. So it really needs three plots. But I'm not very good at it. I need an awful lot of inspiration to think of plots. But if you have that mixture, it makes them very rich.'

Reclining on the well-upholstered banquette, he resembles an extra from one of his own television courtroom dramas: buttoned-up waistcoat, with the deep lenses on his spectacles so bottle-thick they require a formidable industrial-strength frame to hold them in place. 'Up to the age of five I enjoyed the privileges of myopia,' he writes in *Clinging to the Wreckage* (1982), 'seeing the world in a glorious haze like an Impressionist painting'. After a visit to an oculist, 'the world sprang at me in hideous reality, full of people with open pores, blackheads and impetigo'. Although resembling a character in one of his dramas, he doesn't pop back into court on occasion to keep abreast of judicial developments.

'I don't now, but I suppose I ought to. Leo McKern [the actor who plays Rumpole] has never been to a court. I think after whatever I did, thirty years, I sort of know.

'I think I wouldn't like it now because they hand in their

computer printouts of their arguments and it's all become very depressing. Rumpole's really a figure of the past.'

Given his hectic social life and involvement in the arts, I'm intrigued as to how Mortimer finds the time to create such a prodigious output. 'As a writer, do you have a routine? I suspect it might be onerous.'

'I try to get up at six o'clock in the morning, like a farmer, really. I write with a pen on a bit of paper until lunchtime and then I get drunk.' He laughs heartily before adding, 'Not too drunk. But I don't write after lunch. That's a long time. If you write for four or five hours you can write an awful lot.'

'Say with the new novel, *Dunster*, do you put yourself under pressure to come up with a work that improves or tops what you've done previously?'

'I can't really think like that. But I've never written without deadlines. I impose deadlines on myself. Or they're imposed on me. So I have to do it. For instance, in November Leo said he'd do another lot of *Rumpole*. I now have a television company which produces them. I had to finish them by March 1st. Otherwise, all the money we got to make them would … ha ha. So I have to do that. And then I have to produce the book by July. All those things, I don't find unhelpful. I find them very helpful. And then I have a deadline for a novel. I know all those things are very mechanical, but I think there's something very important about them. Like journalism. You have to write to a deadline. You can't just hang around. It's probably better if you have to write. If you're making a speech in court, you can't get up at the end of a case and say, "I've got to make some coffee" and go off. You've got to make the speech.'

At this point I had turned off the tape because of an interruption by the waiter. I suspect we had more drink. Before setting the tape rolling here again, I think it's a good time to mention that, years later, in *The Summer of a Dormouse*, Mortimer's reflections on ageing, the author recalls how his colourful performances in court would often irritate the presiding judge. On one occasion, he writes, 'In one of the better judicial put-downs, a more tolerable judge started his summing-up, "Members of the jury. It may come as a surprise to you to know that the sole purpose of criminal law in England is not to entertain Mr Mortimer."'

Now back to the recording of our conversation in Dublin.

'In *Dunster*, the character who had wanted to be an actor … reminds me of your own early aspirations to go on the stage.'

'When I was a child, the first thing I wanted to do was be an actor. I wanted to be Noël Coward – tap-dance down white staircases and sit at a white grand piano and wear a top hat and white tie and tails with a silver-knobbed cane. But as I couldn't sing, dance or play the piano, it was a pretty hopeless aspiration.

'I did act at my prep school. I acted Richard II. It was the greatest moment of my life. And then I wrote. I wrote prolific plays. When I went to school I wrote a story and got ten shillings for it. From that moment on, I knew I wanted to be a writer. I certainly didn't want to be a barrister. Being a barrister was my day job, like girls who want to be actresses take on a bit of waitressing. The waitressing got a bit too powerful.'

'Do you hold opinions on other actors, the ones you admire and feel should be winning awards? Or not, as the case may be?'

John laughs, tickled I should ask. 'I do. I'm very interested in actors. I love casting. That's one of the pleasures of … I'm very interfering in casting at all times. I have a lot of sympathy with actors. I respect actors. I have a lot of actors who I know.'

'The current crop?'

'Well, I love the actors I've used. The actors in Rumpole and so on. I love Irish actors. I love the Cusack family altogether. I just like actors to give you that feeling of reality plus. My level of realism is about three feet above the ground, so they have to be able to adapt to that manner.'

As he becomes more engaged with the topic, he sounds even more enthusiastic. 'Really, there are actors who can play Shakespeare. If an actor can play Shakespeare, they can play anything.'

In 1977 I was hugely impressed by the ingenuity and humour of the barrister who successfully defended a record shop in Nottingham that had been prosecuted for displaying the Sex Pistols album sleeve. I discovered that the barrister was the one who, six years previously, had successfully defended the editors of the underground newspaper *Oz*, who'd been charged with 'conspiracy to corrupt and debauch the morals of the young'. It was John Mortimer.

I mention the Sex Pistols album case.

John's eyes brighten as he homes in on the daring boss of the young independent record label, Virgin Records, which signed the riotous band who'd already been signed and dropped by both EMI and A&M before a debut album was released.

'I acted for Richard Branson twice in his life. Once, when he was a student, he had a student magazine which had an advertisement for a cure for venereal disease. That was a time when a mention of venereal disease in an advertisement was a crime.

'Then the Sex Pistols had produced a record called *Never Mind the Bollocks* and I had to defend that as an obscene record sleeve before the magistrates. The first thing I did was send the Sex Pistols to the other end of Nottingham because I didn't think the magistrates would like the look of them.

'It also said, "Fuck the Queen" on this record but you couldn't hear that. Then we called the lexicographer from the university and he was a vicar and he gave evidence to the effect that the word "bollocks" meant the rigging of a medieval man-o'-war. So the Sex Pistols got off, and that was the last I saw of them.

'Years later, my daughter, who studied Russian, went to Russia and she was walking across Red Square with a young Russian poet and he said, "It's such an honour to walk across Red Square with a girl whose father defended the Sex Pistols." It had a good effect.'

'What do your legal peers, or indeed magistrates, make of your literary career?'

'I always wrote. I had a job as a scriptwriter before I became a barrister. I'd written my first novel before I was called to the Bar. So they got used to that.

'Most of the Rumpoles I wrote while I was still a barrister. By and large, the lawyers are very grateful because lawyers are much hated in all countries, particularly in England. They are judged with tax collectors and traffic wardens as the most undesirable members of society. Rumpole is a kind of good barrister and he has ideas and doesn't make a lot of money, so I think they're grateful to him.

'But the judges say, "Why are the judges in Rumpole always malignant or twisted and malicious?" And I say, "Well, it's a period drama and you've got to have conflict. You do understand that, my lord?"'

He's laughing again. 'I haven't done a case in court for ten years so I don't know what … I certainly wouldn't ever do one again.'

I'm not attempting to blindside him, but there are a few matters I need to raise before it's time to vacate the table. 'Do you think the British electoral system should be based on proportional representation?'

'I'm very old-fashioned in my ideas. I don't totally understand the Irish system of PR and it may be very good. But we've just had an election in Italy in which there were 250 different parties and the only election question to anybody was, "Who were they going to ally themselves with?" And the government of Italy is in chaos. You know, the idea of it is that if you vote for a certain party, that should be represented. That doesn't happen because the group you've voted for is going to ally itself with any other party with totally different ideas. I have an old-fashioned belief in the British system of a constituency MP looking after all the people of his constituency. I'm a believer in the two-party system and I greatly regret the break-up of the Labour Party into the Liberals. I think that's caused all this rot. But that's a very old-fashioned view.'

As a musician, I'd done the rounds for years promoting new albums. I'd been younger then. I wonder how an author feels about the process at sixty-eight years of age. 'Does the interview trail, the anecdotal trail, take its toll?'

'Oh no. It's much easier than sitting alone trying to think of a bloody plot,' he declares in upbeat fashion. 'I enjoy it. I would never have driven from Cork to Dublin if I hadn't.'

'Do you find interviewers more adversarial these days? You know the trend, the interviewer as superstar?'

'Oh yes, like Lynn Barber? I don't do many of those interviews. I try to avoid them.'

'The *Mail* had a feature on an American *Rumpole of the Bailey* Fan Club. I think you met them.'

'Yes, we did. There's a huge Rumpole fan club. They meet in the Pacific Gas & Electric Building in San Francisco. There's a very obscure character called J.J. McIntosh, and they start proceedings with a blind toasting of J.J. McIntosh. And they have

Hilda Rumpole lookalike competitions. It's rather lovely. I find that very flattering.

'I also write the books very hastily so that they're full of mistakes and they can have long meetings trying to decide …' He breaks off chuckling at the idea of roomfuls of Rumpole fanatics considering the writer's untidy narratives.

'Is the cult of the Rumpole devotee confined to America?'

'That's the Americans. I think they have several in America. When I went there, they came from everywhere. Israel. There are great Rumpolians in Israel.'

'The name Rumpole …'

'I had a different name for him. I can't quite remember what it was, but when I found there was a real barrister with the same name, I changed it to Rumpole.'

'And you've always managed to avoid libel?'

'Yes. So far.'

He's laughing. As I pack up to leave, I wish every day could be as enjoyable as this. And I'm quite pleased to have made John Mortimer, the eminent QC, laugh – even if the man has the enviable ability of finding comedy in almost every situation.

Chapter Three

In the Moment

AN INTERVIEWER NEEDS TO BE versatile.

The studied casual approach I favoured in interview situations didn't always work, as was illustrated by a visit to a male victim of paramilitary punishment beatings in Northern Ireland who'd been persuaded to discuss his life story with me. Despite street sign names on the estate having been removed, I eventually found the correct road, but the numbers had also been taken off all the front doors. As I strolled along conspicuously, I was conscious of being stalked by a group of shaven-headed young men in football shorts. Suddenly, an anonymous voice commanded from a doorway, 'Hey you. In here.'

With holes in the interior walls and doors, the house and furniture displayed signs of having been trashed. This was probably a crime scene. It was a hot summer's day, yet the curtains remained drawn. In boxer shorts, an older man, his tanned skin creased and leathery, lay stretched along a deep sofa watching a racing channel on a gigantic TV screen. Taciturn, his cold eyes betrayed his obvious disapproval of my presence. My host was jittery, springing to his feet at the sound of a car engine and anxiously peering out to check the street. I sat on an outsize leather armchair and, thinking I needed to calm the interviewee down, began chatting, establishing a rapport, finding common ground. Or so I thought.

The interviewee looked at me in disgust. 'Where are your questions?' he barked. 'You're a reporter. Ask your questions.'

He was right. I needed to respect that he was living on the edge, get the facts and get out of there as quickly as possible. 'So when was your last punishment beating?' Already stripped to the waist and wearing snazzy football shorts, he pointed to the fresher-looking scars on his forearms and shins. 'When was your first?' He indicated some livid discoloured weals on his shaved head and yellowing, healed, bullet-wound blotches on elbows and knees. 'Did you not think of leaving the jurisdiction after the first attack when you were beaten with iron bars?'

There was neither time nor need for peremptory palaver or the usual pleasantries. We were here to talk about violence, the causes and results of that violence, and the spectre of further such violence in the future; if the interviewee had a future, which I worried he mightn't have. In this case, I chased down the facts and left as quickly as possible.

Generally, it helps to be encouraging in conversation. However, interviewing celebrities can be hazardous.

While interviewing Van Morrison in a cafe off Kensington High Street, my friend Liam Fay was astonished when the singer, taking umbrage at some innocuous question, demanded loudly that he be given the tape. Sensing Van was about to grab the recorder, Liam reacted quickest. Tape machine in his grasp, he pushed his chair back and swiftly exited the cafe as the frustrated singer bellowed his displeasure. There was a tube strike that day and taxis were impossible to come by. Ten or fifteen minutes later, while waiting for a bus on the high street, Liam was startled to hear wild shouting and, in a cameo that still haunts his dreams, turned to see Van, red-faced and excited, pork-pie hat askew, rushing towards him and swinging his jacket like a whip. Leaping onto the platform of the first passing London bus, the interviewer escaped, tape intact.

I once witnessed a colleague being attacked by an irate film producer. It was not a pretty sight.

I was having afternoon coffee in the far corner of a spacious Dublin hotel lounge when I spotted a journalist setting up for what appeared to be a professional engagement. Having folded his coat over an upholstered chair, he produced a tape recorder, a clipboard, a stopwatch and a reporter's notebook from his briefcase. He meant business. Not wishing to put him off his stride, I remained discreetly tucked behind the pages of a newspaper.

A surgeon entering the operating theatre, his modus operandi was markedly different to mine. I'd simply memorise a few questions which, I hoped, would act as invisible signposts pointing me in a useful direction. Appearing well organised wasn't part of my shtick.

The interviewee arrived. Wearing a shaggy angora sweater, trousers with a loud check, and bright woolly hair, Ken Russell looked as cuddly as Rupert the Bear's grandfather. I felt slightly miffed. Russell was a great director and had a reputation for being truculent, but I'd still like to have met him. Unfortunately, I hadn't known he was in Dublin or why. I had a sinking feeling I'd been scooped.

After the handshakes, the interview began. I resumed perusing the broadsheet. A few minutes later, raised voices disturbed the calm. I glanced to check who had entered the lounge. Rugby supporters perhaps? No likely suspects. I carried on reading.

A voice was raised again soon afterwards and this time it sounded distinctly angry. I peeked out from behind my newspaper and was treated to the spectacle of Ken Russell hoisting himself up and berating the interviewer. 'How dare you … you pup …' He was waving his arms menacingly. Still seated, the interviewer looked petrified. Russell's assistant rushed in and, gallantly attempting to calm the virtuoso director who was doing a passable impersonation of a reawakened Vesuvius, began to usher him towards the exit. Alarums and excursions, the scene was not unlike the Godfather of Soul, James Brown, ending one of his legendary concerts at the Apollo Theatre in Harlem.

Just as he finally appeared to have left the lounge, Russell broke free and rushed back in. His face twisted in fury, he appeared intent on doing damage. Frustrated by the armchairs and coffee table impeding his progress, he rolled up his bumper edition of *Harper's Bazaar* and flung it at the interviewer's head. Around the room, elderly ladies paused in horror over their afternoon iced fancies. Not wishing to embarrass the journalist, I retreated once more behind my newspaper, thankful that the broadsheet afforded me ample camouflage in a crisis.

Calm descended. A few minutes had passed when a smothered cough prefaced a discreet greeting. 'You saw that?' It was the ashen-faced interviewer.

'I could hardly miss it.'

'Don't tell anyone about it, please.'

'Of course not. But you've got a brilliant story there. It'll make a great feature.'

'I won't be writing it. It's too embarrassing.'

'Don't be daft. You've got a fascinating yarn to report. Discuss it with your editor.'

I wasn't being cavalier. I was speaking from hard-earned experience. Some months earlier I had turned up to interview Sinéad O'Connor, who was enjoying a breakthrough moment with her majestic version of the Prince song 'Nothing Compares 2 U'. Unfortunately, I was the last interviewer on what had been a busy day for the singer; she was tired and bored, and announced that she wanted to go shopping with her friend. The interview quickly descended into farce.

Given the bum's rush, I phoned my features editor in distress. 'You're going to have to find another feature to fill the space,' I bleated. As I recounted my tale of woe, the calming tones of my experienced female boss reassured me, 'That's a wonderful story. Write it exactly as you're telling me. It's really insightful.'

When the feature appeared under a sub-editor's headline, 'I don't want to talk about it', a hungry Irish stringer for a London music weekly jumped on an early edition, filleted the copy and recycled many of the quotes. Making headlines in the UK, he had himself a lucrative little earner. I had done the work. He collected the cheque. Every day is a learning day, I guess.

The Ken Russell story did eventually appear in print, which is why I feel I can share it with you. If truth be told, it didn't fully capture the flavour of Russell's volcanic indignation at having been repeatedly tested on allegations of misogyny, which, if I recall correctly, centred largely, if not exclusively, on his bonkers satire *The Devils*, which gave full, grotesque, phantasmagoric play to cloistered nuns, witchcraft, hysteria, violence, cruelty, sex and exorcism.

Some, if not all, interviewers might have left the more contentious questions until near the end of the conversation. There are no rules of engagement, no blueprint for the process. It may be that one interviewer decides to set a no-nonsense tone early on, while another might prefer to get some responses on tape before heading into potentially stormy waters.

I sometimes feel the most effective interviewers are the ones who contrive to make themselves invisible.

BRENDA FRICKER – April 1990

I encountered Christy Brown just once. It was at the celebrations for my uncle Noel Ginnity's wedding – late 1960s, I recall. Luke Kelly was best man and the party in the house, attended by musicians, painters, actors and a cavalcade of colourful characters, was riotous.

Taking refuge in the hallway, I was nearest the front door when someone began pounding on it. Acting as an impromptu concierge, I was confronted by the celebrated author and painter in his wheelchair. He seemed in a frenzy of excitement. I hadn't a clue what he was saying or who was with him. Not that it mattered. Christy sped past me, heading for the kitchen, where drink was flowing and the action was most intense.

Theatre producer Noel Pearson had long believed in the cinematic power of Christy's story, a boy from a large, poor, working-class Dublin family overcoming the disabilities of cerebral palsy to become a successful writer and painter, as told in his autobiography, *My Left Foot*. Having received five Academy Award nominations, Pearson's film, directed by Jim Sheridan, won two Oscars at the awards ceremony in Los Angeles on 26 March 1990. Daniel Day-Lewis was voted best actor. In winning the best supporting actress category, Brenda Fricker became the first Irish-born actor to win an Oscar since Barry Fitzgerald in 1944.

Following a hectic few days in Hollywood after the ceremony, Brenda flew to Dublin. I was probably just checking on her whereabouts when I rang her family home. Her father, Des, who had been a journalist, disarmed me by revealing that his daughter was in bed asleep, having flown in on the red-eye from LAX a day earlier. It was mid-afternoon. A few hours later, Des phoned me to confirm details of our meeting.

He didn't have to, of course. But Des was considerate and obliging. Like father, like daughter.

***

'It was worth winning an Oscar just to see his joy,' says Brenda of her father, when we meet the following afternoon in a quiet suburban lounge.

'Did you find the whole Oscars experience and Hollywood a culture shock?'

'I lived in America for a year a long time ago and I found the culture shock then. I think to go into Los Angeles as a winner, you don't see the real Los Angeles because they are so into winning that you're everybody's friend. I wouldn't like to go in as a loser. Jesus, they'd walk all over you.

'It was interesting. Six weeks ago nobody knew my name in Hollywood and now everybody's queueing up to say hello. That's very weird. And quite frightening. It's intrusive as well.

'I wasn't there long enough to work it out, to learn all the rules of the game, nor even know what the game is, never mind the rules. It was weird.'

'Have you noticed any attitude changes since you came back?'

'No. Not really. Obviously everybody's thrilled and the amount of joy that everybody else is getting. I haven't had time to sit down and ask myself how I feel. Jet-lagged and hungover is about as far as I've got.' She laughs at the idea of her exhaustion. Back in Ireland just over twenty-four hours, she's possibly unaware of the demands that are about to be made on her time.

As an interviewer, it's a relief to be able to be enthusiastic and mean it. '*The Woman Who Married Clark Gable* was genius. I went to see it twice.'

'I'm glad you mentioned that. It was made in black and white, which is my favourite. I love that little film. I think it's one of the best things Bob Hoskins ever did.'

'I heard a rumour that you had to strive to win the part in *The Field*.'

'I had to beg for it because Jim Sheridan said to me, "Noel Pearson doesn't think you're physically right for the part."

'I thought, *What do you mean by that? I've read the script. I can see how she was a kind of gaunt face, but you can do that with make-up. What's the problem?*

'He said, "I'll get Noel."

'I said, "You will not. I'll get Noel."

'I phoned Noel and he said, "You're too fat." [Laughs] Being as blunt as he always is. I got upset and I thought, *He's right*. I phoned Jim back and I said, "I want this part and I never asked for a part before."

'This was around July and I knew they weren't filming until September/October, so I said to Jim, "I'm just going to phone you four times a day until I get this part. And I'll give you my word of honour that I'll lose at least a stone before the time." I was getting nowhere, so eventually I said to Jim, "Do you think I can't act? If you think I can't act, I'll stop pestering you because I totally respect the decision." He said, "No. There's no problem about acting. Do you really promise to lose the weight?" I said, "If I give you my word, I won't break it." So I lost 28 pounds.'

'But you had put on weight for *My Left Foot*.'

Brenda looks at me askance and declares, 'And for *Big Maggie* for Noel Pearson. And then he says, "You're too fat." It's funny, when I had the weight on people were saying to me, "Jesus, you've put on an awful lot of weight." And I was thinking, *Robert de Niro put on four stone and they say, "What a wonderful actor."* You never get that if you're a woman. You just look fat.'

'Those great Irish women parts you've been playing prompt me to ask if you feel Irish women are more oppressed than women of other nationalities?'

'No, I don't. In certain ways they are because they have the Church on their backs as well. They haven't got things like divorce.

'In a play I did six or seven years ago, *The Ballroom of Romance*, which was about a woman who was isolated in the country. I got letters from all over the world from women who were in that situation and identified completely with it.

'There's poverty all over the world. There are Mrs Browns all over the world with underprivileged children, with children with cerebral palsy and all kind of diseases. I don't think it's totally Irish. I think it's universal. Unfortunately.

'There are incredible women who have a very tough life, and I wish I was one-eighth as good as any of them. I play these wonderful women. It's so depressing.'

'Can roles sometimes impinge to such an extent that they become depressing?'

'Playing saints can become depressing certainly,' she says sipping her pint of larger. 'If I was to have the same attitude to acting as Daniel Day-Lewis, I'd be dead. I'd be in a mental home because I couldn't align the two, because I'm not a nice person as many people think I am. I have a very vicious tongue. I have a very fast temper. I haven't got one ounce of the patience that the women have that I play. So I have to keep it at arm's length.

'It can get in on you sometimes. You come home from playing this saint all day and you're snapping the nose off somebody for no reason. On the other hand you can use it positively and say, "I'll try and be more like them."

'Three weeks before I started filming *My Left Foot* I said, "I'm not going to use any of the mod cons in the house." I've no children, but I'd do everything by hand. I'll not use any electricity and just see how tired she will get. I lasted about four days. You try washing sheets by hand and washing the floor by hand and not using the hoover and not using your dishwasher and all the things you're spoilt by; my admiration for the woman went up.'

'The film jolted me into remembering how grim things were in Ireland in the 1950s.'

'She gave birth twenty-two times. Thirteen alive. And having survived in a tiny house. No privacy. None at all. Terrifying. How they came out sane, I don't know. And talking to the surviving brothers and sisters … I didn't do a lot of research. I didn't need to because the script was so good. Chatting about their mother, they said she was good-humoured, intelligent and sensitive. She was strong and patient.'

'One of the nice compliments to you that I noticed, immediately after the awards, the Brown daughters were saying, "We'll grab her and say, 'Well done, Ma!'"'

Brenda beams with delight. 'That's better than an Oscar. You can't get better than that accolade. That's what Daniel said as well. I remember he said he was accepted by the Dublin audiences and the Brown family, and that was all he wanted. He was stunning.'

Brenda's eyes are bright. This encounter is warm and upbeat. The woman seated opposite me, in a discreet lounge bar booth by a window, has the aura of someone on the first day of a summer sun holiday by the Mediterranean, even if the afternoon spring sky in the south Dublin suburbs is overcast and grey.

'Excellent script apart, what difficulties did you encounter playing the role of Mrs Brown?'

'The script was brilliant, and when I read it, I knew I had to do it. That was the first time I ever felt like that. And luckily there was no problem in doing it. Mrs Brown wasn't complex. She had no time to be complex. She was too busy being a mother and a wife. It was all there in the words. There was nothing to do.'

'What struck me was …'

Alert and clued-in, Brenda's antennae are hyper-sensitive. 'Do you mean problems working with Daniel?'

'Well, yes.'

'No. I think some of the younger actors found it [his method] a bit threatening. I didn't know that he was going to stay in his wheelchair all the time. We had two days' rehearsal and he came in in the wheelchair and I was knocked out. It was the first time I'd seen him in the wheelchair. The last time I left him, he was this hunk of a man with the hair flowing. Suddenly he was Christy in his chair. We did a bit of rehearsing and I was looking at him, and then Jim called a lunch break. And he stayed in the chair. We all got a little bit embarrassed, as you do around people in wheelchairs, not knowing what to do.

'Little Eanna [MacLiam, who played Benny in the film] wheeled him out. And I thought, *This is going to go on the whole way through.* And for about ten seconds I was quite threatened by it. I thought, *Can I talk to him as Daniel, an actor? You know, I need to get the job right. Or are we going to be stuck with him being Christy all day?* But that didn't happen at all. You could talk to him as Daniel because he would stay in character as Christy. Which is hard to understand because he'd talk, "Ney nah heh." But talk as an actor. Once you got past the first ten minutes of that, you were away. I have so much admiration for the man.'

'I thought it must have been challenging for Tom Cruise to play opposite Dustin Hoffman's complex autistic savant character in *Rain Man*. So I wondered if you encountered acting difficulties working with such an intense character?'

'No. Not at all. I wouldn't compare Daniel and Dustin at all. I'm not a fan of Dustin Hoffman. I think he's totally technical. He's never moved me. I would admire him in the way that I've said before in the case of Sir Laurence Olivier … he's completely a technician. But at the highest point that you can be a good technician, Daniel is that. But he's all heart as well. He's such a giver. There was no problem with scenes being shot again. He's a good, good team member.'

'The other thing is, your own personal story is a cracker. Disaster after disaster and you're still here.'

'In a way, those hard knocks, as I said before, I don't regret one of them. Because you do learn. You learn to appreciate the heights and walk away. The *De Profundis* [out of the depths]. You can't appreciate the heights without having the other. It keeps your feet on the ground. It's all very temporary. If you want to be happy all the time, you have nothing to balance it up against.

'When people say to me, "How do you feel winning an Oscar?"

I say, "I've nothing to compare it with." I don't know. If I win the second one, I'll know.'

'Do you still get your mood swings?'

'Oh yeah. I think depression is a national characteristic. I have it under control now. There'll be a low after this, I'm sure. There'll be a lull. There won't be a depression, which is a different thing.'

'How did you come to terms with depression?'

'First of all, by using friends. Calling on friends. And giving them a hard time. I'm thinking of two or three friends in particular – I don't know how I stayed friends with them. Honestly.

'You find an inner strength if people believe in you. When people do believe that you're not a piece of shit when you think you are and convince you that they really believe that, that's a terrific starting point. And you do get stronger as you get older. Your need to be liked gets less. You learn to say no to certain things that you were spending energy on that you should not have been spending energy on …

'I still get depressed, but I know the signals now. I can see it coming. And I can avoid it. The black dog on the shoulder as Churchill said.

'You've very little control over it. As I say, you learn the signs. You learn to dodge it occasionally. And then you get maybe one day when it catches you out. But in the last couple of years, I've only had a couple of weeks … Never a full week even. And that's great. Hang in there. Don't be afraid to use your friends. If they're any good they'll stick by you.'

'Now you're having people like me and other journalists coming and sticking their noses into your career and your private life. Do you find that heavy duty?'

'Yeah, I do, yeah. But I promised Noel Pearson that I'd do as much for this film as I could and I've kept my word. It's part of the job I don't like because I'm not naturally talkative about myself unless I choose who I talk to. You're actually being forced to talk to people you haven't chosen to talk to and that's difficult. But it's only when I'm misquoted that it's really annoying. The English press isn't great.'

'Oh, the story about you saying the Oscar was a great advantage because it was going to get you more money …'

'I know, and they said I left my marriage to follow a career. It was lies. And it affects other people. And people accuse them. They don't seem to think about that at all. And then you say, "I didn't say that at all." They slightly believe you, but they kinda think, *Maybe she's gone a bit funny now that she's won an Oscar, y'know*. A lot of people's attitudes change as well. They think you've got a big head now. That can be very annoying. One paper made remarks about my mother. My mother has been dead since 1981. That's hurtful. Because I miss her.'

At this point we veer into a chat about her father. It's an affectionate and hilarious exchange about the person she calls 'a darlin' man'.

I say that I had been thinking of asking if her father had been supportive of her decision to become an actor, but that now seems redundant. What is of interest is why Brenda is an actor in the first place.

She laughs at the enquiry and appears to head me off at the pass.

'It's what I get paid to do. That's a straight answer. It's the only thing I ever got paid for really, so I just went on doing it. But no, he was always supportive in anything, anything at all, that I would have chosen to do. He's totally unjudicial, which is challenging when you're very young.'

I was aware that Brenda had spent long stints in hospital as a teenager. Once when she'd been knocked from her bike, and then when she contracted tuberculosis.

'Apart from later stints in hospital,' I add, probably thinking of those times in my own childhood when I spent lengthy spells bedridden in hospital wards, 'how was it being in hospital as a teenager?'

'I was in hospital when I was fourteen until eighteen. I missed an awful lot of the craic.'

'The formative years.'

'Yeah. And I think that's where the need for privacy was developed. There was this desperate, desperate need to be alone. I have to have it.'

'Were you wildly introverted? You would have been, probably.'

'I had to be. I was in a hospital room on my own for nearly three and a half years at that age and you had to look inwards. There wasn't much there, so I had to develop it. I think that's where the need for privacy comes from. I just have to be alone at a certain point in the day. It's very difficult for people. It was difficult in my marriage. It didn't break my marriage up or anything. But it was very difficult for Barry [Davis] to understand, because people think that you're rejecting them. And you're not.'

'That's understandable. It's just a need, as the Americans might say, to be in your own space.'

'In your own space.' Brenda rolls the phrase around on her tongue and chuckles. 'More and more, I think, with the age we live in, too.'

'It's important in general terms, but you got to it before the '60s generation or whatever.'

'Maybe. But also when you think about acting, one of the main ingredients of acting is communication and you're communicating your emotions all day so when you've done twelve hours on a set you need to go home and be in touch with yourself for a couple of hours and go for a walk with the dog and look at the sky and walk on the grass and just be real for a while. I can't live without it. I really can't. It's really important to me.'

I dredge up something that impressed me as a schoolboy. 'The ancient Greeks had it covered with *gnōthi seauton* carved on the temple at Delphi: know thyself.'

'To thine own self be true. When you take a simple thing like that and really try and do it every day, it's very tough, isn't it. If you can do it for three days out of seven, you're not doing too badly.'

'You mentioned getting lots of letters after *The Ballroom of Romance*. Is it a bit soon for you to be getting them after your Oscars win, or were you already receiving them for Mrs Brown since the release of the film?'

'Boxes of them,' says Brenda, with a sense of amazement. 'Literally cardboard boxes of them. Full. A friend of mine was over and I couldn't open the door. The house is like a flower shop. People are just so generous. To take the time and buy a card and write it and get it stamped. I'm no good at that kind of thing. Put it in an envelope and find a postbox. That's a lot of time and effort. I'm going to have to spend weeks answering them now.'

'You might not have been here and possibly missed it, but something's happened in the Irish psyche in the past five or six years. There have been Irish success stories with the likes of Barry McGuigan or Stephen Roche and now there's yourself ...'

'It gives courage to other people. I was going down Andrew Street the other night to the Trocadero and grown men were coming up to me and crying and hugging me, and that kind of personal touch, you think, if you can do that by the job you're in, by getting recognition from somebody else for doing it, then that's okay by me. It's very moving.'

'Your appearance at the Oscars ceremony had a powerful effect on people. And not just in Ireland.'

'I'm dying to see the video. Seemingly I didn't make a fool of myself, and I thought in that situation I would have. Jane Fonda said it was the most gracious speech of the evening. I thought, *My God, that's very nice*.'

She laughs at what she considers the incongruity of the moment, then adds ruefully, 'I forgot to mention Ray McAnally, though. I was kicking myself. It was the first thing I thought of when I came off.'

'The problem is you've only got forty-five seconds to speak. You need to be on your marks. Time your run, as they say in football.'

'People get cut off. Your heart goes out to them. God, I'd die.'

'It probably seems worse in the room than it's perceived on the TV.'

'The thing I remember most was my name was read out. I can't remember then. I have a blank.

'I remember thinking, *Thank God, the awards are on this side of the stage and I'm just here*. Daniel had to walk the whole way across. God love him, his legs nearly gave out.

'And then you turn around and look out, and every single film star you have ever seen on the screen in your life was looking at you. And I can't remember anything of the next ten minutes.'

She laughs again. A nervous, relieved laugh.

'My earrings were going. I could feel my knees going. I remember putting my two hands on the thing and all I could think of was, *Say something … something … something. Just say something*. It felt weird. Like a car-crash. Terrifying. I'm glad that it didn't come out too bad.

'There's a certain arrogance in not preparing a speech. I hadn't thought of it in that way at all. Maybe it was arrogance. I don't know. It never crossed my mind that I was going to win. This is completely truthful. Daniel was in such a state of nerves. Jim and Noel were in bits. I was going around playing Mrs Brown, calming them all down.

'I didn't even know my nomination was next. My agent said, "You're up next." I said, "Oh that's grand. That'll be over in a minute." And then they said my name. Extraordinary. It is an extraordinary feeling.'

Looking back, what is extraordinary and truly special is that I'm sitting with a woman who has just returned from Hollywood with an Oscar, which is a really big deal. And she's relaxed, in the moment, generous of spirit, and candid and fearless in chatting to a stranger.

I compare this to my experience with a musician whose career I championed and encouraged in the press and on radio, affording him plenty of coverage whenever asked, which prompted his mother to once contact me to say thank you. No need. It was my job, even if other critics scoffed at his babble and bluster. But when the musician won an Oscar, my editor called and said, 'Can you get an interview with that chap you've been writing about these last few years?' I made various calls and said, 'I just need a couple of first-hand quotes.' Each response came back the same: 'Sorry, he says he's interviewed out.'

Seeing Brenda buoyant, with a calm sense of optimism and expectancy, I wonder where she might go from here. 'Have you an idea of what you'd like to do next?'

'I want to make more films.'

'Do you prefer filming to being on stage?'

'I do and I got knocked for saying this. There's an awful lot of snobbery around theatre. There's so much. It's a load of bollocks. I like the immediacy and spontaneity [of filming]. I know people who come to watch filming get bored with the hanging around and doing things over and over again. It isn't [boring] when you're doing it. But for people watching it's very boring. Because you're keeping your distance and you're concentrating and what you're paid to do is when you're in front of the camera. I like that. People say you have no control over it. You have when you work with people like Jim [Sheridan], who lets you go and lets you watch the rushes. You have a chance to do it again if you get it wrong. You can get closer to being better than you can on the stage. You can have a right off-night, and somebody who's paid twenty pounds for a ticket is not getting their money's worth. Yeah, I love working on film. I'd love to do more.'

A sudden thought strikes her. 'Is my face going red from this [pint]?' she asks with concern as she tucks into a second one.

'No. Not at all. You'll probably feel it beforehand. An allergic reaction, is it?'

'I used to be legendary for drinking people under the table. I can't do it any more, though. Ah, but it's good, though. I could be in trouble otherwise.'

She laughs quietly.

Feeling a twinge of guilt that I'm not joining her and that I might be seen as a killjoy or, worse still, judgemental, I blurt out unnecessarily, 'I haven't had a drink since June.'

'And how are you doing?' she enquires with the quiet, genuine concern of someone who has asked this question before.

'Grand, thanks. It's not a major problem.'

She nods her assent. 'It's good to clear your system out.'

'Yes, that's it exactly.' I explain that I've been on a massive sugar and yeast detox, not even drinking tea or coffee – a programme that proved wonderfully rejuvenating.

'I hardly drink at all in Bristol. [Brenda played Megan Roach in the BBC medical drama *Casualty*, which was filmed in Bristol.] There's no time to drink. But this is a special occasion.'

'For sure. Enjoy every minute of it.'

'The Trocadero [restaurant] gave me an absolutely wonderful welcome [home from the Oscar ceremony]. There was champagne on the house. It was lovely. Really nice.'

'Quite apart from anything else, it must have been a buzz to come home from England and headline on stage at the Abbey Theatre in *Big Maggie*.'

'Oh yeah. That was. Twelve years out of the country and nobody asked me to work. And I was dying to work. To go into the Abbey and have the best press in twenty years, that was a thing. The first night of *Big Maggie* in the Abbey was something I will never forget. It was extraordinary.

'When they gave a standing ovation at the end, I really thought – because I'd done that new ending – I don't think it's as strong as the original ending, but I'd chosen to do that because it was the only thing he [John B. Keane] had written in years and it's a beautiful piece of writing and I wanted the audience to hear it. ["I'm alone now. But I'm free. And there's not too many can say that …"] But it was nerve-racking to step out and talk straight to the audience. By the end of it, I was really nervy. And I saw them standing up and I thought they were going to lynch me. I really thought I'd blown it. Then I heard them clapping and I thought, *Oh, no, I've done something right.* Then it was just lovely. That was a very proud moment.

'What have I done to deserve all this? Amazing. Something bad's going to happen.'

She laughs as if acknowledging a ludicrous inbuilt mix of pessimism and superstition.

I protest. 'No, no. You're well-centred.'

Brenda agrees. 'I am well-centred. As I said, my father brought up myself and my sister on this whole thing of self-sufficiency. And then the years in hospital and all that. And the kind of friends I have. It's terrific. They won't take any bullshit from me. And the dogs. I'm happy to get up in the morning and walk them. When your call is for 6.30 or 7, you have to be out on the beach at half five in Bray. That clears the old cobwebs. That's all important.'

Self-aware, she pauses and remarks humorously, 'Oh God, it sounds boring.'

'Should you be tackling Hollywood? Or have you agents sifting through stuff?'

'If you get an Oscar nomination, things are happening very fast even then. And if you win an Oscar it opens an awful lot of doors. I couldn't get a work permit six weeks ago. I want to work in America. And I want to work in London. I'd like to be able to take my father on a world tour or something. That's what you do it for, isn't it? The freedom. And the freedom not to work as well. I don't like working. I'd much prefer to lie in bed with a book all day. That's my idea of a good day, y'know.'

'A good doss.'

She lights up again. 'That's a great word. "A good doss." I haven't heard that word for ages.'

'I'm interested in seeing *The Field*.'

'It's extraordinary. My part is minuscule and they've quite rightly cut out most of it. And I asked Jim to cut even more out of it. But it's a wonderful film. On the other hand, it will keep my name in front of Hollywood because it comes out in August. So I'll go back and have a go at it. Have a bash.

'The thing is, it was such a popular win. It was genuinely popular. A lot of people in America have an Irish grandmother. Everybody I met seemed to be Irish, but apart from that it was a genuinely popular win. I'm not name-dropping, but Gregory Peck came to me and said, "I'm so proud of you. The Academy has grown up at last. They're giving Oscars to people who deserve them." That was a huge compliment. Then he said, "Could I meet the producer and the director?" I went over and got Jim and Noel, and they were like kids. It was a good comment from him.

'And at the party everybody was coming up to the table. It was a really popular win. I think it will be remembered.'

A middle-aged man in a casual sweater apologises for interrupting. Brenda may have escaped the attention of other customers, but this guy is buzzing at the success of this Irish actor. He extends his congratulations and expresses his admiration and gratitude in a dignified manner, then moves on. Brenda takes it in her stride. And is pleased.

She picks up from where she left off. 'I know they spent five million dollars promoting Tom Cruise for an Oscar. We had two million pounds for the whole thing. So Hollywood, as Gregory Peck said, has grown up. They were so generous in their praise, and, in my ignorance, I didn't expect that from Hollywood. That was nice.'

'Did you get much feedback of what the paying customers in the States made of the film?'

'When I was in New York in January it was on just around the block and I thought I'd pop down to have a look at it. There was a 2 o'clock viewing and I couldn't get in. The queue was around the block. I went around at half past four and I couldn't get in. I went at half past eight and couldn't get in. And that was the whole week I was there. A friend couldn't get in in Hollywood either. Now it's open all over America and they're queueing around the block. That was before the Oscar nominations. That's some indication.'

'I wondered if there'd be a cultural divide.'

'And I thought the Dublin accent and everything … so many things. Going to see a film about a foot. You know. We were all wrong. There's nothing. I got a call from a relation in Japan. They're queueing around the block over there. Christy Brown was obviously international, God bless him.

'It's an astonishing triumph. When it was mooted originally, I thought, *How could you make this?* I think it's the man's courage. And the achievement. And his sense of humour. And the fact that Jim didn't show him sentimentally. That's the winner. That's the international appeal. People aren't forced to be sentimental about something.'

'Yes. It's well balanced.'

'Totally balanced. It shows the nasty side of him and the drunken side. And the fighting side of him and all the rest of it. And therefore you saw the whole human being who happened to be Christy. There aren't many of them around. Brilliant. So witty. That language.'

'And it's immensely uplifting. Obviously.'

'Totally optimistic. And it's also Jim learning from the first day. He never directed a film before. He hadn't a clue what he was doing. By lunchtime, he'd cracked it. Extraordinary.'

'That is amazing. Can you recall which scene was shot first?'

'I can. It was the very last scene, when he's going off with the girl, Mary. Jim is amazing. He made a lot of mistakes on *My Left Foot* but, by God, he learned fast.'

'And Noel Pearson, the producer.'

'God bless him. It was his dream. His idea. And it came true. I'm terribly fond of Noel. He's a good man to work for. A good employer. He knows everybody.'

RUDOLF NUREYEV – August 1990

'Khrushchev wants to see you dance.'

Rudolf Nureyev knew he was in deep trouble when he was told that, instead of boarding a flight for London at Le Bourget airport, he'd be flying back to Moscow instead.

The young star of the Kirov Ballet was distraught. He had dazzled critics and audiences alike with the fierce intensity and unabashed self-confidence of his performances in Paris. His artistry had just begun to receive international recognition, but now, surrounded by ruthless KGB agents, he thought, *This is the end.*

It was the most crucial career-defining moment in his life. He needed to escape.

While newspaper headlines spoke of 'Nureyev's leap to freedom', the manner of the dancer's actual defection was more prosaic. On the advice of a friend, who had arranged for the French police to be present at the airport, Rudolf blindsided his minders and approached the policemen, asking for asylum. The physical row that broke out was followed by a diplomatic firestorm, with his Soviet handlers demanding he be handed over. Amid intimidation and accusations of betrayal, an emotionally shocked Nureyev held firm. Although convinced he was 'a traitor' and 'a lost person', he valued the prospect of having more freedom of choice.

Believing he would never see his mother, family or friends again, and conscious of the threat of abduction or assassination by Soviet agents, he made a courageous choice. His defection was an iconic cultural event which defined an era.

Born in Siberia, Nureyev grew up in such dire poverty in wartime Russia that he was known as 'beggar' at school. Later, he trained as a dancer in Vaganova Academy in Leningrad. Following his dramatic defection to the West in 1961, Nureyev revolutionised male dance. The twenty-three-year-old Tatar was an explosive personality who became as culturally influential in Britain as The Beatles, George Best and the entire cast of London's Swinging Sixties arty set. Driven by extremes of passion, his fiery temperament regularly tested conventional manners. In short, he was a sensation.

Margot Fonteyn, the ballerina who was his on-stage partner for over a decade, once explained his outbursts. 'It's easier to dance in rage than in cold blood,' she said. In Byronic style, Rudolf was 'mad, bad and dangerous to know'. For me, he represented a time of great cultural promise and optimistic social change.

So, when he came to Dublin with the Cleveland Ballet in 1990, I requested an interview. My petition was rebuffed by the company's press person. 'Mr Nureyev will not be speaking to the media while in Ireland.'

Initially, I shrugged off my disappointment. But, having joined colleagues for a drink in the Horse and Tram on Eden Quay, where I'd exchange nods with the great Con Houlihan, I had a change of heart. As I was leaving the pub, I remembered the direct-action advice of journalist Derek Dunne.

Months before, I had turned up at the Tottenham Hotspur FC team hotel for an exclusive interview with Paul Gascoigne as arranged by his club's Irish agent, Krish Naidoo, the popular South African-born businessman and philanthropist. Unfortunately, in the aftermath of an embarrassing, tearful incident when England had been beaten in the semi-final of Italia '90 ('Tears We Go' – *The Sun*), the English football star had decided to shun all media contact. I was disconsolate.

'Why don't you just doorstep him?' asked Derek, a proper news reporter, when I met him in the hotel bar. 'Ring his room.' I did, and the ploy worked. Contacted directly, genial Gazza generously agreed to chat.

Although it felt against my nature to invade an artist's space unannounced, I wondered whether a direct approach might work again. It was risky because I didn't wish to antagonise the dancer and experience his withering wrath.

'Nothing ventured,' I thought as I stepped into a phone box (pre-mobile phone days) beside O'Connell Bridge and dialled the ballet company's hotel. I sounded business-like when requesting, 'Mr Nureyev, please.'

'Certainly, sir.'

A moment later, someone with a pronounced Russian accent said, 'Hello, yes?'

Though shocked, I guessed it was the ballet star. I played it straight.

'Good afternoon. May I speak with Mr Nureyev, please.'

'Speaking.'

I briskly explained that I was a journalist and would like to meet and interview him while he was in Dublin.

'What about?' he asked pointedly, a sharp edge to his tone. 'I am not doing interviews.'

Not an expert on ballet, I realised with dismay that I hadn't given this conversation enough prior consideration. Needing to say something, I replied with the first thing that sprang to mind.

'About the mystical power of dance,' I replied airily.

While researching aspects of the hermetic arts, I had the privilege of witnessing magicians and witches raise what they termed a 'cone of power' through ritual and dance. As if by magic, in my moment of need, the memory resurfaced. To many my suggestion might have sounded nonsensical. Not to the ballet star.

'Will you be at the ballet tomorrow?'

'Of course,' I fibbed.

'Come to my dressing room after the second act. We can talk more fully then. Come to the curtain beside the stage.'

'Okay. Thank you. See you then.'

Click.

Who could have imagined that I'd have Paul Gascoigne to thank for meeting Rudolf Nureyev.

***

Thanks to the wonderful Irish promoter, Jim Aiken, I received a front-of-house seat at short notice and, suitably tuxed, rocked up to the old Point Depot where, nose out of joint, the publicity director of the Cleveland Ballet proved petulantly uncooperative and obstructive. 'Speak to Rudolf,' I instructed, 'he's invited me backstage.'

Expecting this to be, at best, a swift meet-and-greet during a break in the company's presentation of *Coppélia*, I'm ushered into the star's dressing-room after Act II. The room is dark, lit only by bulbs around a large make-up mirror in front of which Rudolf sits dabbing himself with a small towel. Clad only in sheer tights, his taut muscular torso glistens with perspiration. He eyes me suspiciously. We exchange greetings. The PR man snatches my tiny tape recorder, which isn't switched on, and barks, 'We allow no recording.'

Rudolf dismisses him curtly and gestures towards a black leather sofa across the room. 'Sit over there,' he instructs in the accent of an imperious Bond villain. 'It's too hot here.'

Notebook in hand, I take my seat and am conscious of Rudolf studying me in the mirror. It's a curious scene. We make and hold eye contact. A frisson of electricity bridges the divide.

I brace myself. Rudolf approaches, casually takes a seat and, unexpectedly, places my tape recorder within my reach. While maintaining eye contact, I switch it on and begin to speak.

Understanding he'll be going back on stage in twenty minutes, I worry that I might upset his concentration. I'm also concerned that, given reports I'd read over the years, he might use my intervention as a spur to psych himself up to a heightened level of rage before the final act. So I apologise for the intrusion and for the upcoming questions.

'It is no problem,' he says with a disarming smile, adding coquettishly, 'so long as you don't harass me.'

My opening gambit is one I've sometimes used with ageing athletes who'd been at the peak of their profession for many years. How do they manage to remain motivated enough to want to continue performing at the highest level?

Rudolf seems stumped, but I reckon it's a question he's asked himself many times.

'I really don't know. I really don't know what to answer. Can you ask David Oistrakh why he played till a very old age? Sviatoslav Richter? Why they still come on stage and play?'

Distinguished Russian violinist and conductor Oistrakh had heroically performed Tchaikovsky's Violin Concerto in its entirety during the Battle of Stalingrad in the harsh winter of 1942. Despite a heart attack in the 1960s, he continued conducting until he died following a concert appearance in Amsterdam in 1974. His friend, the great Russian pianist Richter gave his first recital in 1934 and was still performing in his mid-seventies when referenced by Nureyev. He died seven years later, aged eighty-two.

'Look at the vitality of [Mstislav] Rostropovich [the internationally acclaimed cellist and conductor who was sixty-three at this time]. Obviously they were born with music in them. It is a necessity. They wish to renew themselves in the music. They find fantastic strength in it.'

I don't quite catch the conundrum Rudolf begins to tease out – something about how dancing is not at the same stage of development as music – but he quickly arrives at a firm conclusion. 'Once one is a person on stage dancing, one feels a real person. You transcend yourself. You become something else.'

I think of the sheer physicality of his daily routine and compare it to the lifestyle of friends who are painters, writers and musicians. Only boxers seem to have to endure such a regime of physical punishment and most of them get to retire early. A professional ballet dancer must endure the possibility of arthritis later in life. Why does he continue to put himself through such rigours?

'The other day Alicia Alonso came to see me on my island, and she wanted me to dance with her. She is seventy and I am fifty-two. And we danced.

'Before I or anybody could ask a question she said, "I am dancing because it keeps me alive." So. She is seventy. She did full classes. She rehearsed. She was anxious to have two rehearsals. I wanted to do only one. She wanted to have two rehearsals a day. And she worked three hours at each rehearsal. She worked six hours a day.'

The couple had danced *Poema del Amor y del Mar* in Palma de Mallorca with the National Ballet of Cuba just weeks before we met.

Nureyev's sentences are short. Staccato volleys of wonder, admiration and amazement.

'This desire, this fantastic obsession … I don't think an artist could be an artist if he doesn't have obsession. If you don't have obsession, you cannot be a painter, you cannot be a writer, you cannot be a musician. You have to be possessed by it. There's no remedy except to do it and get it over.'

I'd love to follow this conversational thread but, conscious of my limited time allocation, I know my finished feature demands a change of subject.

'In your travels do you get the opportunity to savour the culture of each country, or do you feel confined to hotels and theatres?'

'Well, I went to China. I staged *Don Quixote*. I was trying to see the Peking Opera, which was denied. They did everything possible not to let me see that company because they thought it was not great in that area.'

Yet again, Nureyev wouldn't be denied. There's a quiet impishness to his tone as he continues.

'But anyway, finally I found where the theatre was and it was a wonderful experience. It was a workers' section. In China it is men who are watching. Like here you have a majority women. It is men. They came directly from factories. Smelly. Stinking. Smokey. They came and sat and enjoyed. They laughed at every line.'

For a moment, he sounds wistful. 'It was wonderful. There was a wonderful bit of dancing at the end.'

And then he's off again, bursting with exuberance. 'Thai dancing is wonderful. They also have a wonderful school. We had an extraordinary experiment. They asked us to tell some story. So I told them the story of *Swan Lake* and asked them to do it in their language.

'They have a prince and princess, and they always dance at the same speed without any climaxes and it's always absolutely even and liquid. Then there's a monkey and there's a giant who could be evil.'

With the light from the bulbs around the mirror across the room creating an aura around his head and shoulders, Nureyev's sculpted signature high-cheekboned features brighten as a further thought strikes him. 'At one point I thought to bring schools together. Different schools, Chinese schools, Thai schools and French, and do the same story told differently.'

Knowing I'm just a random newspaper man in a random city, I try to create a bridge no matter how flimsy. 'I was at the Bolshoi in Moscow earlier this year and my friends say Vladimir Ashkenazy's [Soviet-born pianist and conductor] return to Moscow last year was highly emotionally charged. Have you plans for returning or perhaps filming there?'

'We were supposed to do *The Overcoat*. We were invited there. Nobody from Cleveland Ballet told us and I'm not particularly interested in going back.'

I sense the weight of history descending. There's a lot to unpack here, but just then the backstage Tannoy system crackles with a message. 'Ladies and gentlemen, five minutes.'

The stage manager's piped announcement signals the end of our conversation. I rise, thank the ballet star for his courtesy and shake hands. As Rudolf returns to the dressing-room mirror, I offer him a slim volume of poetry by W.B. Yeats to read on his travels. He smiles, thanks me warmly and turns to inspect his make-up.

As I'm about to close the door, leaving him alone, I glance back and notice, disconcertingly, that this iconic superstar seems unaccountably sad. There's a curious tenderness in the moment, as if the man is contemplating the possibility that even he might not be able to dance forever.

I stepped away aware that I'd been granted an audience with a potentate in his inner sanctum. It felt as if I'd been shooting the breeze with the Pope in his sacristy just moments before he stepped onto the high altar.

I wondered why I had been granted this audience, brief and intense though it had been. It certainly wasn't because the superstar was anxious to share his thoughts with readers of the *Evening Herald*. For months I asked myself, *Why?*

I had suspicions, but I didn't know then that my host harboured a cruel secret. He was seriously ill. Two and a half years later, it was announced that Rudolf Nureyev, the most charismatic and enigmatic person I'd ever met, had died of AIDS.

It was then I understood, that in his torment, Nureyev reached towards one thing that might save him. He had taken the opportunity to reiterate, reconfirm or perhaps simply invoke his belief in the mystical power of dance.

Chapter Four

A Balancing Act

INTERVIEWS ARE NOT INTERROGATIONS. THE interviewee needs to get something from the exchange, even if it is just a plug for their latest project.

Avoiding getting bogged down in too much flimflam about the *projet du jour* can often prove tricky. Sometimes it might be prudent to allow the avalanche of hype at the start of the conversation and then digress. Other times it might feel better to introduce the topic mid-way through the conversation. It depends on how determined the interviewee is to promote their current obsession. You don't have to use any or all of the ensuing waffle, but the interviewee feels better for having done their duty.

It's a balancing act. A trade-off.

If you think the interviewee has wasted too much valuable time selling their product, one silly old trick worth considering is one which might remind you of the fictional television detective Columbo, who, as he was about to leave, would intone, 'Oh, and one last thing …' So, you thank the interviewee and wrap up the interview. This is a relief for those interviewees who've been tense and nervous. As they relax in the knowledge that their ordeal is over, throw in a casual, non-taxing question that might prompt a response. And then say brightly, 'That's great. We should get that.' The dynamic will have changed and you should be able to explore a couple of interesting further angles on the record before finally wrapping things up.

Some interviewers set out to test the patience of their guest; to see how they perform under pressure, how they respond to questions about little-known skeletons in camouflaged cupboards. I tended to avoid this approach, as becoming known as a spiky interviewer could put off prospective interviewees. I'd seen columnists come and go. I was in this for what I considered to be the long haul. At least six weeks or so, I hoped. Three months would be marvellous, I thought. I preferred to simply have a robust chat, and I genuinely appreciated and enjoyed the exchanges. Well, usually.

As the months rolled by and I rolled out to interview people from all walks of life and every stratum of stardom, I came to relish the nuances of those meetings. Some people seemed to enjoy being interviewed – not just the egotistical and self-obsessed. Occasionally I would think the interviewee was using our conversation to take stock, measure their successes and failures while considering their future. Other times, an interviewee's curmudgeonly attitude would suggest this was a chore they'd been forced to undertake against their will and, really, an afternoon of root canal work would be a more enjoyable option.

All I wanted was an interesting conversation – or at least a memorable quote.

Gary Lineker was football's head prefect when I met him in the spring of 1990 ahead of that summer's World Cup finals in Italy. He was holder of the Golden Boot award for the most goals scored in the previous finals and was on message while in Dublin promoting a new razor for men. We chatted amicably at a hotel and, as expected, Gary was professional, charming and every bit the clean-cut sporting hero. Frank Worthington had been his idol as a kid. Answering a query on the balance of intuition and craft a striker should have, he explained, 'It's basically about finding space in the penalty area, or making runs, losing defenders. The thing is not to follow the ball but to hope it comes to you. So, when it does, you're on your own.' Great stuff.

People described Gary as being 'very nice'. I didn't pass on the opportunity to travel in the back of a car with him to a supermarket in a suburban shopping mall. That's when the conversation became less formal. I didn't need to remind him that he'd failed to score against Ireland in Stuttgart two years earlier in the UEFA European Football Championship finals. But, as we were being driven across town, I did.

This was at a time when Ireland was benefitting handsomely from a combination of FIFA's Article 18 and Irish citizenship rules, which meant that second-generation players could 'declare' for Ireland. As the conversation swung from Ireland's English manager, Jack Charlton, to the Irish squad, Gary got a bit tetchy: 'A lot of Irish players are basically English people ... I think it's regarded as a bit of a joke really.' At this point I reminded Gary that England star John Barnes was Jamaican. Checkmate.

'Oh, he is,' he responded tartly, 'we can't grumble.' And then, revealing that football's so-called 'Granny rule' was still a sore point, added sarcastically, 'I went to an Irish dentist. I've an Irish filling.'

With the England v Ireland match just weeks away in Sardinia, and football matters high on most people's agenda, his irritation made front-page news. Confident of his position and views, Gary was aware of what he was saying. He wasn't stupid. He understood it would be in print the following day.

Equally smart and refreshingly self-aware, actress Britt Ekland was entertaining and forthright when we met in 1991. Looking back at the time in the mid-1970s when her partner was Rod Stewart, the renowned Swedish beauty said without acrimony, 'I think [during] that whole period of my life I was pretty much taken advantage of, which I didn't realise for many years afterwards. I didn't realise that all these stories that were put out were all fabricated to give him more publicity. That's how naive I was.'

Britt had published *Sensual Beauty*, a book of beauty hints, so I broached the subject of Ivana Trump's facelift. Describing the result as 'beautiful', Britt enthused, 'I know the doctor who did it. He's a very popular LA doctor. I'm sure everybody goes in and says, "Can you give me an Ivana?"'

Ivana had received an uncontested divorce from husband Donald Trump five months earlier and was reported to have received a 14 million dollar settlement. According to Britt, top-of-the-range cosmetic surgery wasn't cheap, adding, 'That's what money can do for you.'

Once the interview is over, that's usually the end of it for the interviewee, for better or worse. Only once during my many years of interviewing did someone attempt to have copy approval. And that was a politician. This was after I'd interviewed a colourful, high-profile public representative, whose business dealings had been under scrutiny in the media. And, in Ireland back then, there were quite a few to choose from. My own sources indicated there was no smoke without fire, so I thought it might be useful to rummage around and see where it might take us. Given my music business background, I was unlikely to be viewed as a threat. I presented as harmless and stole a march on political correspondents and eager newshounds by landing a face-to-face interview.

It was a fascinating encounter, not least for the choreography. Having been greeted as gregariously as a visiting dignitary from a far-flung principality, I was led through portrait-adorned corridors of power to the official's office, where I discovered my seat was much lower than the man behind the grand desk. As I placed my battered cassette recorder on the empty desktop, the elected official reached over and, with a flourish, placed a state-of-the-art flip-top mobile phone beside it. Mobile phones were largely still clunky at the time, but this expensive, sleek machine was at the height of cutting-edge technology. It represented the future. A traveller from an antique land, I was under no illusion as to who was top dog here.

The interview went well and we covered a lot of topics, including the major issues that were exercising the minds of political and business journalists. For background information, I had earlier raided the newspaper's extensive cuttings library and assembled an array of pertinent questions, which I nonchalantly slipped in amid the high-flyer lifestyle shtick.

Afterwards, I rushed back to the office, transcribed the interview and, working closely with the features editor, narrowed down the responses, highlighting the contentious subjects. Next, we had the copy checked by the company's libel lawyers ahead of our deadline.

The following morning I was at my desk, in the corner beside the cartoonist Scratch, when, sometime after 10.30, the phone rang. 'Good morning, Eamon,' boomed the voice of the politician. 'I really enjoyed our little chat yesterday. Oh, by the way, would it be possible for me to read the article before it's printed?' I detected a nervous anxiety behind the bonhomie.

'Aah,' said I confidently, 'it's a very entertaining read. A double-page spread. Very impressive photos. You should be able to pick up the first edition on the street in about twenty minutes. It went to press overnight.'

I swear I could hear the politician's heart plummet like a stone as he wondered if he'd given me a lifechanging hostage to fortune. 'No problem,' he managed, with some further pleasantries before ringing off. I scrutinised the feature immediately and wondered if, perhaps, the various dates and timelines concealed an explosive booby trap. However, there was no negative feedback, no repercussions.

I did get to interview the politician again. This time it was a genuine scoop.

It was some years later; the day after he'd been released from prison. He wasn't meeting members of the media. But when it was explained to him that he'd be wise to do one flagship in-depth interview to help get the newshounds off the hunt, he agreed to meet me at his luxurious home, where I found him somewhat chastened but as spirited and bullish as ever as he protested his innocence. There had been a scandal. He'd been disgraced. He'd been punished. But he was resilient and still in the game.

J.P. DONLEAVY – October 1989

I'd been in the same room as J.P. Donleavy once before.

It was sometime in the mid-1970s and the room was an all-but-empty first-class lounge on a car ferry to Wales. The author was surrounded by a number of attractive, young, American women who hung on his every word.

Cold, tired, hungover and a member of Horslips, I was on my way either to a series of gigs or a lengthy recording session overseas. As the author's rich, sonorous baritone filtered across, I wasn't alone in wondering how it was that a middle-aged, bearded man should be accompanied by a coterie of female admirers. I mean, he wasn't even in a glam rock band: pale, spotty and in need of a hot meal.

As fate would have it, at the end of the next decade, just as I was coming to grips with having to deliver a weekly high-profile newspaper interview, the editor passed me a note about J.P.'s new book. And so, on a dull autumn evening, I'm ushered into a hotel suite on the upper floor of the Shelbourne Hotel, where the glow from the table lights is low and J.P. is seated in a comfortable chair in a well-upholstered study off the main bedroom.

He's on the telephone when I enter, accompanied by his publisher. I take a minute to study the man who, according to his publicists, has sold over twenty-five million copies of his most famous novel, *The Ginger Man*.

'That might be slightly more than reality,' J.P. chuckles later.

He's wearing a dependable three-piece tweed suit and sturdy, well-polished brogues. At sixty-three, he retains the erect, flexible figure of a fit middleweight boxer. Under the misguided impression that my host has a reputation for being spiky, I approach our meeting with a degree of trepidation. Any concern that he might prove austere quickly evaporates amid a welter of affable pleasantries.

'Did you ever regret having unleashed *The Ginger Man* on the unsuspecting Irish?'

'No. I rather, somehow, rejoice in this work. People often ask me am I sick of hearing about *The Ginger Man*, but I must insist I never am. I did become conscious some years back now that, as one saw Ireland transforming in front of one's eyes, I thought, *My goodness, I hope* The Ginger Man *has something to do with it*.'

'Was there a danger of becoming trapped by the myth?'

'I suppose one, as an author, capitalises on the myth, but it isn't largely recognised that a lot of my readers, who have got younger and younger over the years, have never heard of *The Ginger Man*. They come to [*The Beastly Beatitudes of*] *Balthazar B*, [*The Destinies of*] *Darcy Dancer* [*Gentleman*] and so on. As my other books got released, they each found a new following. One most peculiar following is the following of *The Onion Eaters*. That's the most strange one because men appear to love this book and maybe some women do.'

Set in post-war Dublin bohemia, Donleavy's rumbustious debut novel was published by the Olympia Press in Paris in 1955, under its pornographic imprint: Traveller's Companion Series. Donleavy was furious. It was banned in Ireland and the United States for obscenity.

'*The Ginger Man* has become an identity tag which one wears. You know, "Here comes the Ginger Man. Screw down the furniture. Put your chastity belt on your wife." That kind of thing.

'I dedicate this present book, *A Singular Country*, to Gainor Steven Crist, who many people thought was a model for [Sebastian] Dangerfield, which in some effect he was, because both our lives were identical when we came to Europe, attended Trinity College, married English wives and so on. *The Ginger Man*, I'm delighted with its existence. And it appears to sell as well now as it did years and years ago.'

'Given the hubbub at the time – the outcry, the censorship, the backlash – how did it affect you? You were out of country, I think?'

'It came surreptitiously. But remember, the Irish who may feel there's censorship in the country and so on, are very avid readers. The book actually received quite a good reception from people who were intelligent and enjoyed reading. Everybody who had gone to England in those days would come back with three or four copies of the book. And, of course, they were handed around, hand to hand. It did finally dawn on me that of anyone I met, no one owned a copy of *The Ginger Man*. Everyone who had one and who read it, had it stolen. Its dissemination must be extraordinary. The times it's been set up in type and reprinted, it could be about ninety times now.'

I had read a battered copy of *The Ginger Man* as an innocent and impressionable young teenager, and found the adult world it portrayed to be terribly depressing. 'Its accounts of raffish boozy womanising may well have reinforced notions of male chauvinism, no?'

'Oh, unquestionably. Yet when some young lady would read the book pre-marriage, they would be of course outraged because all their dreams and myths about the husband they were about to marry were shattered. But then any woman who was, say, over thirty and had been a bit through the mill in marriage, all seemed to grin and quite enjoy it. There are two sections of ladies. Those pre-disaster marriage and those post-disaster marriage.'

'Would you like to have been born a woman?'

'I can't say that I would. I don't think I would. No. Women are to me the source of a lot of one's information in life. Their responses are much more real to what happens in the world. And so women actually are psychically a great kind of reservoir of observation and information which men aren't. Men pretend to have this kind of sham image, in effect, which they establish about themselves. Unlike women, who are very practical and dig into what the realities of life are all about. So I have a great affinity for women and don't strike them or abuse them. I think I can fairly say that I don't think I've ever been struck by a woman either.'

He chuckles into his beard at the image he's conjured up. Born in New York in 1926, the author's father, Patrick John Donleavy, was from County Longford. At this time, J.P. was living in a rambling old house close to Lough Owel outside Mullingar, not far from his father's home county. I wonder if he resembles his father in any way.

'I don't think so,' he replies, considering the question. 'In one respect, yes. He was a great lover of going for walks. And when I was growing up in America, I was fascinated. He was full of curiosity about everything and anything. I can frequently remember walking with him.

'We used to go travelling throughout the United States in the summer. It was quite strange. It would be 2,000 miles long and we would go from town to town and visit various places. We'd do this all summer long. He was fascinated with the United States. Always stopped to enquire and would ask people what they did and who they were. Unlike most Americans, they're not awfully interested because in America you're supposed to keep your mouth shut. If you want to talk, you pay a psychiatrist and it costs you 200 pounds an hour.'

He laughs at the idea of spending hard-earned money on

psychotherapy and then adds, 'That's the whole thing in America. Everyone's desperate to say something in America and everyone is desperate to tell them to shut up. My father would ask questions of people and actually listen. So that was in one respect I resembled him.'

He muses for a moment and then a thought hits him.

'Some years ago, someone heard me giving a radio interview and I mentioned that my father wrote poetry and so he was listed as a Westmeath author [presumably because J.P. lived in that county]. The difference with him as a poet was that he could remember and recite all his poetry. It was as if the record machine's within him. He would recite his poetry to my mother's great embarrassment. He would also tap dance. He'd, impromptu, get up on a table and tap dance, but since he was built like … Tyson, is it? What's Tyson's first name?'

'Mike. "Iron" Mike.'

'Mike Tyson. Yes. My father was actually built like Mike Tyson and was immensely powerful. He could lift a man up in the air in the palm of his hand. And put him down. So if he tap danced on the table, there were great risks. In that sense, I resemble my father to some degree. He was straight out of the bogs of Longford and I'm back in the bogs.'

The conversation is flowing along nicely. Reminiscing comes easily to J.P. I press on. 'Do you feel at home in the Irish environment?'

'Yes, I probably do now. Because almost most of my life has been spent here, when you take from my starting point at Trinity College Dublin until now. The fostering as an author clearly happened here. When I think of my contemporaries, like say Brendan Behan being the first ever to read the manuscript of *The Ginger Man*, all of these kind of things in one's background still concern one a lot and you come back to them. I'm discovering through David Byrne, my publisher, who's here, that I'm unaware how much I might know about Ireland or how much I feel about the country and so on.'

David is in the room, which means we have an audience. He's riding shotgun for his client and, admirably discreet, only interjects once (on future plans) when drawn into the conversation by J.P.

'So Ireland has become very large in one's whole concern, probably. I know that one feels now that one would love to see an economic wonderful thing happen and, indeed, this is the case with Ireland. Ireland is a unique country now, on the tip of Europe, politically the most sensitive area there is in the world perhaps, just outside the fallout from the next big bomb that someone might let off. You know, it's a very unique situation, which, I suppose, the Russians and the Americans recognise. And so, even from my own point of view, I think this is the centre of the world. As I did think many, many years back. I think the expression is even in *The Ginger Man*, "lying on my back, looking up out of the world". In other words, from Ireland. Nothing else mattered outside in the world then, especially. It was quite amazing.'

It becomes obvious that, from his 200-acre estate in Westmeath, J.P. has given plenty of thought to Ireland and the condition he considers 'Irishness'.

'I think this is the thing that makes Irish people come back to this country. It's the identity and the power that life can give your own life here. That's a question that's been asked in England so many times. That the Irish, generation after generation, haven't even been to the country and are maybe third- or fourth-generation English, and yet you see them there, never been to Ireland, and they're Irishmen, total, complete. Listening to the music. Knowing all about it. Fanciful about its images.'

He's on a roll now. It would be rude to interrupt.

'That's the big question now,' he continues, even though I'm unsure of exactly what this question is. 'It's very rare to find anyone who holds out here without having to leave with his tail between his legs, literally. Where I find that quite pronounced is in this building we're sitting in now. The Horseshoe Bar [on the ground floor of the Shelbourne Hotel, which attracted a mix of artists, writers, musicians, politicians, prominent business figures and the "horsey set"]. It's quite interesting. I very rarely come to Dublin. If I do, I'm always elsewhere, but I'll always stop off at The Horseshoe Bar. And then I'll see a whole new set of the same variety and the same thing, and they're living on this high, this thing, before they get driven out. Whatever they're doing. You know, entrepreneurs. Their big dreams all shattered. Bankruptcies down some side street. Some little business and so on.

'That's the other wonderful thing about Ireland; you can get nowhere here.'

J.P. chuckles at this *bon mot*. Whether it's impromptu or carefully cultivated, I'd probably have to re-read his *A Singular Country* to find out.

As an urbane outsider who arrived in Ireland in the mid-to-late 1940s, Donleavy would be ideally placed to chronicle five decades' worth of great social and cultural changes in Ireland.

'That's right,' he says brightly. 'I witnessed all the changes from the so-called "unspoilt" Dublin. When I first arrived here, Dublin would have been as it had been right back 200 years. There were no neon lights then. The granite pavements were all intact. What was present then, which is no longer the fact, is the appalling, unbelievable slums and poverty in Dublin. That was all still here. One has gauged and watched the changes come to it.

'I suppose in *A Singular Country*, it's full of my being aware of this long transition period that Ireland is undergoing. That's how I regard it as being the most extensive revolution in effect to hit any country on the earth. And all of this came dramatically from television, which revolutionised the country. Overnight. That's never happened anywhere. And it's all artificial. The Irish had nothing to do with it. The foreign transmitting thing that came in was immediate, available to every family, intimate in every house. This has brought around this incredible transition.

'You would never imagine, in the case of *A Singular Country*, if someone said, "This book is an insult to morals and religion," which used to be shouted about *The Ginger Man* when it was onstage here. "As an Irishman, I object."

'Or, as Patrick Kavanagh put it, "As an Irishman and a fucking eejit, I object."'

He's laughing now. If laughter can sound melancholic, then I'm thinking Donleavy has the patent.

'I'm famous for being able to put words in Brendan Behan's mouth too. I'm able to quote these people who left us, and it doesn't seem inappropriate at all because they would have said it had they been able to think it.'

The chuckles are coming thick and fast. So I reckon it's time to dip into Dublin's old literary milieu, rumours of which fascinated us when we were growing up in the 1960s.

'Living in Mullingar, do you miss the old Dublin social scene? Trinity, McDaids, the Bailey, The Palace Bar and so on? Has Irish culture lost something with the departure of characters we associate with those haunts?'

'Maybe it has. Unless we discover they have come back to populate the streets again. I remember one or two journalists here that one ran into – journalists are writers in effect – I'd be a reporter here now if I was more expert with the language and could write more quickly, which I can't do.

'So you find these people about, and these characters. The poet who stands in front of Bewley's now. I spoke to him the other day when I was passing by. He sells *In Dublin* magazine. I stopped to chat. I said, "What on earth brought you to Dublin in the first place? You're from Yorkshire." He said, "Well I read a book called *The Ginger Man* and I said, 'That's the place for me.'" So he set off for here.

'There are still the kind of so-called characters around.

'Imposed upon that might be the fact that there's an international kind of thing, like Joe Dolan or these successful pop groups. And they're producing their own sort of poets and characters. Is it The Pogues? They were naming one of their songs after one of my books? *Fairy Tale of New York*. They sound like a lot of characters and look like them too.

'So I think that must still be the case here. Indeed, really if you think of it, Ireland right now must be, for young people growing up, the most vital, wonderful setting imaginable. Walking around the streets last night, they had this most marvellous band on the walkway. The talents were incredible. Girls sitting on the pavement. Maybe about 150–200 young people playing. All quite talented. That's part of poetry and being a character.'

There's a train of thought working its way through Donleavy's mind that eventually pulls into the station.

'As for writers and poets, it's a tough world and they become slightly academic and withdrawn. Novelists especially. You don't see them. They live rather less-available lives. Even in the days of Behan and Kavanagh, I would venture to Dublin only seldom from County Wicklow. If I met Kavanagh, as I've described it, it was always brief.

He'd walk on the street like a battleship whamming through the waves as he whaled along Pembroke Road or somewhere, and he'd see you and meet you and his greeting often was, "Have you got a pound?" "For lending," I think he'd add. And you'd say, "No." "Well fuck off then."'

J.P. laughs at the memory. 'He wasn't quite that rude to me, I must say. But ...'

Lapsing into private reverie, he looks so content in the half-light of the side lamp on the desk that I'm almost afraid to disturb him in what feel like Gothic shadows. Almost. But having heard stories of himself and Brendan Behan fighting in the pub or on the street, I'm anxious to separate myth from reality and wish to hear a firsthand account of their encounters. Even reclining in an armchair, Donleavy is an imposing figure. Combine boxing skills with his athletic physique and you'd have to think Brendan was foolhardy for getting into a scrap with his friend.

'Yes, indeed. In the middle of Fleet Street. Stopping traffic on either side. Poor old Behan just could not fight. And especially not without a broken glass in his hand. He was pretty helpless. But Behan up a dark alley with a couple of broken bottles would be something else.

'I remember in the middle of the fight ... it's quite interesting. There were words. "Don't you try to kick me in the balls," I think were some of them.

'When the fighting began, I remember just waiting for him to let go a punch and having been a trained wrestler, as well as a boxer, as I moved forward like this, I remember my leg coming up like that in the middle of actually landing the punch. I remember this distinctly. And Behan could see this knee coming up and said, "Don't you try to kick me in the balls."

'And I said to him, "I'm not trying to kick you. I'm stopping you from kicking me." [Laughs] I was blocking what I thought was a natural situation that Behan would actually kick you in the balls.

'People were terrified of me. Literally. It became like a poisonous snake that they would be mesmerised and terrified because my reputation with my fists had got to such a peak that people would say, "My God, stay away from him."

'Behan was concerned that it had come to fisticuffs, knowing what was about to follow. He was promptly laid out on the street.'

The image of Behan prone on the road fresh in my mind, it seemed time to switch back to the present.

'Do you consider *A Singular Country* to be a romanticised history of Ireland?'

'It's romanticised undoubtedly. I'm constantly bringing up this Anglo-Irish thing, which in effect had vanished from Irish life. Because it's so funny in a way. I tend, as you've noticed, at first to write about Ireland in the perspective of all those years, that stretch of thirty years of all the changes. So that does bring in a lot of romanticising about it.

'It's a state of mind, Ireland. As anybody who lives in Dublin knows. You walk around with Ireland in your head when you go up and down the streets, either avoiding people and so on.

'Ireland goes through stages of the day. As the day wears on, you become more and more optimistic. Then you get … not perhaps more optimistic but less depressed as the day progresses, because the pubs are going to open at a certain time, and you get into the pub and the optimism develops as the drinks increase. Until about 10.30 everybody is again back on good terms, talking, laughing and carrying on.

'And you know Ireland would go like that in gaps. And then the gloom and despair of the next morning and "How am I going to get out of here?" "What's going to happen to me? Us?"

It may be an effect of the subdued lighting, but I'm beginning to feel like Bram Stoker's Jonathan Harker meeting a reclusive Transylvanian nobleman in a castle in the Carpathian Mountains. Worried that J.P. has been spending too much time cooped up on his estate, I switch to other work.

'Have you any major projects on hand at present?'

'One other one that I've tucked away is called *The Unexpurgated Code of Growing Old*, which is very funny.' J.P. brightens. 'An irreverent book of etiquette.'

'From the vantage point of being widely published, is there any advice you could share with our writers in Ireland today?'

'Yes, I suppose I could. There was a review in *The Guardian* of *A Singular Country* which was quite fascinating. He [the reviewer] now declares me "the world's heavyweight champion stage Irishman". I've now taken on this mantle.

'What he's pointing out is that presumably young Irish writers are getting very serious and grey. And yet I, in *A Singular Country*, have probably, pretty presumptuously, never hesitated to take on the Irish vernacular. And I've become an Irishman talking as a stage Irishman about Ireland, which I suppose makes *A Singular Country* quite amusing.

'I thought it best written from the vantage point of assuming that one was an Irishman, whereas I know nothing really about Ireland, and facing an Irishman and the gigantic reservoir of what I know is his psychic condition, I still wouldn't be able to figure him out.'

'Do you have a vote in Ireland?'

'Yes, I do. I'm an Irish national. I'm even ready if there's a war to be appointed as, let's see, Admiral of the Fleet. Having been in the US Navy, I'm hoping they'll give me a prime position.'

I'm the one giggling now. Guard lowered, here's evidence of the genial, mischievous Donleavy that seeps from the pages of his books.

'I remember witnessing a confrontation at the American Embassy here, which was a marvel of protocol and diplomacy. One of my … he was at that time a fan of mine … John Lehman, former secretary of the US Navy and the ambassador here, gave a party and he was asked who he'd like as guests and I was one of the people asked to come. So I came, and the thing that was so fascinating to me, having been an ex-naval person in the US Navy, was being face to face with the secretary of the US Navy, and I had a very low rank during the war.

'He was face to face with his counterpart in the Irish Navy and there they were and I could see his face creased with interest and listening devoutly to the naval man from the Irish Navy and he had 600 ships and the battleship *Iowa* has 18-inch plate across the deck. If you took the weight of the deck of the *Iowa*, it would weigh ten times more than the entire Irish Navy.

'It was a wonderful moment of diplomacy. But if there's a war and the Irish go to war, maybe the Orangemen will put to sea in some small boats and there'll be a battle. Well, if they did, I'd like to be appointed as a naval commander of some kind.'

J.P. DONLEAVY – 2008

I didn't meet J.P. again for almost twenty years. And probably wouldn't have done unless a recently appointed young features editor, intrigued by the man, asked if I could arrange and write an interview piece.

As he hadn't published any new books in recent years, and appeared to have been leading a quiet life, it seemed like a long shot. But I established contact and was delighted when, through his secretary, he agreed and suggested we meet in the Merrion Hotel.

On a sunny June morning, J.P. is in good spirits, welcoming me as an old friend. This is a very different experience from the first time we met. We chuckle a lot in his bright, airy, expansive suite. I'd never have guessed he's eighty-two. He seems younger and appears tickled at my suggestion that he bring the spring water, as good as from a Holy Well, from his Westmeath estate, Levington Park, to charm the host or hostess on American TV talk shows.

'I'm intrigued by your writing regime. Do you write every day?'

'I don't seem to specify and work out times. I let myself gravitate into working periods. If I've got something to do with a deadline, I've got to make sure that every day I go to work. I tend to work later in the day, and I find sometimes I might leave it until four o'clock to do anything. I treat it in various ways.

'I have a couple of work rooms. I have a library where I sometimes go in to sit and work. And I have my room itself. And I have a large sitting-room where I sometimes go as well. That keeps me moving around and changing the scene. The house is a marvellous house and it provides all the variations that I can take advantage of.'

'It's certainly a long way from the cottage in Wicklow I've heard so much about.'

'I should think so. I have two gatehouses, which is very unusual. And either one would be bigger than my cottage in Kilcoole and certainly a hell of a lot more modernised, with running water and electricity.'

'They were different times. It wasn't a case of being carefree.'

'No. In those days it was just a matter of coming down to basic things. As Kenneth Donoghue, who's Kenneth O'Keeffe in *The Ginger Man*, has said, "The land is the basis of everything." And then take it from there. So I said, "Right, I'd better go and buy myself some land."

'And an old pal of mine then was Tony Macken, who recently died. He was one of the IRA people and a friend of Brendan Behan's. He had a small inheritance and he thought he'd buy some land in the country, which was my idea for a proper use for his inheritance. But, instead, he took a party of people and went off to Paris and paid the bills. That got rid of a lot of the inheritance. When it came time for him to go and see some properties, I went with him, and he didn't want to go ahead with any sale. I saw this place and thought, "This is quite a pleasant place." And I made an offer for it and that's how I got my first place.

'It was inland from the sea by about half a mile. But you were in sight of the sea. Behan spent time there. He came visiting when I wasn't there and broke a window to get into the cottage. Blackened all my cooking apparatus. I wondered who the hell had done all this damage, but it didn't take me long to find out, because when I went out to my studio there were two manuscripts lying on a makeshift desk that I had there. One was *Borstal Boy* and the other was *The Ginger Man*. A unique situation. He'd gone off to the pub.

'The one mystery I faced when I returned to the cottage was the absence of all my shoes. As an American I had about twenty or thirty pairs of shoes. I couldn't understand it. Most of them had gone. I said, "Brendan, what's happened all my shoes?" He said, "There's nothing more I hate than getting my feet wet, especially in the countryside. So I took a bag of your shoes and I let them get wet as I walked up the lane and put on a dry pair every hundred yards." That's how he got to the pub.'

I'd read that Behan had amended or annotated the manuscript, a fact that J.P. gleefully confirmed.

'Yes, indeed. He'd sat down and went over the manuscript, which was quite an astonishing thing for him to do. The first words I remember him saying were, "You know, Mike [the name his Irish friends used for Donleavy, from his confirmation name Michael], that manuscript of yours is going to go around the world." We were in my car and I thought to myself, "My God, Behan doesn't hesitate to exaggerate and flatter." But I often remember that. There was no question in his mind. He simply said, "This is going to go around the world."'

By coincidence, I'd been up by Behan's statue on the Royal Canal recently, when I'd suggested it as a location for a photo shoot with a band (Republic of Loose). I mention this and say, 'Who could have foreseen such a development back then?'

'I wouldn't have imagined he thought there'd be a statue of him one day. But I feel Behan was aware of his own brilliance, and so on. He knew this. He was very quick to recognise anybody else. He was very generous. Although there is, I suppose, a naughty story about him. He was put in charge of the offices of *The Bell* magazine in Dublin and it was a very cold winter's day and there was no central heating, of course, and he decided to keep himself warm and just took a whole stack of manuscripts and started to burn them in the fireplace.'

I tell J.P. how I'd recently recounted the story he'd told me previously of his scrap with Brendan outside McDaids. Calmly, the author sets the record straight. I'd conflated two episodes, which leaves me wondering if my memory can always be trusted.

'We didn't actually fight that time. We went out, but Behan very wisely said, "Look not one of them has bothered themselves to come out of the pub to watch us fight so we're not going to put on a fight now, we've no audience."

'But we did end up having a fight in London in the middle of Fleet Street. Behan couldn't really fight. But I was a skilled boxer. And so this one punch, the only punch I threw, hit him squarely on the nose and laid him out in the middle of Fleet Street.'

The admiration in which J.P. still holds his friend Behan is obvious. Both men were maverick gunslingers on a literary scene that boasted a legion of intellectual sharpshooters.

'He was a great companion and a fascinating man. And full of horrors about his life. There were so many terrible things that had happened to him. In fact, some of the things connected with Behan I have never been able to tell anybody. They are so horrifying. I've never divulged these things. I was always sympathetic to the idea that he had this raging worry of his life. He was concerned with a lot of troubles.'

A friend of mine, Comtesse Joan de Frenay, who was very fond of Brendan, told me she came down the morning after her wedding to find him asleep on her kitchen table, stark naked. Joan lived in a room at the legendary late-night Dublin drinking den that hosted a motley crew of scamps, wastrels, blackguards and scoundrels, which J.P. dubbed 'The Catacombs'. I share this yarn with him.

'I went down to Nighttown [Monto, the red-light district in Dublin, was dubbed 'Nighttown' by Joyce in *Ulysses*] with Behan and some relatives and people he knew very well from down there. He introduced me to these getting-elderly ladies, and he'd say, "Mike, give her a good hug. She's spent thirty years of her life selling it down on the quays."

'Behan was very strange. He'd fill up a pint glass with a dozen different things in it and drink it right back. He literally fell down like a tree after finishing it. Since I was with him and brought him to the party, I was asked to remove Behan. So I had to pick him up off the floor, throw him over my shoulder, carry him out and throw him in the back of my car and drive back to Wicklow with him. I forgot that Behan was left in the back of the car, and it wasn't until the next morning that I saw this figure wandering around the cottage. But he was trying to feed this really nasty bull with some grass that he'd pulled up, not realising he could get killed. Luckily I saw this and rushed out and stopped him.'

'That cocktail story reminds me of my friend Shane MacGowan, who is very talented, with a heart of gold, and reminds me of Behan in a way.'

'Oh, Shane. He's controlling himself a lot more, isn't he?'

The fire alarm rings out loudly and stridently.

J.P. is unperturbed. 'They're testing the fire alarm.'

'I read somewhere that you've never invested money, opting instead to only earn money through your own work. I find that admirable. Have you stuck with that?'

Downplaying his principled stance, J.P. makes light of the topic. 'Yes, I have. Of course, if you own some land and the price, as is happening these days, is escalating and I have a couple of hundred acres on the outskirts of Mullingar, one realises … I have a neighbour who also owns land and he'd drive by in the car and shout out the window what the current value was.'

J.P. is laughing loudly. 'He'd say, "Ten million now!" This is awfully amusing that he is counting his chickens.'

'Remembering when I began reading your books in the 1960s, you've maintained a consistent vision and have stuck to your guns in the face of some critical belligerence.'

'I'm even surprised right now that I sit down and just focus on what that book is going to be without any regard as to whether it will sell or whether anyone will want to publish it and so on.

'At the moment I'm writing a similar book, which is a similar length to this one. [He produces an elegant US imprint of his 1995 novella *The Lady Who Liked Clean Rest Rooms*.] They are two stories set in New York. This one has an underground thing that people hear about it and come across it. It's a simple story about a funeral parlour in New York and a lady who goes in out of her own feelings. She wants to take a pee and was so desperate that she went into a funeral parlour knowing the lavatories would be clean in there and to use it. But she was spotted doing this and she didn't want to be arrested as an imposter invading the funeral parlour, so she rushed in and pretended that she was a mourner. The story is quite unbelievable because in order to perfect her position of being a mourner – there was nobody in this little room, but the deceased was in his coffin and so on – when the person was going down the hall to check, she immediately went over to the guest list and wrote her name in it. She wrote her name and put her address in it and thought nothing about it. This man who was deceased was hated by everyone who knew him and they were delighted he was dead.' He's chuckling at the idea now. 'He, being still a bastard in his behaviour, wrote in his will that his entire wealth be shared between the people who came to his funeral and signed the register. She'd signed because she didn't want to be caught simply using the restrooms.

'These I enjoy writing.

'There's a thing I'm writing now called *The Dog on the Seventeenth Floor*. There's an amusing thing. I was in New York with the manuscript and one doesn't want to drop people's names, but the fact of the matter was that one of the few people who came into the room – I was in a club in New York called the New York Athletic Club – I had a manuscript there and this gentleman pointed at it and said, "What's this?" I said, "Well that's a manuscript I'm working on called *The Dog on the Seventeenth Floor*." He was absolutely intrigued with this and said, "What's that about?" I started to tell him the story. Now the man I'm telling this to is Johnny Depp of all people.'

And he's slapping his knee and laughing. 'Anyway, these are short pieces that I'm doing now.'

I'd been noticing over the last few years that J.P.'s paintings have begun to filter into the art gallery system. I hadn't realised that he had such a huge body of work until a Dublin gallery hosted an extensive exhibition of his work. I mention this to J.P.

'It's for my own personal entertainment. I enjoy doing drawings and seeing what comes out. Damien Matthews [art dealer] is someone who likes to overcome difficulties and he put on these exhibitions. I leave everything to him.'

'I'm intrigued by the work itself and what it means to you,' I tell him. 'It's not a bagatelle.'

'Indeed. I'm conscious of what one's doing and also take an interest, as you usually follow what you've previously recently done, and from there it goes down into another category [style] but influenced by what the recent work was like. I let that happen. I sit down and do a drawing. Sometimes it's quite a good thing for me to switch into doing that. It quietens you down and you relax.'

'It's clearly not just a hobby you took up late in life.'

'Yes. From my early days in Trinity College, I started taking myself seriously I suppose. My rooms in New Square, you could see my light on from a distance away. One of my neighbours living nearby was Jean-Marc Heidsieck from the Heidsieck champagne family. He was out of his comfort zone in Ireland, being from a French background and an elegant life that he lived. But if he ever saw my lights on, he could see an easel up at my window and I'd hear a knock on my door and he'd say, "Would you mind awfully if I came in and just sit?" He'd just sit there and we'd spend maybe a Sunday … and he'd been out in Dublin going through this ordeal, as it became for him, of [being] one of the most sought-after bachelors available in Dublin. He looked like a glamorous movie star and was charming as well, so he was sought-after in Dublin, and so he'd come back weary and see lights on and come up. He'd sit and I'd go on painting. He could remember the name of the girls whose parents were trying to get some romance going with him.

'We were in Paris when the champagne company held this great celebration and had invited people from all over the world. I was invited and went over. Jean-Marc and myself were talking together about the old days at Trinity, and about various women whose names we could both remember, and where he would be put on display on Sunday for the daughter of the house and go through this ordeal. There was this girl listening to us recalling those days and I looked at her and tears were streaming down her face. She said she'd never heard anything so touching and sad. She thought it was profound and sad that we could remember the names.

'We have great recall. Unlike with the majority of people in America, I find people in Ireland carry the past and memory with them as if it's the present. It doesn't have the time to happen any more – life is too fast and the competition between people.

In those days neither of us in that conversation had anything to gain from the other except their company and social interest in one another. People can't afford to do that any more. They have to make themselves known and what they might be there for and how the people present can take advantage of their coming together.

'Would you like to have a glass of water?'

This is such an unexpected query, I think perhaps I'm about to be shown the door. But there are sparkling glasses and branded bottles of water on a tray on the coffee table beside us. However, J.P. produces a French-style table bottle with an airtight hinged stopper lid from a bag beside his seat.

'I have a wonderful spring on the land,' he begins as he pours me a glass. 'People have probably never tasted anything like that. It has no surroundings. It is just alone by itself with fields around it. My neighbouring farm has the same.

'This water has hardly any foreign influence in it at all. This water would be as pure as you could get. I bring it to Dublin when I come.'

The water is clear, pure and crisp. I take a sip. It's refreshing.

I tell him, 'This reminds me of water I drank from a sacred well in County Meath [two wells in fact, St Kieran's and also St Bridget's] when I was a child.'

'We do have a sacred well. Not on my land but not that far away. It is a sacred well. It's been there for centuries. And people still come and take the water. I travel into town with my water.'

It's then I suggest that J.P. bring his 'sacred water' on tour to offer to his hosts on television chat shows. We find the potential scenarios amusing.

'What's the state of play with regards to a possible film of *The Ginger Man*? Apart from Robert Redford and producer Sam

Spiegel, I've heard Johnny Depp mentioned in relation to a movie being green-lit.'

'One finds in the film business that is largely a talking matter. It becomes a social matter. My social life in years going back was always on the basis that somebody was concocting some plans to do something. I had actually signed a few agreements years ago and they would elapse and so on. As *The Ginger Man* circulates, it always comes up frequently enough, I think less and less focusing on Dangerfield.

'But people forget that I'm also a playwright. People have performed in the plays. My particular favourite was *Fairy Tales of New York*. I loved that. And *Balthazar B*, I found I couldn't go and watch that any more because it's so sad. It's ending was cataclysmic. It was being performed in some city in America; Baltimore, perhaps. I remember it coming to the end; I went to the lobby somewhat affected by it because I had only sat once in rehearsals years before, and a woman came running out of the theatre saying, with her friends waiting for her, "The party is off. The party is off." She was in tears.

'My son was with me and the woman sitting next to him with her husband broke into tears and began sobbing. It was always in my mind that it might be banned because of its sorrow.

'They are over the hurdle of my dirty overtones and shocking references. Now it's sorrow. Sadness.'

Chapter Five

Leaning in Gently

I NEVER SET OUT TO give an interviewee a hard time. That would be rude. And probably counterproductive. Yet some interviewees could prove to be guarded, controlling or even adversarial. On occasion, attitudes would harden and exchanges become abrasive or confrontational. So I needed to be prepared, when necessary, to become assertive; combative even. I would remind myself that this was a professional engagement. I had a responsibility to the newspaper's readers. From time to time, an inner voice would chime, 'Expect the unexpected.' If I wasn't prepared to be bullied, I would need to give as good as I got and hope that, perhaps, I'd get to expand on the fundamental narrative that was embedded in the public consciousness.

Only very occasionally did an interview assume the air of an inquisition. One such occasion was when Anita Roddick was promoting her autobiography. Her PA was professionally apologetic when I arrived on time. Anita would be here soon, she assured me. It was midday and Ms Roddick had had a busy morning. While I fretted about my own schedule, which was hectic that day, I learned that Anita was in the local park communing with nature. Yes, the woman whose Body Shop empire stretched to 600 shops around the globe needed to hug some trees before meeting me. The revelation was presented half-heartedly as part of the wonderful enigmatic persona of a dynamic industrialist whose personal fortune was estimated at £40 million at the time.

Despite the intervention of the St Stephen's Green trees, Anita, on message, displayed a brusque, business-like demeanour. The interviewer can sometimes be regarded as a small cog at the interface of a PR and news-reporting machine that spends vast amounts of money creating and maintaining a client's public image. Occasionally you might find yourself kicking against that inescapable fact.

Overwhelmed by a flotilla of overly practised soundbites and sales spiel, I hastily adjusted my line of enquiry. There were occasions when, if given the run around, I targeted the Achilles' heel. Here was an example of the interview as a war game.

Trying to avoid more guff about tribal people who had 'catalogued 300 extra species of bees you never knew existed', I asked pointedly, 'Do you miss having Margaret Thatcher around?' It was 1991, and the Tories' 'Iron Lady' had been ousted as leader ten months previously. Roddick was aghast. Bull's eye.

'I hated her. Why would I miss her?'

'You seem to be a product of the Thatcher era.'

'No. I'm not. Bloody right, I'm not ...'

Here we go, I thought, as the tycoon's faux hippy charm was quickly replaced by hectoring business-like aggression. Game on. Anita became more agitated as we progressed. At the time, the slogan that adorned Body Shop branding declared 'Against Animal Testing'. From animal rights activist Niall McGuirk of

Dublin's Hope Collective, I'd learned the stark reality that beauty and skincare products were tested, in horrific circumstances, on animals. Along with other major toiletry and cosmetic companies, Ms Roddick endorsed what was known as 'the five-year rolling rule', which, Niall had explained, meant that the Body Shop could use ingredients which had been tested on animals up to five years and one day previously. Opting not to look me in the eye, Anita leaned in, tugged at her hair neurotically and pointedly directed her considerable energy towards my little tape recorder on the table. 'You can't say we've never used ingredients which have been tested. Bullshit. It can't be said.' She may have been campaigning against animal testing, but this clearly didn't equate with a company ethos that accepted ingredients which had been tested five years previously.

A conversation about animal cruelty was not what Anita Roddick wanted. 'The biggest challenge now is large corporations who have been running companies on less than ethical lines,' she declared before abruptly turning her back; deciding to cut her losses, she rushed from the room without even a glance in my direction. I'd been dismissed.

That same year, Archbishop Cahal Daly was another who pulled rank. Theologically conservative and strong on evangelisation, his unequivocal doctrinaire approach left me under no illusion as to my lowly place in the hierarchy of souls. The Archbishop was nothing if not dogmatic. Like Ms Roddick, he had a firm to promote and protect. He also had a disquieting habit of creating a whistling sound when speaking passionately. In response to a question on the possibility of an integrated education system helping further the cause of peace and understanding between communities in Northern Ireland, he was in danger of sounding like an amateur flageolet band. The gist of his barked argument was summed up in his dismissal of such a preposterous idea, which claimed that, despite 'a great body of research', there was no evidence of 'any significant effect on social attitudes and on, particularly, intolerance, peace and reconciliation'.

I also asked Archbishop Daly how he viewed suggestions that the use of condoms could help stop the spread of AIDS. Contraception had been banned in Ireland until 1980, and it was not until five years later that the Health (Family Planning) (Amendment) Act made condoms and spermicides available to over-eighteens without prescription, if only through restricted outlets. At the height of the AIDS epidemic in the mid-1980s, they were still not readily available in Ireland, so I arranged for a band to give away a free condom with every copy of their new album on Hotwire Records, an indie label I'd set up to encourage bands who'd been ignored by the mainstream. It was a Situationist prank designed to highlight the ludicrous nature of the law.

A few years later, I knew this initiative had been justified when the Department of Health's Deputy Chief Medical Officer, Dr James Walsh, told me in interview, 'A good condom used intelligently reduces the spread of infection. And as a public health doctor I would advise it.'

How did Dr Walsh reconcile advocating safe sex and condoms with his Catholic upbringing? 'I don't believe an autocratic type of attitude towards people is helpful and it's not very republican,' he said. 'I feel [iconic republican Theobald] Wolfe Tone probably would have used a condom if he had it.'

Archbishop Daly, who was due to be promoted to the rank of cardinal the day after our interview, bristled with conviction as he brushed aside the recommendations. 'I cannot see the widespread availability of condoms as in any way contributing positively to health preservation,' he declared. 'I can see it, rather, as encouraging and persuading people to take risks.'

It wasn't until the following year that the Bishop Eamonn Casey scandal, sexual and financial, made front-page headlines. This was followed by the news, two years later, that Fr Brendan Smyth had been jailed for four years for abuse of children in Northern Ireland. While my interview with Cardinal Daly in 1991 had been hard work – it felt less like a conversation and more like a sermon from the pulpit – had the encounter occurred a few years later, we'd have had even more pertinent matters to discuss.

You never know how an interview is likely to turn out. My mood was upbeat when meeting Christy Moore in August 1991. I'd first met Christy in the late 1960s when I was reading poetry at the Traverse Theatre in Edinburgh. The event organiser told me that he'd added a fellow Irishman to the bill as guest. Although I'd keenly observed the 'ballad boom' in Ireland, I hadn't heard of Christy, who, it transpired, having found himself out of his day job as a bank clerk during a lengthy strike, had relocated to England where he was making his way as a folk-singer. That evening in Scotland, the Kildare man sang a heart-wrenching a capella version of 'An Bonnán Buí' (The Yellow Bittern). Dating from the sixteenth century, the song is about a man who, while struggling to stop drinking, finds a dead bird by a frozen pool where it died for 'want of drink'.

Christy's performance was a tour de force. Afterwards we went to the pub, became friends and corresponded by letter for a few years. Christy never went back to his job in the bank. Instead, through his talent, he created his own institution.

I was looking forward to our meeting in Dublin as Christy had been out of the public eye for four years following a health scare. I'd heard from a mutual friend that he'd embraced meditation, fitness and a macrobiotic diet. This represented a dramatic lifestyle change. A similar regime had worked for me in the 1980s, so I thought we'd have plenty to chat about.

When greeting Christy and remarking on how well he looked, my mistake was to jokingly enquire, 'What's all this vegetarian craic then?' Perhaps assuming I was being sarcastic and mocking, Christy snapped, 'It's not vegetarian craic. It's holistic healing, macrobiotic food…' There was a cutting edge to Christy's harangue. I was shocked. I didn't need this stinging rebuke in the penthouse suite of a posh hotel from someone I considered an old friend. 'A joke,' I protested. But the damage was done. I had underestimated how emotionally fragile and sensitive Christy was. While I knew he'd come through a personal crisis, I didn't think of myself as the enemy.

Throughout the interview, arranged by his promoter to help sell tickets for gigs, Christy, his mood having darkened, remained tetchy and disapproving. In the hardscrabble world of Irish showbiz, where you're either with us or against us, by becoming a member of the commentariat it appeared I'd sullied my flimsy artistic bib. However, I believed my role was to act as intermediary between the interviewee and the newspaper's readers. As interviewer, I posed questions I believed the public would like to ask if they had the opportunity. His team had requested the interview and now Christy wasn't helping. I wasn't prepared to be treated as part of his problem. I had a job to do.

There was only one thing for it. Resorting to the Gaelic football coaching I'd received from Cavan stalwart Jim Duignan, I leaned in gently with the shoulder.

'Speaking of holistic healing, how do you think your support for the armed struggle squares with the laws of karma?'

Silence.

'I notice you came out recently and criticised the Provisional IRA.'

'Oh, yeah.'

'That's unusual for you, isn't it? Where do you fit into the picture now?'

Christy remained shtum. Swivelling his head away, he stared out the window at the sky.

Silences in interviews can be tense and off-putting. Known in radio exchanges as 'dead air', such pauses appear unprofessional. They can sometimes be embarrassing. A year earlier, insecure and anxious to keep the conversation going, I'd have blurted out a follow-up question. But I'd learned that silences can be revealing. They also allow time for the interviewee to gather their thoughts. So I let the tape roll. Only when it appeared we'd reached an impasse, I continued.

'I know it's a big canvas. Do you feel the need to address it?'

'You're the one who's addressing it.'

'Well, I'm the one who's raising it.'

'I was very, very critical. Basically, what I said recently was that I can no longer handle the violence. It frightens me … I don't know where it's going …'

It may have ranked as one of the most uneasy, and at times defensive, interviews I ever did, but, in allowing me to glimpse the conflict within the character, it gave an honest picture of the unflinching soul-searching Christy had put himself through. Not for the first time, it transpired the balladeer was in tune with the public mood. There was something in the air. Three years later, after a bloody campaign that had been waged for a quarter of a century, the Provisional IRA announced 'a cessation of military operations'.

Curiously, I came across an interview that a former colleague, Mary Carr (no relation), did with Christy a year later. Those 'comeback' concerts had been a sell-out and he was set to repeat the trick. Under the heading 'Moore the merrier', the feature explored how Christy's dramatic lifestyle change had affected the performer. 'I was a bag of resentments,' he revealed. 'I used to carry them around with me, but now I realise that resentment is a lot more damaging to the carrier than the person it's aimed at.'

While not suggesting there's any connection to the foregoing, I'm happy to take this opportunity to correct the widely reported perception that it was I who described Planxty's album *The Well Below the Valley* as 'The Well Below the Average'. I can attest that it was not me but Horslips' Charles O'Connor who, on hearing the title of the folk group's album for the first time, delivered the off-the-cuff Wildean quip. It was an innocuous gag from a man who had played with legends Tommy Peoples and Liam Weldon before forming Horslips. No harm or slight was intended – just a jocular piece of wordplay that would have been forgotten had it not been so witty.

SHANE MacGOWAN – November 1989

In 1989 Faber & Faber, the publishing house renowned for a roster of talent that included Ezra Pound, T.S. Eliot, Seamus Heaney and W.H. Auden, launched *Poguetry*, the collected lyrics of Shane MacGowan. Sipping from a pint glass that contained a Coke topped up with double measures of vodka, gin and rum, the author was on a roll at a boisterous launch reception in the Irish Club in Belgravia. Having released four exciting albums in five years, his band was at the peak of its powers. And now, Shane's lyrical genius was being officially feted.

I hadn't foreseen this development on the first few occasions that I'd met Shane. Back then, in the late 1970s, he was a shy and socially awkward youth working on the Rock On record stall in Soho Market. Owned by Dubliner Ted Carroll, who'd moved to London as road manager with Skid Row a decade earlier, and his business partner, former Queen's University Belfast graduate Roger Armstrong, the stall was an outpost of the famous Camden Town vintage record shop Rock On. On Thin Lizzy's song 'The Rocker', Philip Lynott sang, 'I bought my records at the Rock On stall.' A magnet for young punks, indie bands, fanzine creators and collectors of rare vinyl, the stall was a vibrant counter-cultural oasis, and Shane, when on duty, was a laconic, supremely knowledgeable, irascible and insightful host.

It was my habit to buy new indie releases and bring copies, including 'King of the Bop' by Shane's band the Nipple Erectors, when I'd visit America with Horslips. Indeed, I was the first person to play The Pretenders' debut single 'Stop Your Sobbing' in the US, when I produced the vinyl from my bag while on air at KSAN, the influential countercultural San Francisco music station, which first exploded in popularity in 1967 during the psychedelic era.

The market in Soho became a multi-storey car park and employees Stan Brennan and Phil Garston took the franchise, re-branded as Rocks Off, to Hanway Street, off Oxford Street. Both Shane and Cait O'Riordan worked shifts behind the counter. Bradley's Spanish Bar next door became a favourite haunt of all in Rocks Off's orbit.

Still recovering in the aftermath of a decade of music and business intensity with Horslips, I'd initially declined Shane's invitation to attend rehearsals for the new band he'd been working with. But I was taken aback by the power and purpose of the band's debut single 'Dark Streets of London', which Stan Brennan helped them produce.

When I dropped into the shop some days later, Cait explained that Stan had been called to meet Dave Robinson, head of Stiff Records. A phone call to Stan that evening confirmed a deal with Stiff Records had been agreed. This story was too good to waste. And so, the first newspaper feature on The Pogues in Ireland appeared in the *Evening Herald*. Under the headline 'It's punk o'ceili', it was written by a mysterious stringer called Edward Cash.

During those halcyon years I was one of a coterie of devoted friends and fellow travellers and, along the way, spent some late nights socialising in Shane's company. The band's gigs were riotous, poignant, inspirational and life-affirming, and I was delighted to champion such explosive talent. My friend Philip Chevron later joined the group. Pioneering Dublin folk stalwart Terry Woods also became an important part of the team. Terry and manager Frank Murray, who I'd known since his days as tour manager with Thin Lizzy, urged me to join them in a visit to Shane in hospital when he'd been knocked down by a taxi when leaving a restaurant in Queensway with film director Alex Cox. It was suggested that, seeing as I'd survived the hedonistic seventies rock scene, Shane might heed some brotherly advice. As if.

Though bruised and scarred, his leg and arm encased in plaster, Shane was in high spirits and chuckled throughout our visit, while I marvelled at the array of bottles of Seven-Up and Lucozade that surrounded his bed. A couple of nights later, I was in the Devonshire Arms when a deathly white Shane was carried into the pub, feet first, by a gaggle of drinking buddies.

I first heard the epic 'A Rainy Night in Soho' on a rough mix cassette when staying with American producer Craig Leon, who would produce the band's 'Haunted' for the soundtrack of *Sid and Nancy*. It was thrilling to experience the band in its earliest incarnation, driving an audience of fifty or sixty demented and to have been on hand to witness their full flowering as they galvanised audiences of 6,000 in the great public halls. Sadly, due to prior commitments, I was unable to deputise for drummer Andrew Ranken on a Scandinavian tour, but I did get to sit in with the band when he missed his flight to Dublin for a TV appearance of The Pogues and The Dubliners performing their hit 'The Irish Rover'. That was fun.

By the time Shane's *Poguetry* was published, I'd been hosting my weekly celebrity interview series in the *Evening Herald* for a couple of months. The opportunity to afford Shane a double-page platform in Ireland was too good to miss. Frank agreed. Shane, however, seemed somewhat reluctant. But he obliged and, after some delay and prevarication, turned up at Frank's office armed with, if my memory is correct, two bottles. One was Jack Daniel's, which I've never been partial to, and the other may have been Goldschläger. I may be conflating some of our other get-togethers, but vodka may also have been on the menu.

I appreciated quickly that this interview might be difficult for Shane. Our comradely acquaintance was being transformed into something ostensibly professional. Boundaries could become blurred. Highly intelligent, Shane was aware of the tricky transaction. He'd have suspected I knew too much behind-the-scenes stuff and was probably concerned I'd be digging for dirt. If it wasn't for the encouragement of lighting engineer Paul Verner, our mutual friend, Shane might have cancelled.

On the afternoon we met, it struck me that this mightn't be a good idea. Shane and I had known each other too long and were possibly too close for this to work.

When the tape machine was switched on, I got an immediate impression that Shane was set to filibuster or play a dead bat in an effort to avoid engaging seriously. So, acting on instinct, I attempted to make him feel more at home by matching his insouciant air and adopting a mildly sceptical and quizzical punk fanzine attitude. I was delighted when my initial tease about it possibly being 'poncy' caught him by surprise.

Like everything Shane undertook, this interview has its own unique flavour; the back and forth is terse at times, vaguely anarchic, tense, jarring, defensive in places. And yet, as I listen to the recording I feel a mixture of awe and great sadness. I miss Shane's knowing sense of humour and poetic soul, his encyclopaedic knowledge of music and literature, and my appreciation of the man's generosity and obliging nature simply multiplies.

**

SMacG: It's a nice book, innit?
EC: Yeah, and it's about time your work has been compiled like this.

Why do it in the first place?

SMacG: I didn't do it. I'd already done those lyrics. They [the publishers] did it. It was their idea. In fact, I was quite surprised to see the print on the front 'cos what I was told was that it was going to be all the names the same size. 'Cos Steve Pyke is a famous photographer. John Hewitt is a famous illustrator and I'm a famous piss-artist. [Laughs]

EC: Do you think it's a bit poncy?

SMacG: Poncy? What? I didn't do it. I mean, if I was dead would it be poncy? Do I think it's a bit poncy? Nah, I don't think anything about it except that it looks good. The layout and the graphics are good ... can't be bothered to read the rest. [Laughs]

EC: Are there other writers who have influenced you?

SMacG: You're not talking about lyric writers?

EC: Not necessarily.

SMacG: Why not?

EC: Not songwriters. Not exclusively. Just writers in general.

SMacG: Lou Reed, Jim Morrison, Jimi Hendrix, Laura Nyro.

EC: Someone mentioned the other night that The Pogues might be playing in Italy during the World Cup.

SMacG: Yeah, we're trying to get that together. Do you wanna drink?

EC: No thanks. Will there be a conflict of interest if it comes to supporting Ireland or England?

SMacG: Nah. Don't be ridiculous.

EC: Who would you be supporting?

SMacG: Ireland.

EC: I know your parents are Irish, but are you Irish?

SMacG: I've got a passport that says I'm Irish. I spent a lot of time there when I was a kid. I don't want to get into ... gimme a break. All this stuff has been done.

EC: I was talking to Gerry Conlon and he says that the Irish in England don't get a fair deal from the law.

SMacG: Well, you know that.

EC: Has that been your experience?

SMacG: I haven't been kept under the PTA [Prevention of Terrorism Act] or anything like that. No. But I know people who have.

EC: Has the BBC officially banned your Birmingham Six song ['Streets of Sorrow/Birmingham Six']?

SMacG: I'm really not sure exactly what the ban means. I know they're not going to play it any more. And they took out the last verse when we played it live on ITV a year or two ago. I know we're on some kind of list. But it's sort of bureaucratic jargon. I don't really understand it and I haven't got time to fucking think about it. It happened when we were doing something else, but I stand by it completely. But they won't be playing it anyway seeing as it's an old record.

A few weeks before we met, four innocent people jailed for bombings in Guildford and Woolwich were cleared of all charges and released from prison after serving fifteen years. During the hunt for the bombers, the police had made a dawn raid on the house I'd been living in with Horslips in London at the time. Our nocturnal comings and goings, Irish registration plates and moustachioed roadies who vaguely resembled crude identikit images led them to staking out the place before swarming in early one Monday morning while everyone was asleep. Thankfully, we had cast-iron alibis. The so-called 'Guildford Four' weren't as lucky.

EC: Do you think the Birmingham Six have a chance at this stage in the light of the Guildford Four's result?

SMacG: Yeah. But I don't want to say anything about … that might … I think if they admit one thing, they ought to admit to another. But I don't know whether they will 'cos you can't tell what these bastards are going to do.

EC: Do you think Mrs Thatcher will hang on and get in for another term?

SMacG: Probably, yeah. I dunno. Maybe not. They're televising the House of Commons now. Maybe she's had it. I think she's had it. She might have had it and she might not. I couldn't tell you. I'm not … For a start, I don't read. I just think of it in terms of Conservative and Labour, right wing or left wing. I'm left wing. Apart from that I can't really say much about politics except this is the worst government that I've ever lived under.

EC: You've done your bit, but do you reckon the Labour Party has done enough for the Birmingham Six?

SMacG: Nah, I don't think so. It's all come from the street, hasn't it. But I'm not criticising Labour.

EC: Were you away when the Guildford Four were released?

SMacG: No. I'd just got back. I was really surprised.

EC: Did you notice any hypocrisy or politicians taking credit or political backslapping?

SMacG: Nah. I don't think anybody's got the right to … have they? I don't really watch the news that carefully but, in saying that, if something like that comes up then I notice it. I couldn't give a bollocks what some politician's got to say.

Six months after this chat with Shane, I spoke with journalist and justice campaigner Chris Mullin, who published his research into the Birmingham pub bombings in his book *Error of Judgement: The Truth About the Birmingham Bombings*. He said, 'I thought that after the release of the Guildford Four that they [the British authorities] would begin to look seriously at the possibility that they have made a mistake in the Birmingham case, but in fact, literally within an hour of the Guildford Four being released, the British Home Secretary, Douglas Hurd, was on his feet in the House of Commons explaining why the two cases were entirely unrelated and why Guildford had no implications whatever for Birmingham.'

Discussing Lord Lane and the appeals process, Mullin added, 'British judges and British lawyers in general are a very self-satisfied body of people. They believe that British justice is the best in the world, that our police force is the best in the world. There is this chauvinism about Britain that's not always supported by the evidence.'

Declared 'unsafe', the case against the Birmingham Six was quashed in March 1991. The innocent men had spent sixteen years in prison.

EC: When you started The Pogues you were planning things on a week-to-week basis. You're now having to plan things a year ahead. Does that put a strain on you or compromise you in any way?

SMacG: Not really. How could it?

EC: Well, trying to figure out where you're going to be in a year's time. That sort of stuff. After The Nips, when The Pogues thing was starting up, you obviously had some objective or goal. You wanted to do it. Do you think you've succeeded in what you set out to do as a unit?

SMacG: Yeah. Basically. Yeah.

EC: Is there still stuff you feel you want to do?

SMacG: Yeah.

EC: I wonder if it's been your experience that the level of popularity or fame or the attendant situation where you have a fair amount of money by comparison to when you were starting, if that in any way has had a detrimental effect on the original ideals you had when forming the group?

SMacG: We're not politicians. We're musicians. You know about that.

EC: How do you cope with that?

SMacG: What do you mean?

EC: I just want to know if the thing that drove you to get the band together in the first place, that spirit …

SMacG: We all got the band together. I don't know what drove other people. I think we had a basic thing in common, which was the disgust with the complete lack of live music in London at the time. A love for the music, for all good music. And a sense of humour. That's what we had when we started. That's all we had when we started. The objective was to make a good living for all of us out of playing music. That objective still stands, but I think we've already achieved it to a certain extent, but I think we've been hindered by a lot of things [Sighs] which aren't to do with music. Various things to do with prejudice, intolerance, bigotry. Just people. People who try to make you and break you and do it maybe not understanding what we are doing. It's not something I think about much because I'm not part of the management or I'm not a politician or I'm not a bloody freedom fighter, you know. If I was, I wouldn't be sitting talking to you.

EC: That sounds heavy. You mean there are people who would want to stop you?

SMacG: No, look, I'm talking about a general thing that applies to record companies and the press to a certain extent. Although they've been very good to us. It doesn't really apply to the public at all. That's the point. The people know what it's about. They understand. But there's a lot of people out there playing good music that never get past anywhere. They're still borrowing a tenner to get a drink.

EC: When you said recently that you liked acid house, a lot of people couldn't understand it. Some people in the press had a problem with you enjoying acid house and being a member of The Pogues. As if the two couldn't go together. What is it that appeals to you about acid house?

SMacG: That's their problem. Acid house is what it is. You can't explain it in words any more than you can explain Irish music in words. Or rock'n'roll in words. Or jazz in words. It's all a waste of energy talking about music. It's good or it's bad.

EC: Since you wrote and recorded 'Dark Streets of London', the streets seem to have got worse.

SMacG: Yeah, that's true. But anybody can tell you that London's a shit hole. Maybe that wasn't true before, but it's obvious now. It's a zoo. It's like saying that … looking back it seems to me that it's like a sub-Lou Reed song, know what I mean? Like the sort of songs he writes, which are just the truth about reality. It's not a big deal. It's not a statement. It's just a bloody song.

EC: But do you think kids read your lyrics and take them seriously?

SMacG: If I thought about it, then I couldn't write.

EC: But does it worry you that perhaps you might be giving young fans a bad example?

SMacG: Nah. Maybe as a person I'm giving them a bad example, but there's nothing in the songs which I don't think is the truth.

Not even the heavy truth, just the lightweight truth. Just what anybody can see.

EC: Yeah, but what about your image?

SMacG: What image?

EC: Like Lou Reed had a distinctive image, you've an image of being a man who drinks a lot.

SMacG: Well I AM a man who drinks a lot. I'm not saying anybody else has to. You could also say I was giving them a bad example by thinking and writing and playing. But that isn't a bad example and you know it. Nobody needs to convince them that having a drink can make you feel good and too many drinks can make you feel bad. It's not what it's about. There's nothing in particular in the songs about drink more than anybody has a drink anyway.

EC: Surely it's been suggested to you that by drinking as much as you do that …

SMacG: I don't say I do it. People ask me if I drink and I say, 'Yeah, I drink.' But I don't drink that much on stage. It's my business how much I drink. When I drink it. How I drink it. Who I drink it with. It's also a social thing as well. But that's not an excuse. If I want a drink I can have a drink. It's legal.

EC: You've probably heard the stories of Brendan Behan being brought into pubs and put up against the wall and his drinking cronies going through his pockets …

SMacG: I've read Anthony Cronin's *Dead as Doornails*, but I don't remember that.

EC: Do you think people take advantage of you?

SMacG: Nobody goes through my bloody pockets. I don't get that drunk. I don't get drunk enough for people to steal money off me. If I was getting that drunk then I'd … er … slow down. I mean out of my pocket. I mean cash.

EC: But there are other ways for people to rob you.

SMacG: What can I say? If you think that, you think that. What? You want me to start worrying about it? I'm not worried about it and I'm not going to start. I've got enough to worry about.

EC: Surely it's been said to you that, like Behan or Dylan Thomas …

SMacG: I'm not Dylan Thomas. I write pop songs. I don't write novels. We're lyricists. Like Ian McCulloch or Jim Reid or Van Morrison or whoever. Or Charlie Rafferty.

EC: I'm not saying you're Dylan Thomas.

SMacG: I'm not sure you have. In some ways I wish I was though. He's brilliant.

EC: But it's been said to you that punishing the gargle as you do is going to destroy your liver.

SMacG: My liver's all right. I had it checked out a while ago. It is. Otherwise I'd be yellow. What are you at? If I deny that I drink you put that down. If I don't deny it then you put that down, you know. I drink what I've always drunk.

EC: But what would you say to the person who sees you on the box or hears a record and thinks, 'That Shane MacGowan is a good lad but the poor divil is going to kill himself?'

SMacG: It isn't true. I'm a victim of publicity. [Laughs]

EC: I thought your single 'Yeah, Yeah, Yeah, Yeah, Yeah' sounded closer to the idea of your original band, The Nipple Erectors, than to what people might expect from The Pogues.

SMacG: The Nipple Erectors never had an idea in their life. [Laughs] We have more of an idea what we're doing in this band. But then this band was made up of older people.

EC: Do you have any fresh musical surprises in mind for fans?

SMacG: There are eight people in the band, right. There are no changes in musical direction 'cos I don't know what musical direction means. You can't play music unless it's natural, yeah? If you start thinking about musical direction you should be doing something else, like being a music critic or something. You can't think about it. In words. It just comes. Whatever you happen to be playing at the time. And it develops naturally, organically. And everybody in the band is involved in it. Just because I'm the singer and I write a lot of the songs doesn't mean I know where we're going or where we've been. If I did know that it wouldn't be any use to me or anybody else.

EC: So your love of music isn't being dampened by the business?

SMacG: No. I knew it was a shitty business. But, obviously, none of us knew how bad it can get. But that's got nothing to do with music anyway. I'm not counting how much I'm making per minute when I'm on stage. I'm counting beats. Pretentious statement of the year. [Laughs]

EC: How much pressure does the business put on you and on The Pogues?

SMacG: You know the pressures that are put on you. And nobody can tell whether they're going to be able to handle it or not, day by day. At the moment we're still handling it. If I started thinking about the future that's about as constructive as thinking about the past. Which is completely non-constructive. Interviewers are always trying to make you think about the past or the future.

EC: If what you're saying is that you concentrate on the present, you're sounding very Zen Buddhist, very West Coast.

SMacG: [Loud laughter] Nah, sorry. The West Coast has nothing to do with Zen. The East Coast has a bit more to do with it. How to buy a bottle of [amyl] nitrite without getting mugged in New York. [Laughs]

It was evident from Shane's discomfort and evasive demeanour that all was not well. He seemed unhappy. Out of deference to my friend, I avoided asking the obvious question or questions. I didn't wish to put Shane in a position where he might feel he had to lie.

The interview appeared in print on 30 November 1989. It came as no surprise when, within six months, The Pogues informed manager Frank Murray that they weren't renewing his contract. In the autumn the band released *Hell's Ditch*. It was the last Pogues album to feature Shane MacGowan. The centre couldn't hold. In the memoir that's credited to himself and Victoria Mary Clarke (*A Drink with Shane MacGowan*), Shane reveals how he'd felt 'like a prisoner … Only God knows why I wasted all those years on the road. I'm frightened of change, and I knew it was going to be a big change, if I left.'

BRIAN BEHAN – March 1990

When he was eleven, Brian Behan was sentenced to three years in Artane Industrial School for shoplifting. Twelve years later, in 1950, he emigrated from Dublin to London with a knapsack of troubles.

A rangy, scarecrow figure, the Brian I meet in 1990 bears little resemblance to the figure his brother Brendan's biographer, Ulick O'Connor, described as having 'a head of heroic proportions, well cut features and a mass of wavy, copper-gold hair'. At sixty-three, the firebrand of old has a face that resembles a melting wax effigy of his infamous older brother.

His mother, Kathleen, who'd been a courier for Patrick Pearse and James Connolly during the 1916 Rising, had died six years earlier and Brian had published the memoir *Mother of All the Behans*, described as 'an autobiography of Kathleen Behan as told to Brian Behan'.

Although he lives in England, author and playwright Brian is back in Dublin for Peter Sheridan's stage adaptation of the book.

'I get two and a half per cent,' he announces bullishly. 'Now they're going to do a film of it. I wanted to memorialise my mother and capture a slice of Irish history. In the last years of her life I went to see her and she said, "Brian, who made the world?"

'I said, "God."

'She said, "Well, who made God?"

'I said, "You've got me there."'

While well-practiced at setting up a gag, Brian is also master of the myriad skills of the seasoned raconteur. When the listener might be expecting a follow-up quip or wisecrack, Behan can hit a note of harsh realism. 'It was disturbing for me that at ninety-three, she was giving up religion when other people were fuckin' running to it as a form of insurance. She was a very strong woman.'

Raised with an acquaintance of poverty, it was incarceration in Artane that scarred him for life. Emigrating to England in 1950, he worked as a labourer on building sites and joined the Communist Party of Great Britain, which he quit in protest following the brutal suppression of the Hungarian uprising by Soviet troops and tanks in 1956. A militant trade unionist, his direct-action campaigning resulted in prison sentences in 1951 and 1958.

I meet the author in a crowded, noisy, smoke-filled lounge bar in the Liberties, and for over two hours listen as he runs me ragged with a non-stop torrent of irreverent, mischievous, bizarre and often objectionable ranting.

Initially, when I feel he is being flippant or showing off for the benefit of those friends in surrounding seats, I think I should attempt to get his undivided attention. Knowing he was two years older than his brother Dominic, who had been a fellow columnist in the *Evening Herald*, I enquire if, in light of Dominic and Brendan's fame, he thinks he might have an inferiority complex.

'That didn't bother me because I was famous in England before them,' he retorts. 'My photograph was on the front page of *The Observer* in 1951, standing with Mao Tse-Tung reviewing the troops. I'd be shot for that now.'

He laughs at the surreal spectacle.

'In London I went with Brendan once to see *The Hostage*. We went with the Guinness family, Lady Oranmore and Browne. Brendan knew them. They took him on like a rich person's pet. As we were going along in this Rolls-Royce with my mother, our Brendan turned around and said to me, "You renegade bastard, you've left the Communist Party."

'I said, "It does seem odd to me that your ambition is to be a rich fuckin' Red. You're sitting between two millionaires and you're attacking me for betraying the working-class movement."

'My mother then said, "Stop the taxi, I'm getting out. I'll walk. I don't want any more of this." That shut Brendan up. She was very dignified. A very strong woman.'

Dominic had died just seven months prior to our meeting. 'Did you go to Dominic's funeral?'

'No. His wife refused to allow any of us to go. The whole thing became something of a farce. They cremated Dominic in Glasgow and came to bury him on the banks of the canal. [Seán] Garland [of the Workers' Party] raised our Dominic's ashes aloft to ceremoniously fling them into the canal near Russell Street and a fuckin' gust of wind came and blew the ashes all over everybody.

'They were picking lumps of Dominic out of their eyes. It's a horrible tale. I never made it up with him because he took himself too seriously.'

'Ah, yes, but that was just for stirring it up, surely?' I venture.

'Yes, but that was something Brendan envied. He said to me during the big dispute, "I'm very proud of what you're doing." It was a side of him and Dominic which was never developed. Dominic would pretend to be a revolutionary, but he wasn't. In the end he became a kind of poseur.'

At times, I suspect Brian is winding me up. Yet he also seems sincere in his beliefs, even if they sound outdated, theatrically cranky or repugnant. Oddly, his intransigence and humorous belligerence remind me of many of punk rock's more entertaining practitioners in the 1970s. He certainly doesn't care what people might think of him. 'I like a bit of stick,' he declares. 'It doesn't do me any harm.'

'You've had serious health issues lately. Wasn't there a colon cancer scare a few years ago?'

'I was terrified. All I did was meditate out of desperation because I'd been told that if you did this self-visualisation and try to get the positive energy of the body to the affected part it would cure it.

'A lot of my trouble was because I had a divorce from my wife. She had rung up and said, "I'll kill myself." I'd gone off with another girl. She was pregnant. My whole nervous system was shattered. But at least I'm still here. Another thing I learned from my mother was laugh and the world laughs with you. Weep and you weep alone.'

Following a work-related accident, he became a mature student at Sussex University and graduated in English and history. He later lectured in media studies at the London College of Printing. His play *Boots for the Footless* had a successful run at the Tricycle

Theatre. But given the social and economic problems that afflicted Britain at the start of the new decade, I wonder if writing a farce was an easy option. Had Brian thrown in the towel?

His response is another colourful swerve. 'I've tried to do a play on male liberation, but it met with a savage response. I've tried to argue that men need to be emotionally developed in order to meet the new right-wing feminists of whom Thatcher is a prime example … I think we should have mixed prisons where men and women could live together in free sexual harmony. I see change not in political terms but in terms of human relationships.

'The real war in Britain now is the sex war. The sex war is much more total than the class war. All an employer will want to do is exploit you between the hours of eight and five o'clock. With the wife, the battle is twenty-four hours.'

'You're another lad who spent time in the Artane Industrial School.'

'It fucked up my sexual life. The Brothers conducted two wars. One against impurity, but they were bendable.' He laughs without joy. 'The other was against communism. I wonder why they never said the Reds were impure. They never connected the two.

'Look at the structure of the Communist Party and the Catholic Church. They're identical. Centralist organisations ruled from above.

'It was a very severe regime. Father Flanagan came from Boys Town and said, "The rule of the boot and fist predominates." The reply of the Brothers was that he was obviously a communist agent.' He emits another garrulous laugh. 'It took me a long time to get my sex life untangled.'

It is forty years since Brian left Dublin. How would he rank the changes he'd witnessed in the city over the four decades?

'Immense. I find Dublin a clean, lively, bustling town. The centre of it seems to be flattened. Nevertheless, there's an immense reconstruction. My mother claimed that all cities had to renew themselves.

'I like Ireland. I may come back, partly because of the poll tax and partly because I'm anxious to dodge the English divorce laws. I'm married again …'

It's likely that Behan doesn't require an open microphone to prompt him. All through his life, this lecturer in media studies has displayed an ability to grab the headlines.

But is this the real Brian Behan or a performative caricature? I leave the pub thinking that perhaps, as was sometimes the case when meeting public figures, I need to search between the bravado and the bombast for my answer.

Chapter Six

Into the Lion's Den

FAMOUS OR OTHERWISE, MOST PEOPLE are more complex than we might initially think. It's impossible to say we fully know an individual. People we've known for years often surprise us by doing something considered 'out of character'. Interviewing someone offers an opportunity to get a more in-depth understanding of the individual.

In the mid-1980s, when I was still actively involved in the music industry, working in the studio with some excellent cult bands including The Sting-Rays, I tended to live at the Irish Club in Belgravia, where, among the members, was a man whom a resident remarked 'looked like a dentist'. On those occasional nights when I might arrive back early, 'the dentist' could be found in the TV lounge with an ever-present sketchbook in hand.

I recognised Paul Costelloe, international fashion designer, who, more often than not, would have a client appointment the following morning, quite possibly at nearby Kensington Palace with Princess Diana, a great admirer of his creations. Paul was amused by the dentist description when I recalled it in 1990. While we'd often chatted at the club, it wasn't until we engaged in a formal interview that I discovered the question of identity wasn't entirely a light-hearted matter for Paul, a Dubliner who'd been educated at Blackrock College. It was something he took seriously.

'It was mentioned that I have a problem with my identity,' he noted firmly. 'I don't have any problem. They might have a problem about identifying whether I'm British or Irish. I have no problem.'

While discussing the lack of high-end training and job opportunities for young designers in Ireland, he revealed, 'I'm self-made in that sense. I didn't go through college. I worked in different countries [France, Italy and the USA] and developed that way. That was probably a lot easier back in the late '60s than it is today.'

The interview process is often an essential component in the career arc of famous people. Most crave publicity when struggling to draw attention to their work. Later, some find they can't live without the oxygen media coverage supplies, while others, accepting the interview process as intrusive, reluctantly accept it as a chore, a necessary evil.

It's not always possible to put interviewees at their ease. Maintaining eye contact and being seen to be fully engaged in the conversation helps. To that end the reassurance of having a tape recorder proved useful. Initially, I used a Pro Walkman cassette machine. But no matter what technology you're using, accidents can happen.

In the back of a taxi after an enjoyable and generous interview with Emmylou Harris, I pressed 'play' and discovered I had only the first ten minutes of the conversation. In a panic, I immediately scribbled shorthand versions of all the quotes I could remember from our chat. Luckily, I'd enough to fill an interesting article, but from then on I began to use a backup dictaphone. 'To be sure, to be sure', I'd joke lamely, hoping to break the ice.

In hindsight, considering what came after, some of the interviews are fascinating. Five years before he became the monstrous Fr Jack Hackett in the sitcom *Father Ted*, satirist, TV and radio voiceover artist, and recording star, who'd appeared on *Top of the Pops* with his hilarious 'Twelve Days of Christmas', Frank Kelly had told me of those occasions between jobs when he'd 'trotted into the labour exchange many, many times'.

'They all nudge each other in the queue and say, "It's yer man,"' he recalled. 'It's very funny. People pay lip service to socialism, but when somebody goes to collect what is their right, their social insurance, it's "What's he doing in here?"'

He wasn't the only future member of the Craggy Island crew to know how precarious an acting career can be.

I loved meeting Dermot Morgan who, bursting with live-wire ideas, would always launch into a rapid-fire series of gags, impressions and hilarious insights, much of it stuff he'd be working on. He'd then use me as an audience as he tried out new material. I dreaded having to interview him in 1991, knowing that it would be like trying to pick up mercury with a fork. But, yet again, Dermot surprised me with his candour and the courage he showed in airing his insecurities.

He was riding high at the time with his acclaimed contribution to the satirical radio programme *Scrap Saturday*. Reminding me that he'd first achieved national celebrity a decade earlier with his appearances on *The Live Mike* television show, he said, 'I'm a great believer in television'. But this success had been followed by some heartbreaking failures, particularly an attempted TV series with scriptwriter Barry Devlin that fell at the first hurdle. Dermot couldn't hide his bitter disappointment. After analysing what he believed were the reasons for this setback, he declared, 'It's time to put up or shut up as far as I'm concerned. I don't know whether it's the onset of mid-life crisis but for me everything is now shit or bust.'

With the determination of the superstar football strikers he admired, he stuck with it, won a Jacob's Award for his work on *Scrap Saturday* and, five years later, won a BAFTA and achieved genuine iconic status in his role as Father Ted.

Dermot wasn't the only interviewee capable of conjuring up surreal scenarios. Zig and Zag, the alien TV celebrities in Ireland and Britain who had a smash-hit single, presented a challenge. Perched on the back of a sofa, with their voices appearing to emanate from the cushions, they remained resolutely in character, as I had hoped. 'Prince always rings us,' Zag revealed after telling a caller to phone back later. 'He's the same height as us. Three feet.'

I wondered if the pressures of the intergalactic emissaries' hectic schedule might result in musical or personal differences that could, as with so many pop groups, lead to a split. While Zig insisted, 'We're a team,' Zag confided, 'He's got my Dinky cars in a drawer so I could never leave.'

Deftly switching topics, they homed in on what they considered a serious political issue. 'Dáil fashion,' they chorused. Zig, the lanky one with the close-set eyes, said, 'That's going to be the next big thing.'

Zag continued the prediction, 'Everybody will be wearing it. They'll all be going around with, "Hey, I've got an Alan Dukes tie." It's all about fashion, Eamon. It's the ties we're interested in.'

Their prescience foreshadowed the national debate sparked some time later by the casual approach to tailoring of an incoming gaggle of unconventional TDs.

Some of the more uncontrollable laughs I've had in life were enjoyed while listening to the surreal ramblings of Peter Cook and Dudley Moore during the 1960s and early 1970s. Relocating to Hollywood, Moore starred in a string of successful films, including *10*, *Arthur* and *Micki & Maude*, for which he won a Golden Globe.

Early in 1992, on the release of *Blame it on the Bellboy*, he was subdued. Worryingly so. 'I think there's a period of your life when you're not quite sure who you are,' he ventured. 'And where you are and maybe you pay a lot of money to people to find out. I don't think you can have a nice cup of tea with someone and get it all out. I'm certainly an example of psycho-analysis working.'

Contemplating his openness about his mood swings and bouts of depression, he added, 'I sometimes think, *Oh God, maybe I shouldn't have talked about that*. But I'm not a politician so I can be as sick as I like … what's important to me is expressing myself but I'm just getting on with it rather than talking about it.'

It was never less than intriguing to be offered a glimpse behind the veil and get to hear details, either serious or trivial, of the irritations that sometimes bedevil people whether famous or otherwise.

When Hanif Kureishi was young, in the mid-sixties, there was anti-Pakistani sentiment in his area of south London and a constant threat posed by racist skinheads and the National Front. Talented and industrious, at eighteen, Kureishi was writing drama for the Royal Court Theatre.

I'd met Kureishi briefly at Faber & Faber's launch of Shane MacGowan's *Poguetry*. By the time we next met, in Dublin, he had followed the success of *My Beautiful Laundrette* with the award-winning novel *The Buddha of Suburbia*. While responding to an enquiry about his family's response to his work, he admitted, 'I had an aunt who'd write me letters abusing me. She'd ring up my dad to try to get him to stop me writing. [Laughs] As if there was anything he could do. My family and relations respect writing. It's only the English who don't respect writers. The Irish, the Scots, the Welsh, the Indians and everyone else respects writers. In England, they think writing is a funny way of life.'

Ireland's 'Queen of Showbusiness', Maureen Potter, told me of when, as a child, she performed with Jack Hylton (the English composer and band leader known as 'The Ambassador of British Dance') in Germany, and Adolf Hitler came to a show. 'He marched into Austria in 1938 and we were playing in Berlin. We got home very quickly because nobody knew what was going to happen.'

She actually met Hitler on the night; he presented her with a wreath. 'When my mother saw it, she put it in the bin. "That man," she said. "You mean to say you accepted something from that man." Boink! Into the bin it went.'

When I met Jennifer Johnston on a promotional tour in 1991, I didn't remind her that she had taken the title of her Booker-shortlisted novel *Shadows on Our Skin* from a lyric I'd written for *The Táin* album. ('Now we've got time to kill!/Kill the shadows on our skin.')

However, in conversation, I was slightly taken aback by flashes of the author's indignation and impatience when discussing other writers, the political situation and the problems of juggling family matters with a writing career. Perhaps registering my unease and checking herself, Jennifer explained, 'The thing about doing five or six interviews a day is that you find yourself saying the same things over and over again. You think, "Jesus Christ!" You get a sort of aggravation in your voice and you have to soften it. I've had my bellyful this week.'

RALPH STEADMAN – March 1991

Ralph Steadman is already settled at the bar when I arrive at his Dublin hotel. In front of him sit a tumbler of whiskey and a pint of beer.

Remembering his crazed anti-social adventures with Hunter S. Thompson, I fear for my sanity, if not my safety. Hadn't *Fear and Loathing in Las Vegas* begun with the line 'We were somewhere around Barstow on the edge of the desert when the drugs began to take hold.' That trip, and other sordid, if hilarious, escapades had been undertaken on a diet of whiskey, beer and hallucinogenic drugs. The evening is young. Where might we end up, I fret? In some filthy jail shouting for a solicitor? Or in the damp casualty ward of a Victorian mental hospital somewhere in the midlands?

Thompson's concept of 'bad craziness', which Steadman gleefully chronicled with a series of urgent, scratchy drawings, may have been our watchword in the zany rock'n'roll 1970s, but I've long renounced that helter-skelter, hedonistic lifestyle.

So, it's with not a little trepidation that I introduce myself to the fifty-five-year-old Welshman with the piercing eyes who, disconcertingly, explains that his wife is having a bath. I'm shocked. It feels as if this disarming individual is someone I might meet on a package sun holiday for retirees. However, being familiar with Steadman's volcanic, often grotesque, ink-spattered cartoons, I still suspect I'm stepping into the lion's den.

There's only one thing for it. I beckon to the barman.

'An Irish whiskey for me, please. And another pint and a short for my friend.'

There's so much I could speak to the artist about, including his work with poet Ted Hughes, Frank Zappa and The Who. Or his thoughts on having illustrated Flann O'Brien's *The Poor Mouth*. But after a bit of chit-chat, I steer the conversation towards Steadman's most recent venture, an exhibition in London of large-scale images inspired by the Gulf War.

Operation Desert Storm had been launched with an aerial bombardment of Iraq in January 1991. Nightly TV news bulletins transmitted near-apocalyptic footage of burning oilfields, incinerated army and civilian vehicles and the awful destruction caused by precision-guided missiles and bombs. There's nothing ironic, jokey or clever clogs about this nauseous and terrifying set of Steadman images, which I first became aware of when I saw some reproduced in the *Independent on Sunday*.

'It was shortly after I saw a clip on TV about the war artist who was commissioned by the Imperial War Museum to cover the Gulf War that I saw your work reproduced in the newspaper,' I say.

'It was so quick,' replies Ralph. 'I just happened to show them to Richard Williams, the editor, and he said, "We'll do it. Next week." It was as quick as that. So we found a gallery in London who'd put a show on. I took them in and José, the Mexican owner, wasn't there, but they hadn't anything planned for the next month so, over the phone from Mexico, José said, "We'll do it." He hadn't seen it.

'We'd been lobbed so much media stuff, all this imagery, I felt I was going crazy. There was so much media stuff. What can you do with it? You can't sit down and do careful drawings. You can't digest it all. There's too much of it. You just simply suffer from an overload. So I decided to lob it back in a sense by throwing it at these sheets of pure linen. I just went for it like a bull in a china shop.'

I know Steadman, born in Wallasey in 1936, would have been old enough to register memories of nights spent in an air-raid shelter as German bombers unloaded their cargo over nearby

Liverpool and surrounding areas during the Second World War. But I don't interrupt.

'You had to respond like the violence we were feeling,' he continues. 'Violence is the total negation and breakdown of everything. Because I'm certain that, when they were watching those black and white video replays of the bomb sites, a lot of people knew instinctively, even though they couldn't hear, that inside that puff of smoke there was carnage. We all knew it like an animal instinct. But we tried to treat it like a video game, as though it wasn't really happening. There may have been a few who thought it was wonderful. But I felt that all we were watching was a muted result of total scorched earth policy.

'I likened it to chemotherapy, where they try to get the cancer out of a body by laser beaming in on the one thing but not getting the cancer but killing the body politic. If you think of it like that, they've done a lousy job. Like a spoiled child who couldn't have the toy says, "If I can't have it, you can't have it either."'

At this point, Ralph opens a satchel and produces photocopies of some of the work. We look at it together. It's impressive.

'Why is it there are so many wars?' he continues. 'Where are all these people who commit the crimes? They're everywhere. But they're nowhere. It's a strange paradox. Everyone talks of peace. Everyone is pleasant. You meet people and they're pleasant. But they are those who commit the crime.'

While aware of the sometimes oblique anti-war statements implied in much of the work of First World War artist William Orpen, I suggest, 'I think the concept of the official war artist is essentially to capture the jingoism of the moment.'

'Yes, I think so. I don't know why others would want to do that, in a way. I didn't want to think about it. I wanted to react. There was an energy there that I had to get rid of. So I used it. In the space of three weeks, I did over thirty of these pictures. Which is a lot, because I don't do that many pictures. And then it dies with it. One could say that from an artistic point of view, war is a good thing.'

He laughs at the irony and adds, 'Or a bad thing. But it produces imagery of a kind which doesn't ...'

As his voice tails off, I raise the matter of *Private Eye*, his old alma mater, lampooning him when his war paintings appeared.

'I expected that from them. They're so bloody philistine. Schoolboy philistines. It's the worst kind. Never mind. When I worked for them in the '60s they wanted me to carry on doing pastiches of old artists like H.M. Bateman and [John] Tenniel.

'I felt I had my own things I wanted to say. Richard Ingrams [the editor] was never interested in that. So I had to go.

'Then I went to America and met Hunter Thompson and found that screaming lifestyle running through the whole of America.

'I hate it and I love it. It's a strange thing. I find that one gets into a rather creative mode when you're surrounded by hideousness. Why is that? Why aren't I stimulated by cows in the meadow, I ask myself? They're lovely to look at, but I don't want to draw them.'

'And yet you're not a jaundiced individual.'

'No, I don't think so. People say, "Oh, he must be a violent person. He does violent pictures." But the violence is the reactive response. It's the shock in my own system which generates energy that has to be expended. Either you beat up old ladies or you do pictures. And I do pictures.' He's laughing again.

'I can't think for a minute that I'm a violent man. Over the weekend, I tried to save a lamb. We have sheep in the orchard. And one of them had three lambs. It was obvious after a few days that she was rejecting one. The other two were coming on in leaps and bounds. The poor little bugger, every time he tried to get to the teat, the mother walked on and he fell over. So I took it and bottle-fed it, like it was my own baby. I was getting up every three hours over the weekend. We had an Australian staying there and he said, "Ah, you've got to put a raw egg in there. A raw egg will do it a world of good. You need a bit of protein." But on Monday morning it wasn't working. I was trying to save it, but I didn't know what I was doing. I was trying to save it, but I was killing it. The poor little thing was probably saying in its own mind, "Please leave me alone." Anyway, I took it to the vet and he gave it antibiotics for a stomach infection.

'With all this killing going on, all this hideous stuff, I would love to do something just like save a lamb. Just a symbol of something towards positive thought.

'People say, "Why would you bother saving it? Because in a few months it will be slaughtered." But I wouldn't. I don't have them to buy and sell for meat. I only have them there to keep my orchard down. They have a good life. If they keep their head down, they do alright.' He laughs at his gangster persona.

'I don't want to have them put down. But at ten-thirty yesterday morning this little one gave up the ghost. Gave a strange little bleat then it was gone. I was very sad for a while. I have to tell you, I wept a little.

'I thought, what a terrible arrogance to think that we can go out and zap others. Food for thought. It only confirmed everything I've ever thought about violence. I think in the first paragraph the United Nations call it, "To protect the world from the scourge of war and to consider war to be the breakdown of diplomacy." They did try this time, right till the very end.

'But there's something where we seem to demand a cathartic experience. And someone goes to war because of that. There have been heightened moments during history, times when the human race seem to require a purgative.'

We're joined by his wife, Anna, a teacher and artist, who is clearly a reassuring and stabilising influence on the artist. The couple have been together since the early 1970s. I wonder how she felt when Ralph was schlepping around America with the notorious Thompson. But it would be unfair to put her on the spot. So I ask Ralph if, given the reach and impact of his work with Thompson, he'd felt in danger of being typecast.

'Since I've met Hunter I've always been regarded in America as his buddy, his sidekick. But, in another way, it's opened doors. They're interested in what you do when you do something on your own. Hunter always said to me, "Aah Ralph, don't write. You can't write. It's all gibberish. Gibberish." [Laughs] But I said, "Look Hunter, I can write better than you can draw." So that's something. He says, "I warn you, you'll come to no good trying to write."

'You suddenly hear yourself taking yourself very seriously, so you puncture it, somehow. It seems to me a necessary part of it all. It's an instinct thing. With this, I went with it. I thought, *I'm an artist. What does an artist do at a time like this? Does one just indulge in interior decoration?* So I did this. I could imagine, in a hundred years' time, if these images still exist and we're all still on the planet, they'll be looked on at least as a historical document, if not art. What made him respond this way? It becomes intriguing, doesn't it? It seems to me to be a reasonable response to it.

'It's not unlike the way Robert Capa [the war photographer] responded when he came ashore at the Normandy landings. He just shot in all directions and had all these pictures of soldiers slightly blurred. That's what he wanted. He didn't want clear pictures. It was real.

'So not thinking about it is a better way. So there they are. They exist where they wouldn't have existed had I not set the question, "What would an artist do in times of war?"'

'I haven't seen the new book, *Tales of the Weirrd*, yet. But I gather it's quite a change from *The Big I Am*, which has the quality of fine art.'

'Would you call *The Big I Am* fine art?'

'Yes, I would.'

Oops! We are several rounds of drinks in now and I worry that I may have offended the artist. By clumsily invoking 'fine art', have I implied the rest of his work is of lesser merit? Of course not. But it's tricky. I can't back down.

Ralph adds, 'One of these days people will say, "My God that's an interesting thing to do."'

Noting his scepticism, I press on, hoping to repair any damage. 'I don't mean that as a disparaging remark. I hesitate to use the word "sophisticated", but maybe superficially more sophisticated or something ...' God, I'm making this worse.

Ralph clears his throat and thinks for a moment. 'It wasn't sophisticated at all. What it was is the history of the US, as we know it, in a funny kind of way. We all know somehow the Earth came into being, so I made a little legend of what might have happened. The biggest insult I could heap upon the Earth was to say that it was a vomit and a screaming ball of unreason, and then God cried because of the hideousness of it and then he killed his wife. So he had this resentment and this terrible despair and he wept. And the tears fell upon this screaming ball of unreason and turned it into a muddy scum. And out of the primeval mess, little things started to appear. Something which resembled life. Then evolving.

'I thought I was making some point when it came to the figure like an orang-utan getting up – which was a creature completely puzzled by everything around it, screaming into the blackness, believing only in itself. And then five minutes later everybody bowing down to a graven image. It has to believe in something. It's too much of a quantum leap to just believe in yourself. You have to have something to believe in. So we have to create the gods. And we create them in all shapes and sizes.'

(Here we digress into a discussion on Freud, Jung and anti-Semitism, much of which is indecipherable on tape due to increased background bar noise and social chatter.)

I pick up the conversation with Ralph ruminating. 'This rise in jingoism – I thought we'd killed it after the Falklands War. I thought we couldn't possibly go through that again, but in fact it came up again like another new boil. Now people are conscious of being jingoistic.'

'Why did you decide to stop drawing political figures?'

'I know people think it's silly, but one of the biggest political statements I could ever make is not to draw political figures. Who wants to draw bureaucrats?

'Now John Major is walking on the mild side. [Laughs] These people have been schooled for the last twenty years in a new kind of bureaucratic government which isn't the man of fire any more. Maggie Thatcher had fire in her belly but for different reasons. They're honing their image to catch votes. It's nothing to do with ideology any more. It's careerist.

'If you have socialist feelings you have to vote for the ideal. You're trying to find what is best for everybody in the community.

That's what I always thought the simplistic version of socialism was – that you were voting for the good of the community. You weren't voting so that it would be good for your bank balance. But that's what everybody does now. They vote for their bank balance. I find it a bit upsetting.

'I had an ideal of human nature in which the bad would see the error of their ways and that suffering, hunger and poverty would become things of the past. Now suddenly boils are appearing all over the place in ways one would never have imagined.

'I just want to be an artist. What's wrong with art now is that people try to market commodities which are acceptable. If you can imagine a Sotheby's in the 1920s, when George Grosz was painting the Weimar Republic, which now would fetch big prices but then was totally unacceptable. It needs time to pass to get these things into an art perspective. The German Expressionists were regarded as the decadents at the time, including Marc Chagall [the Russian artist spent time in Berlin before basing himself in Paris].

'Maybe we've made some progress, but we still haven't made it in terms of today. We still have that attitude that we want to be comforted. We want to know that we're okay and that we're doing the right thing. So the art should reflect that and make us look good. The fact that it doesn't make us look good, it must be decadent. There must be something nasty about it.'

Ralph is fully engaged and speaking with a deep passion. 'It's like *Piss Christ* [American artist Andres Serrano's 1987 artwork *Immersion (Piss Christ)*]. I almost feel the man is probably religious. It wasn't, "How can I make myself notorious?" In a way, once it's gone through a process, it's a comment that we could level at our society, that we've shat on everything decent in the name of business or anything else.

'Art always only ever responded to the raw edge of human activity. They simply see it and respond to it and that's what generates the energy.'

He pauses for a brief moment before carrying on. 'Maybe I should be an artist rather than just a cartoonist. I prefer to put it another way and say I'm a cartoonist trying to extend the parameters of cartooning, to include the rest. In fact, Picasso was a cartoonist. Goya, Leonardo da Vinci, [Honoré] Daumier, Otto Dix were cartoonists, but as they get nearer to our time, they [as artist-cartoonists] start looking less and less like artists. It's only Picasso who pulls off the full trick where he's somehow creating interior decorations at the same time as making comment. Most people think art is about something that goes with the wallpaper. It's not. It's something that's a little uncomfortable to live with in the time it's created.

'It's a great problem and Maggie Thatcher has tried to create an environment where that kind of art cannot survive. I'm a little upset about trade unions who never talk about art any more. I thought that trade unionism wasn't just about more money but about a better quality of life. But they only ever talk about more money. "We've got the best conditions. We don't want to know about art. We want bingo. We want Gazza."'

It's easy to engage with Steadman's polemic. I reply, 'You've homed in on two things there, motivation and ambition, that intrigue me. And you don't rest on your laurels.'

'Why do we do it otherwise? Is it just a way of making money? Or is there some other purpose to it. And that's why I asked myself the question when the war began. That frustrated me and what can one do? In a way, you lash out blindly. This [his Gulf War images] was just to do something.

'Someone said it's blood money. But a third of the proceeds are going to the Red Cross and a third to the gallery. And I might get something out of it for doing a day's work.

'It's always bugging me. I'll probably never reconcile with it. I'll never feel happy that it's just art for art's sake. I'm never more happy than when I've got a hook in something. That's when I really come alive.

'But you can't expect it every week. Or every day. But you feel some strange urge and power that you can do something. You can feel almost self-righteous. So maybe that's a good thing to feel. It's not a self-righteousness based on smugness. It's because you've grabbed something that's troubling you. It legitimises art. Instead of it being the thing you do when you can't do Latin and mathematics.'

I hadn't expected this level of discussion before I arrived. But now we seem to have reached the core. This begs one key question. 'What is it that keeps you cartooning?'

'Cartooning is never a space filler. Just something to put in the paper to titillate the eye for the sake of filling a space every day. I can appreciate the fact that somebody starts a strip cartoon. People want to see what happens next. It helps sell papers. That's one kind of cartoon. But I think it's a limited idea of what the cartoon is or can do.

'It can encompass everything. It's a way of thinking. It's not a rather shallow job you do because you can't do anything else. It really has a stimulating intellectual purpose and I don't mean that in a kind of highfalutin' way but simply that it makes you think visually through your intellect. And some people might be stimulated by that. There are things you can say in pictures that you can't say in words.'

'MAD' FRANKIE FRASER – February 1997

The London criminal known as 'Mad' Frankie Fraser, one of the most feared villains in London's underworld, hadn't been on my radar until I got a heads up from a mutual friend that he was coming to Dublin and would be happy to meet. I established contact. But our planned get-together was postponed indefinitely.

Then, out of the blue, I received a call. 'Would I be free to meet with Mr Fraser this evening?'

And so, the deep hues of the flock wallpaper in a discreet reception room at a city-centre hotel create the ideal ambience when I meet a well-dressed gent and his girlfriend, the charming Marilyn Wisbey, daughter of Tommy Wisbey, one of the men sentenced for the Great Train Robbery of 1963.

After we've exchanged pleasantries, I produce my little Pro Walkman tape machine. As I switch it on, I become concerned at how Frankie's eyes narrow and appear even more remote. He remarks on the little red light that lets us know it's recording. I say that I could cover it up with a bit of gaffa tape, as I'd normally do if I was bootlegging a music gig or something.

Frankie seems relieved. He and Marilyn laugh, then smile at each other. 'A bootlegger.' Taking this as a sign I've been accepted, I apologise for not being well prepared for our interview because of the short notice. Given that he's familiar with all manner of techniques the English police use, some covert, others more robust, to get suspects to talk, my palaver is nothing he hasn't encountered before. The first thing I'm curious about is when he got out of prison.

'I came out of prison in 1989. Eight years now,' he says in a hushed, unhurried, calming delivery that's oddly alarming.

He'd been in and out several times over the years for a variety of offences, none of which were trivial, hadn't he? This proves to be a delicate understatement.

'Yes. I spent over forty years in prison. Not all in one go.'

I attempt a quick calculation of likely remissions. Frankie is seventy-three. 'Your actual sentences would probably have added up to a lot more because you probably got time off for …'

Frankie cuts me short. 'Well, no. I always lost my remission, didn't I,' he says in a kindly manner. 'I always got in bags of trouble.'

I find it difficult to associate this seemingly mild-mannered man with the shocking violence that earned him both various custodial sentences and the frightening appellation 'Mad'. I have to remind myself that Fraser earned his reputation over decades in a gang world populated by people regarded by society as monsters – people such as the Kray twins, the Richardsons and their ilk. 'You seem such a soft-spoken gent,' I remark.

'That's true, but it's the facts of life, innit,' replies Frankie in a matter-of-fact tone. 'Only because I learned through experience that that was the best way to talk, if you was making an offer that you didn't want anyone to refuse. I always thought it went over better like that. They knew you really meant it.'

He ponders the dichotomy and continues, 'Or else you'd come over as a bully.'

Delivered *sotto voce*, Frankie's authentic old-world East End speech patterns and cadences have a unique salt-of-the-earth, neighbourly charm that I associate with classic Ealing comedies, those British films made in the late 1940s and early 1950s when people, even hapless criminals, seemed good-natured and optimistic after the war. I remark that, by comparison, people shout a lot these days. There's a lot of anger about.

'I couldn't fault you there. It is a different ball-game.'

Marilyn points to the case of her father, who received a thirty-year sentence. 'After my sister died in a car crash, the Home Secretary [Reginald Maudling] refused my dad permission to come out to support my mum at the funeral, while he allowed Myra Hindley, who helped to murder all these children, to have a day out. And yet my dad never killed anybody. He just stole the Queen's money. And wasn't allowed out for the funeral.'

'Aaaww, it's ridiculous,' snorts her partner.

Reared in a tough, unforgiving East End environment in the 1930s, street fights were commonplace in Frankie's manor. 'Bloodthirsty but honourable.' When he was nine, he began working as a runner for the notorious Sabini brothers, a family gang that controlled racecourses and night clubs. Three years later, he was caught thieving for the first time and sent to an approved school. A deserter during the war, he was in and out of prison on a regular basis. After the war, he set up what he dubbed 'the Friday club' – coshing people who were withdrawing cash to pay weekly company wage bills.

An exchange in the 1971 film *Get Carter* plays on my mind. When Michael Caine's character (Jack Carter) says to a former associate, who's now working as a chauffeur for a crime boss, 'I've always had your welfare at heart, Eric. Beside which, I'm nosey.' Eric replies, 'Well, that's not always a healthy way to be, is it?'

Frankie and I have been chatting for some time, recalling incidents and episodes that resulted in his incarceration, when I ask if there was anything he'd do differently if he was a young man today.

'Of course. If I could look into the crystal ball, if I was starting out, I'd be different. But you must remember what was against me. My mother was Irish. My father was Canadian. My father's mother was a Red Indian. He came over in the First World War, a seaman on a convoy. He met my mother in London, fell in love and later married. He was about thirty-five then. He lived to about eighty-eight. If he was alive now, he'd be 116. But when he was born in Canada 116 years ago, how many white women would he have met in Canada? I'm not going off about colour or anything. It's just the facts. I'm the youngest of five children.'

No mistake, Frankie feels hard done by. He voices his complaints. 'But they were both straight. They were two of the most honest, hard-working people you could wish to meet. I had no help from them in crime, did I? Or any of the family. My older brother was decorated for bravery in the war. He's a nice man. Not into crime or nothin'. But he understands. He knows that but for the grace of God, it could have been himself. He saw active service in the desert.

'The only other relation we had in England was my mother's brother, Denis, who was also Irish. You couldn't go to places then like you can now. You couldn't go on a plane and go here or there. It was impossible then. So we had no help at all.

'When I got into crime, I had to start right from the bottom and work me way up, with no help. So, therefore, I did make a lot of mistakes. Whereas if my father had been into crime, or my mother, they'd have an idea. "Don't you go doing that. If you're going to go into crime, do it like this." Advice like that. But there wasn't advice, so therefore I did get a lot of prison sentencing when I was young that I most probably wouldn't have got.'

As the waiter arrives with tea and biscuits, we switch from Frankie's lament to consider, instead, Marilyn's career in show-business.

'At the time of the accident, I just lost interest,' she says. 'It knocked the stuffing out of me, losing my sister. Eventually, I got back to singing in pubs and clubs. Mostly in America. I met Frank Sinatra with my father. And Tony Bennett. Then we managed to get Frank's book published. And now we're doing shows in theatres. And it's been accepted for a film about Frank's life story. Jocelyn Brown, an American singer, is coming over to record a song for it. We'll try and make a hit of that. It's called 'I Still Believe in You'. I wrote it.

'I was with Frank when he got shot by the undercover outside Turnmills Night Club in '91,' Marilyn adds.

I look at Frankie, his cold eyes, unblinking, betraying no emotion, and offer a colloquial euphemism. 'You weren't being a naughty boy, were you?'

Frankie perks up. 'Naw. They knew that my book was in the transition stages. I'd been approached time and again to write a book. I said, "No. No. No." But eventually I said, "Alright, I'll consider it." And they realised that there could be a lot about corrupt policemen. Unfair convictions. Whatever. And the British police's reputation for the last few years, after the Birmingham Six, the Guildford Four, the Tottenham Three, the Bridgewater Four and so on, has gone right down the pan. And they thought, "Well this so-and-so is about to push us down even further so we'll shoot him and put it down as a gangland killing."'

The hardened criminal credits the 'bent coppers' with being smart, for once. 'I can't blame them for a good idea. But when they done it, one of them bullets went in here, in my 'ead, and went all the way round … one of them bullets, very clever, it's not powerful enough to go right through.'

Indicating the point of entry, he continues. 'So it travelled looking for an exit and in travelling it goes to your brain. Or if it's here, it goes to your heart. It's a clever bullet. Luckily, it went from 'ere and stopped there. And she saved my life. She was marvellous. It didn't knock me out or nothing. Only because we'd gone out for a drink at eight o'clock in the evening, one of them drinks, and it's now four in the morning and we're just going 'ome. Well, by then I'm not legless but …'

'A bit of an anaesthetic, no?' I propose.

'A bit of an anaesthetic, yeah. A baby could have crept up and done it. When it hit me, boom, I'd seen the flash, as you do, and I went for the flash. Nobody's had that luck with me.'

He's sounding indignant that, after a lifetime at the cutting edge of London crime, someone managed to shoot him. He's back there now, in the moment. 'She said, "Why don't you fall?" and pulled us back and the next two bullets missed. Then I pushed her away and managed to run into the car.'

'The second bullet ricocheted off the front of the car,' says Marilyn.

Frankie resumes his account. 'From the word go, when the police said, "Who done it?" I said, "Undercover police." They had armed police around my bed. I said, "You've already shot me once. You want to shoot me again?"'

Knowing he's speaking to someone inexperienced, he explains, 'When you get shot, if you're in Britain, I don't know about Ireland, or are somehow or other attacked, the police are duty bound to ask you for a statement. If you refuse and you're in hospital, they call a nurse or a doctor, and they say, "Mister Smith, I'm asking you once again. Would you please make a statement. Your recollections of who done this. Mister Smith does not answer once again." So they're in the clear, aren't they? They give you the opportunity to make a statement and you refuse, or whatever. In my case, when they asked who done it, I said, "You. Undercover cops." They went and they never ever asked me for a statement. The top surgeon in Britain, a neurologist, a lovely man, a gentleman, came in. He asked, "Who done it Frank?" I said, "I've already told them. An undercover cop done it." And he said, "You know, Frank, I've never trusted the bastards." That was his assessment.'

Wandsworth, Pentonville, Brixton, Wormwood Scrubs, Strangeways, Bedford, Parkhurst, Lincoln and Durham are just some of the prisons Frankie served time in. While his career became a thing of record during the war, with repeated custodial sentences for robbery, it wasn't until the 1950s that he began to achieve new levels of notoriety for violence. This was a time when a cut-throat razor was his preferred instrument of retribution, although it's claimed this seemingly easy-going man also tortured people, electrocuting them or pulling out their teeth with a pliers.

Clearly he's lived a chequered life. With the enthusiasm of someone remembering their first holiday abroad, he recalls, 'I was on the run over here for the Jack Spot one. A very amusing story.' He has my full attention now. Jack Comer was known as Jack Spot because, it's said, he was always 'on the spot' when the London Jewish business community needed protection. In 1955 East End kingpin Spot was involved in a legendary knife fight in Soho with Albert Dimes, six foot two inches, of Italian descent, who loved sport and religious processions. Albert was the right-hand man of rival underworld boss Billy Hill. Despite Spot and Dimes being badly slashed, expert defence on both sides saw the two men acquitted in court. 'The Fight that Never Was,' says Frankie. 'They were both found not guilty, weren't they.'

According to Frank, 'It was arranged that Spot should be done, but Bill and Albert were worried that I might kill him. And the death penalty was about. We did him.' Frankie slashed Spot with a razor, which, after Spot had 'broken the most important code' by naming his attackers to the police, he later lamented had been too lenient. ('He should have been killed.')

Frankie recalls that while he was in Ireland, 'Around 1954 they 'ad a famous world title fight in a bus station in Donnybrook. Billy Hill rented a doctor's house, furnished. We used to drive to the mountains just outside Dublin. I was 'appy 'ere.'

'Wicklow,' I say.

'Yeah, Wicklow. Lovely, innit.' Lost in rose-tinted reverie, Frankie continues, 'I never smoked. And this guy with me, he didn't smoke. But Billy Hill smoked like a top. Moving backwards and forwards from England to here, to see how I was getting on and letting me know what's happening back there. Every so often we had to phone England, and you could only use certain coins then. I don't know. So we'd drive up the mountains and go into one of the little village shops and buy cigarettes. We said to the guy, "Could you give us the change in whatever coin." He never give it to us. So we bought another packet of cigarettes and said, "Could you please give us the coins." So we tumbled it was an old rebel from the 1916 Rising. So we said, "Look, we're on your side. We hate them an' all. Don't worry about us." And he was smashing. He opened the door to us. He gave us the coins. We had a good chat with him.'

So Frank Fraser, Scotland Yard's 'most wanted' lay low in a safe house in south Dublin?

'Yeah, it was safe over here, but all of a sudden two friends of mine got arrested in London for another gangland thing that I was on the run for. So I flew back to London to help them, knowing that they were two good friends of mine. But I phoned up London to let them know and the phone was tapped, wasn't it? So they were waiting for me at London airport and I got seven years over Jack Spot. He gave evidence against us and all. He was a horrible man. Evil.'

'You worked closely with Hill, didn't you?'

'I did, yeah. Lovely man, Billy. Best gangster of all time.'

Frankie also knew and had dealings with the Kray twins. 'They'd been to see me in Dartmoor, Pentonville and Birmingham,' he says in his book. 'I think perhaps the Twins were jealous, most probably that we had a better edge in the West End than they did.'

An entertaining raconteur, Frankie recalls one of the highlights of his career. 'I met Lucky Luciano in Rome in '55 or '56. A very likeable guy.'

He also did a bit of work for the American crime boss. 'How did that come about?'

'Through "Italian" Albert [Dimes] and Bert Marsh, who also was an Italian. Bert had been a boxer in the '20s.'

From my memory of boxing stats, Bert was Pasquale Papa, who fought at bantamweight and had a busy career before retiring and setting up a security company business offering protection to racecourse and greyhound tracks, which essentially involved demanding money with menaces from on-course bookies.

He was another of Frankie's role models. 'He was a top Mafia man in this country. Sorry, I mean in England. Lovely man. He's dead now. And "Italian" Albert. They're both dead.'

There's a certain wistfulness in the recollections of this dapper, diminutive version of The Rolling Stones' Charlie Watts – a genial remembrance of times past that makes it easy to forget Frankie's reputation for volcanic and destructive retribution. I find it difficult to imagine that this man could bite off a prison warder's ear and flush it down the toilet. But he did.

Frankie would have witnessed a lot of social and cultural changes during his time as a career criminal. I'm thinking of the growth in London of the Triads and Yardies. And a generation brought up on violent movies and TV shows. How did he think the London police were dealing with the changes?

'It's been quite reasonable in London considering all the movements that go on. With the Triads, Yardies and all that,' he says in a gentle, measured tone. 'They've got to get a living, haven't they? They can't all get jobs, can they?'

Marilyn agrees. 'Crime's gone up because of the population. The population's tripled. When you look at it logically, when you have more people there must be more crime.'

We're having our conversation in February 1997. 'There must be twenty million more people in Britain now than there was sixty years ago. They would never admit that because that means they've got to go on about the immigrants. They would say there's been an increase in populations but maybe not the expense.'

'Are the police as clued up as they'd like us to think they are?'

'They are. Don't worry about that. With the population going up like that, you've got a lot of loose cannons about. By that I mean who would give evidence against their own mother. And yet they would still be getting up to mischief themselves. And they would be letting the police know what the police want to know. And so these people would have their ear to the ground and they might hear the odd thing they shouldn't hear and that would be relayed back to the police. They are a bit more clued up now than what they normally would be. They do get a lot of help from a lot of these immigrants who know no difference. They've got no real loyalty. Some have but most haven't. They'd shop their own mother.'

In Frankie's heyday, there was a code of honour among

criminals. And heaven help those who broke it by becoming police informants. Frankie 'did' anyone who grassed him up. He cut them up, slashed them to ribbons. The bloke who 'fingered' him for slashing Jack Spot, which led to the seven-year sentence when he returned from Dublin, had his leg blown off. As Frankie recalls in his biography, 'Everyone thought it was me and they were quite right. He deserved it. I never done him any harm.'

To this day he holds the police in contempt. 'They're evil. Always have been. It's nothing new. It's been going on since I was born.'

Even after his shooting, the police were investigating him. 'As part of their inquiries, they suspected me of two murders, where a guy had pulled up on a motorbike and, on each occasion, shot someone dead. They tried to make out it was me. Which wasn't, in fact, the truth at all. They found nothing, of course.'

Whether it was a case of trouble finding Frankie or Frankie finding trouble, he considers his extensive conviction record and adds, 'You must remember, my record, in prison and out, was always help the underdog. Very few people have gone through it like I went through it, which I'm proud to say.'

As we get up to leave, I pick up Frankie's smart dark Crombie overcoat, which happens to be on top of mine on a nearby armchair. On instinct, I hold it out for him to slip into. A simple courtesy to an older person. Our eyes meet and for the briefest instant suspicion registers in Frankie's eyes. As he slips his arms into the sleeves, he chuckles and says softly, 'You're doing my old job.'

I'm puzzled. He's smartly dressed and well-mannered. Although amid the contours of his mask-like face evidence of past violence can be discerned – nose breakages, stab wounds and bullet holes – I assume rashly that at some stage Frankie might have been a maître-d'? Not quite.

'I often helped people on with their coats,' he reveals. 'It made it easier when I was kidnapping them. Throw them off guard. Put them at their ease.'

Chapter Seven

Striking a Chord

IT WASN'T UNTIL MUCH LATER that I came to fully appreciate how meeting such a broad range of talent had proved so educational. If sometimes only on a subliminal level, my enquiries had often led to insight. Had I the time to dwell on the previous week's work, I'd have noted how many of the conversations I had were instructive, carrying life lessons (as well as the headings of potential seminars, keynotes of masterclasses and private tutorials!). You'll find the seeds scattered here, some beneath the topsoil of tabloid demands.

Something I hadn't expected was the lasting effect many of those weekly exchanges would have on me. Even now, over thirty years later, the psychic subtexts of encounters with Josephine Hart, Rudolf Nureyev, Brenda Fricker and others continue to echo in my subconscious like the mood of a poem or half-remembered aria. Inspiration can be taken from each individual's story.

From time to time, a memory will surface unannounced. For example, was I really imagining nuanced signals and pointed undertones when interviewing Dr João Havelange, the formidable president of FIFA, who insisted on speaking with steely gravitas through an interpreter, one of his imposing and expensively tailored coterie? It was a rare interview, set up by a mutual friend. Football was big business. A lawyer and astute businessman, Havelange had driven the growth of the sport and its revenue. Steering global sponsorship deals and bidding for TV rights, the Brazilian helped make the World Cup tournament the most lucrative show on earth. With an interpreter conveying my questions in Portuguese and then, after a *sotto voce* debate, relaying the boss's responses, I found myself wondering what was actually being said. I suppose I could have had the tape analysed, but I didn't have time. It wasn't until after the president's retirement in 1998, after twenty-four years in office, that it was revealed Havelange and his son-in-law had been in receipt of millions of Swiss francs in bribes.

My equally memorable early morning hotel meeting with Jonathan Irwin in 1990 was what they once termed 'a power breakfast'. The man who'd transformed the Irish bloodstock industry, was fronting a syndicate that had ambitious plans to form a new Dublin-based Association Football club that would play in the Scottish league. Later, when Jonathan's baby son Jack suffered permanent brain damage at birth, the remarkable, charismatic executive worked tirelessly to set up the Jack and Jill Foundation, which continues to provide much-needed respite services to families whose children require round-the-clock care.

It was one o'clock in the morning in an empty function room in a motel somewhere in County Clare when Gerry Adams finally sat down for an in-depth interview. He'd been travelling around Ireland since early morning, coping with winter floods and traffic diversions, speaking at meetings and attempting to persuade Sinn Féin followers and the public of the political benefits of the peace initiative. Gerry's message was simple and persuasive. 'There's very much common ground at the moment,' he insisted after over twenty years of bloody conflict. 'Because there's a common acceptance and hope that this peace process can build into a peace settlement.' Time was of the essence and after our lengthy chat, which took place seven hours later than scheduled, Adams climbed into a car and was driven to Belfast via Dublin in icy conditions by his alert security detail who had sat a discreet distance behind me throughout our interview. For him, the work never ended.

I was reminded of the caveat a similarly industrious David Ervine of the Progressive Unionist Party had sounded to me days earlier on the Shankill Road describing his efforts to bring the doubters and hardliners on board the movement towards peace. 'There isn't much point in either Adams, myself or anybody in any other party marching to the end of the pier and turning around and finding there's no one behind them. People have to be brought along.'

I was equally impressed by the attitude of someone faced with potentially life-changing injuries. 'The car got metal fatigue,' croaked Martin Donnelly casually. He may have shrugged. But propped up in bed, surrounded by pillows, hoists and medical apparatus, it was difficult to tell. A ward in the Royal London Hospital in Whitechapel in February 1991 was where I met the Grand Prix racing driver who had survived a horrific 170 mph crash in his Formula One Lotus in Spain the previous September. The car had smashed into pieces on impact and Martin was thrown onto the track forty metres away, in a broken heap with the remnants of his seat still strapped to his back. A bloody mess from a burst artery, he had suffered two skull fractures, leg and shoulder bones had been shattered, muscles on his left side had been ripped from the bones and he wasn't breathing when the first responders reached him. His kidneys packed up. Yet he'd made a miraculous, if slow and painful, recovery.

An enormous bouquet of flowers dominated the spartan room. They were from Elton John, whose 'I'm Still Standing' had been a hit eight years previously. While I was present, Martin was taken to have the plaster cast removed from his leg. Smiling on his return, he was determined to regain fitness and race again. That might take some time yet, I thought, considering the infections that had hampered his recovery and the bed-bound months of muscle wastage. 'I wouldn't mind getting up on a pair of crutches and seeing how I get on,' he said gamely, his cracked voice still hoarse from weeks on a ventilator.

Admitting it had been 'touch and go for a while', the race ace attempted to brush off the profundity of his near-death experience claiming, 'It was just one of those things.'

On the fifth anniversary of my friend Philip Lynott's (36) funeral, shortly before I interviewed Martin, I met Ozzy Osbourne, who also ruminated on the fickle nature of life and death. He told me, 'I saw him [Lynott] a few months before his death and he looked pretty unhealthy at that point. But Steve Clarke [the thirty-year-old Def Leppard guitar hero] just died from an alcohol overdose. It's just kicked me in the arse again. There but for the grace of God go I. I've been abusing alcohol and drugs for years. By some miraculous reason I'm still here. I don't know why I should be here and they should die.'

JOSEPHINE HART – October 1992

'Damaged people are dangerous. They know how to survive.'

The often quoted tagline from the novel *Damage* played on my mind ahead of meeting Josephine Hart. I hadn't read the bestseller or seen the film, which, primed for release, had already received plenty of tabloid publicity if only because viewers were afforded a sight of actor Jeremy Irons' bottom. I had, however, read Hart's second novel, *Sin*, which I found gratifying and stylistically intriguing.

'There is no irony in the book. It's written without a hint of irony,' Hart explained.

Before we met, I'd seen her in action at a book launch. Dressed in chic black and white, with jet-black hair and fire-engine-red lipstick, she cut an imposing figure. When she addressed her audience of mainly women her own age, fifty, she was as precise and accommodating as I remembered hospital head matrons to be in my childhood.

I knew something of her back story. But an astonishing surprise lay in store.

As Hart, from Mullingar, had been about to finish boarding school in Carrickmacross, Co. Monaghan, in the early 1960s, her sister died. Six months later, caught in an accidental explosion, her young brother Owen also died. Instead of going to university, Josephine felt obliged to stay with her parents for the next four years. Eventually, her parents urged her to leave and find a career. In 1964 she moved to London – 'To a society where no one knew anything about me or my background. That was a release.'

A scholarship at the Guildhall School of Music and Drama seemed a possibility, but Hart opted to work anonymously in the telesales department of Thomson Newspapers. From there she joined Haymarket Publishing, successfully supervised a variety of titles and became a member of the board. Her first marriage, to fellow Haymarket director Paul Buckley, lasted seven years; in 1984 she married Maurice Saatchi.

***

When we meet, we sit by the window high in her suite in a swish, modern hotel overlooking the rooftops of Georgian Dublin. I wonder if she recognises the city she passed through on her way from Mullingar to London at twenty-two, almost thirty years previously.

'Mam used to come over to me three or four times a year, and I used to go over, but because I had two small children, I'd only be staying for a few days.'

Josephine moves seamlessly from the personal to the public and is comfortable in sharing her observations of the changes she's noticed. 'The thing I see as an immediate change is how prosperous it seems to be. Dublin seems to be a very European city. Much more European than London.

'London's still deeply English in its psychology. Dublin's very European. That I find very interesting. Dublin's been able to make a quantum leap towards the concept of Europe much more easily than English society. It seems to me to be very cosmopolitan and it seems to be very well off.

'Now, I know England's in the depths of an appalling recession for years, but you've suffered much less in this recession. There's tremendous self-confidence about cultural matters, as there should be. You've had a kind of renaissance, particularly in theatre.

'These things go in phases. There was a time in the late '50s when great playwrights were English. You had Pinter, Wesker and Osborne. There was a fallow period. Now you have Brian Friel, Tom Murphy, Frank McGuinness and extraordinary successes. Not only here and in London but also in New York. *Dancing at Lughnasa* is extraordinary. Tom Murphy's *The Gigli Concert* is … I always wanted to put it on. I think it's an extraordinary piece.

'You also have, which I'm less familiar with because it's outside my age group, but from my son I'm familiar with this incredible blossoming of popular music in Dublin. Dublin is full of self-confidence, which wasn't there when I left Ireland.'

In 1992 there was scant biographical information to hand on Josephine Hart. She'd lived a life largely under the radar. Since her marriage to Maurice Saatchi in 1984, she had been organising poetry readings and had produced a number of plays in London's West End, all notable box-office successes.

'Did you attend Trinity College?'

'I didn't go to university at all. I left Carrickmacross [she attended secondary school at St Louis Convent] and we had a number of tragedies in our family. And I went home and stayed with my parents for four years. These things happened in my last year in school, and I did my Leaving Cert, but instead of going on to university I stayed at home for four years.'

Josephine has lowered her voice. An unsettling hint of sadness has crept into her tone. 'Then they were better and I left and went to London.'

Remembering when local day students from the town of Mullingar came into class and told us about a local teenager who'd died in an accidental explosion, and now knowing that this was Josephine Hart's younger brother, I'm about to say something.

'Fireworks …'

Josephine cuts me short. 'I never talk about that. I don't ever refer to that. My sister died six months before that and Owen died in an accident and that's all I ever want to say about it.'

'I'm sorry.'

'No, no, no. I'm not criticising you at all. It was such an appalling tragedy. Apart from anything else, I've never been able to translate it into something that was positive. And because of that it seems to me to be better to keep it to myself. Maybe someday I'll find a way of seeing it all in a useful way for other people. But at the moment I don't try to talk about it to satisfy curiosity.'

'What sort of emotional baggage did you take with you back then in terms of the emerging, young, self-confident Ireland?'

'My life had nothing to do with self-confidence or society then. My life was absolutely devastated. I went because my parents said, "You've stayed for four years. You have got to leave. We are better now. You have got to go." I was very distressed. But also, they were completely wise. Had I stayed, I was living in a very abnormal way. Because my mother was insane with grief and it took four years for her to get over it.

'I have to say, as encouragement for other people, she did get over it. And not just meandered away for the rest of her life. Herself and my father were incredibly, positively happy for the rest of their lives. They were very determined that I had to save myself ... my mother was very good to me. She said, "You know, it's been a terrible sacrifice what you've had to do for four years." She didn't ask me to do it. I knew I had to do it. And they are crucial years. I know that ... In a sense, they've come back to me now ... I was in a daze. I was in a complete and total daze, as you could imagine.'

'But you emerged into the Swinging Sixties?'

'Yes, London was a thrilling place. First of all, it was thrilling to me because I went to a society where no one knew anything about me or my background. And I never told anyone. When people said to me, "How many brothers and sisters do you have?", for a very long period of time, I said, "One." Because there's only one remaining after that, my other brother. And that, for a start, was a relief.

'I went to the Guildhall School of Music and Drama as a part-time student and when they offered me a scholarship ... I must rephrase that. They said to me, "Would you like to try for a scholarship? You could be good." I then decided, "No." I just completely turned my back on it and went into a business career. And I was absolutely right. Because I realised that trying to do, and I wanted to do, the great classical parts, would have just tipped me over the edge. So I went to the Sales Department of Thomson Newspapers and after a very short period of time, about a year, I joined Haymarket Publishing and I turned myself completely around and I became a very successful businesswoman. I went on the board. I never worried. I ran fifteen magazines. I ran all their business magazines. All their medical magazines. Not immediately. But over a period of years, and I worked incredibly hard. It wasn't intellectually challenging, but it required no emotion whatsoever. It was the best thing that ever happened to me.'

Feeling comfortable in herself again, Josephine enjoys the memory of her time as a publishing supremo.

'The greatest worry in my life was what to wear to the board meetings. People used to say, "Josephine, you're launching a new magazine, aren't you awake at night, biting your nails? They're investing three million pounds in this magazine." "No!" I would work very hard. I wasn't going to let anybody down. But nothing of emotion went into it. That actually was wonderful for me. It was only very tentatively I went back to have anything to do with … I agreed, because it was Maurice who said I had to stop doing this and I went back and started organising poetry readings. Then I did the theatre. But all the time, I had all these characters in my head, and ideas and writing, and eventually he said, "You're getting too old Josephine. If you don't do it, you're going to die." Eventually I did break my own rule. Because I'd made my mind up that I wouldn't write or have anything to do with the theatre.'

The trajectory of her career is fascinating. I find the pale, intense woman sitting across from me, dressed as if she might be a high-powered legal counsel, albeit one with vivid red lipstick and impeccably styled hair, quite heroic. I say nothing.

'It's a very interesting and very long journey. I'm not going to go into my age. And if you ask, I'm not going to tell you, but I am very old to be writing. Forties is not the time people are writing their first book.

'We've all known people who, even before they go to college, are saying, "I want to be a writer."

'You have to know something about life. What is your contribution going to be? But of course, you can turn that on its head and there are a lot of brilliant things written by people in their twenties. Interestingly enough, poets are often at their very best very young. And novelists, though there are a number of exceptions, are very often at their best in their middle age. Middle age is the most interesting time of life, because you're on a plateau facing both ways. And you really do know, finally, that you are not immortal.'

Bright and alive to the topic, Josephine continues enthusiastically. 'Martin Amis said a wonderfully funny thing in an interview I read, where he was saying, "Up until forty no people die. Indeed, the vast majority of people do eventually die, but we are also certain that in your case an exception has been made. After forty, no exception has been made. Not even in your case."

'I think that is very good. The forties and fifties. My mother always said that they were the most interesting time in life. I do think they are very rich in knowledge. Because everything that you're experiencing, you also have all that depth of reminiscence as well. I hate to say this in front of you, because you're probably in your twenties, but I wouldn't go back to my twenties for anything.'

Sitting back, she laughs as you would if you were among family friends. No doubt she knows that she's obligingly shaved about twenty years off my CV. Time to change the subject.

'I'm so intrigued by the compactness of *Sin* that …'

'I do work very hard on the editing. Cutting. Cutting. Cutting. To make it very formal. Some people hate that, but it's something I admire. It's something I like, that whole highly stylised, unnaturalistic kind of writing. They don't like it at all. I sympathise with that to a degree.'

I mention that something of her terse use of language reminds me of the Greeks – Sophocles, Euripides and other playwrights.

'It's interesting that you should say that there is that, because they have a very formal style. I've always admired that.

'When I used to produce plays, it struck me as terribly interesting that all the Greek tragedies that have come down to us use an extraordinary economy of language. Also, they were very short, with no intervals. I think one of the things the theatre could benefit from a great deal is having plays that last an hour and a half. Maybe then you'd have a series. Each one an individual. That's what I was trying to do.

'I'm not being coy when I say I was genuinely astonished that

Damage was successful, because that kind of writing is terribly unfashionable. The kind of writing that is fashionable … I did a programme called *Books By My Bedside* [Thames TV]. I was reading a lot of books, so I knew what worked and what didn't. I was looking for a kind of street credibility. The rhythm of catching life as it goes.

'I still say, they are very unfashionable. Yet somehow or other they seem to have struck an odd chord.'

At the time, I found the manageable size of the hardcover copy of *Sin* and the clear typeface a delight. No surprise then that the woman who'd successfully launched the advertising and media magazine *Campaign* had a deep appreciation of presentation. 'That's all Sonny Mehta, the president of Knopf, who's known in America evidently as the Dark Prince of Publishing,' says Josephine, laughing. I learn the typeface is Bembo, a facsimile of a Venetian typeface from 1495.

She's laughing at her 'Dark Prince' remark but is alert to the possibility of tripwires when I remark, 'I wondered if your knowledge of contemporary literature combined with your background in publishing might have created subliminal marketing.'

'Actually, no. Because if I'd wanted to … first of all there's the actual physical thing of having been in *Campaign* and also married to somebody in advertising. It was Knopf's design and also they are famous for design. I always give the girl's name. There's a tragedy that she designed both of these covers which have been so commented on. The woman who designed them is the design director of Knopf, Carol Devine Carson. She didn't even talk to me. I'd never written a book in my life before, and my publishing career, of course, was in magazine publishing.

'As far as the literary thing – and I've always been a passionate reader and I've put on plays and everything – as I said, had I sat down and thought, "Now that at last you've allowed yourself to write," although I was writing in my head for years but wouldn't put it down, "let's go and make this a success", *Damage* is not the book I would have written. Because I could have done two things. I could have done an autobiographical, "Irish girl comes to London" or I could have done a super-cool kind of street credibility English businesswoman or something. When I say could have, the truth of the matter is, I couldn't have, because I can't write like that. But that is what I would have said would have been much more fashionable.'

It's fascinating to witness her sharp mind in action, clarifying, attending to detail, micro-managing, leaving no room for ambiguity. No wonder Josephine Hart was a powerful success in publishing.

'The writers who are very successful in England, who I, personally, greatly admire, like [Martin] Amis, Ian McEwan, Julian Barnes are enormously successful. But their style is very ironic, as opposed to tragic. They're very clever. They're very funny. As well as everything else. There's a lot of irony running through it. So to write a formal tragedy, without a note of humour, as one reviewer said, "In Ms Harte's book, nobody lets the cat out." And I understand that criticism is the very antithesis of what I would have said was a fashionable book.

'I can honestly say to you, certainly, that I was very lucky getting Chatto and Knopf. But Sonny at Knopf always believed, from the minute he read it. I certainly didn't. When I heard what they thought they were going to do in terms of the number of books they were publishing, I had sleepless nights saying, "This is terrible. You can't possibly do this." He said, "I have a feeling."

'*Damage* ends without a ray of hope. It ends with a man sitting in a room which is all white and is actually a white coffin and everything in his life has been destroyed. That is not what I would regard as a potentially popular success.

'If you are truthful, you can only write what you can write. And trying to move out of your world, it's not going to work. You can write it, but it won't have any energy.'

'There may be some readers who feel the author of these books perceives life to be nasty, brutish and short. Are your novels autobiographical in terms of emotions if not details?'

'They're not,' says Josephine patiently. 'They're certainly not autobiographical in terms of any situation that I have seen. They're not based on any characters, which I find surprising. There is a line by Flaubert which is, "You don't choose your subjects, they choose you."

'I believe that everybody is capable of the most extreme heroism and the most extreme evil. When I say the most extreme, let's leave out the monsters of history: Hitler, Stalin and so on. You only have to pick up the paper any day to see people whose mother loved them and whose father was good to them, who do appalling things.

'If you think of Eliot saying, "There's time to murder and create in a minute." Our minds and our souls contain within them the possibility of profound evil. Every day we make choices, sometimes very minor choices: the betrayal of a friend over a drink, perhaps. At least in our head, the potential seduction of somebody who is not for you, murderous thoughts of somebody who crosses your path, deep and profound envy – not the kind of innocent forms of envy, "oh, he's better looking" or "she's richer" or whatever, because that's childish, but deep, deep envy, a desire for destruction.

'I'm convinced that it's a quantum leap of imagination because we never know anybody else. But my logical conclusion is that we would not understand the great works of literature and the terrible characters in them if we did not know that it was possible to do that. I have such a reverence for literature, because it is the geography of mankind. Infinitely more than any book of non-fiction ever written. And it's all in us. It's all there in us.

'Therefore, what was difficult with Ruth [in *Sin*], is that I had to connect and go deeply down into a psychology that had decided to allow evil to predominate. This is a highly intelligent woman who could have decided to be good, but she didn't. And, therefore, staying with that character and going to the extremes of destruction that she is capable of was very disturbing, but she was actually looking for a unity with Elizabeth [her adopted sister] and, in a sense, Elizabeth was the great love of her life. That is the paradox of envy, that you do not envy what it is that you don't love. That's why it divides you against yourself.'

The author has clearly given this thorny subject a lot of thought.

'There's a great price to be paid, which you decide on,' she continues. 'You start with small things and you decide on a path of allowing the meannesses and cruelty in yourself to dominate. We have a choice. It's very horrifying. Choosing to do what is right. There's not a word for it, other than within yourself. It doesn't always work out best in the end. Virtue is not its own reward in that sense. But it is the only way if you are going to find a peace, if not exactly happiness.'

At an appearance in a book shop in Dublin, Josephine spoke of 'know thyself', a term that we're familiar with from the Greeks. I wondered if this commitment to self-awareness stemmed from her religious upbringing or from meditation.

'No, I didn't do any meditation,' she states. 'I've never been psychoanalysed. Though I'm profoundly grateful for having had a religious upbringing, I'm not at all religious now. But one of the aspects of a Catholic upbringing is that while you should examine your conscience every night, self-involvement was very naturally curtailed. I didn't understand. Self-involvement is a very bad thing. It's boring, absolutely appalling. But self-knowledge is something different altogether. I think that my upbringing made me believe that thinking about yourself, who you were, was completely unnecessary.

'I do think that can be very dangerous, because until we know ourselves, involving ourselves with other people in serious relationships can be very dangerous. I have two sons and one is too young to know what I'm talking about, but the other is sixteen now and all his life, gently, I've been saying, "Really do try to understand yourself, Adam," because finding out who you are too late is a very … you'll have harmed a lot of people along the way. It's terribly important.

'I think the Greeks were right about everything. There is a little tribute in that conversation about the difference between the pagan and the Christian virtues. Of course, the pagan virtues are the Greek virtues – justice, temperance, prudence and courage. They stand up pretty well against the Ten Commandments. I'm not saying I'm anti-the Ten Commandments. But those qualities are of enormous power and importance.'

'Having explored envy and lust earlier, you don't have an agenda, do you?'

'I don't. I never saw *Damage* as a book about lust. I see it as a book about erotic obsession and the connection between erotic obsession and death. Because erotic obsession is a desire for complete unity and in *Damage* the man keeps saying pleasure was an incidental.

'Lust is driven towards pleasure, and it's driven by the eye, and no one should be surprised when lust dies because the eye tires. It's no surprise, and people's hearts are broken over and over again because of that.

'Whereas erotic obsession is rooted in the psychology and it's expressed physically. And the expression is a desire for complete unity. That desire for complete unity is actually a desire to be lost in the other person. Which is a kind of death.

'I don't know whether you can print this in an Irish newspaper, but the French call orgasm "la petite mort". And that is a very good description. It is a loss of self.

'That is what I was trying to examine in *Damage*, the connection between erotic obsession and death. That's why Anna is not an archetypal femme fatale. There is very little description of her physically. There's virtually none. We know she's tall and that's about it. But there is a great deal of exploration of her psychology. And why her psychology would be so fatal for this man. Absolutely fatal.

'So I'm not working my way through the seven deadly sins. I couldn't work as mechanistically as that.'

The promo build-up to the release of *Damage* in the cinemas has already begun. Has Josephine seen the rushes? 'Have you any involvement in the film-making process?'

'No. When he [director Louis Malle] bought [the film rights], we spent a weekend together going through all of the characters. And the character he found most difficult was Anna. Because she was so strange. Also, he was very worried as to how he could keep an audience with him. There is a scene in *Damage* when the man is found dead, and Anna just walks straight past him. That was difficult. David Hare did the script, and I spent some time with

David as well. They were very good. I got every single version, as well. As you know, Jeremy Irons' favourite line is "a scripted work is progress on a movie". And they did send that to me.

'I was very pleased with 85 per cent, and on the things that I wasn't, I wrote about exactly why. Sometimes we agreed and sometimes he didn't. But it's Louis' movie and I am very honoured that Louis Malle is doing it. I went on set, but I was so disassociated from it. He's going to show me the movie when I go back. I'm going to America [after here] and when I get back – he didn't want me to see it in the kind of rushes stage. He wants me to see it with the music and everything perfect. Maybe it's because ... I don't know. It's probably a strange thing to be showing a movie to the author of the book. So he's waiting until it's right.'

'How was Jeremy Irons in the film?'

'Jeremy's perfect to me. I know Jeremy anyway. He has a complete understanding of this man. Jeremy has got an extraordinary intelligence. And also, he's someone who's very daring. He does explore the dark side. Did you see *Dead Ringers*? I think his is one of the great performances in cinema history. It's extraordinary. And the Claus von Bülow is amazing. Very daring. That's a very dangerous and difficult thing for Jeremy to do, I would have thought. So he has no fear. He's a fearless actor. He's a man of extraordinary ruthless integrity in relation to what it is that he wants. So I couldn't think of anyone who would have been better.'

This seems as good a time as any for a conversational gear change. I remind Ms Hart that her home town of Mullingar was described by Ivan Fallon, biographer of the Saatchis, as 'that unlovely town on the edge of the Irish bog'.

'I'm very cross with him,' replies Josephine, betraying a slight irritation. 'Mullingar is a wonderful town. Maureen Cleave in *The*

Telegraph said it's so unfair because Mullingar is very gentle and soft and it has five lakes around it. I'm a great defender of it. It's not dramatic. It's very soft. I had a very happy ... various unhappy things happened but, generally speaking, it was a wonderful town and very good to my family. I love it.'

'Did you have any fear or a sense of trepidation going back to Mullingar?'

'None at all. I've always kept in great contact. I don't have any family left. My mother died in 1988. No. I feel great sadness when I go back to Mullingar. The man who runs the Bazaar [a bookshop and stationers at that time], John O'Donnell, I go out swimming with him. When my mother died, Buddy Shaw, who is the undertaker, I went to school with him. I could never fear Mullingar because it's a wonderful town. Some of the girls there I've known since I was four. No. I do feel great sadness.'

'I used to pass your family garage on my way to the football pitch.'

'That football pitch was opposite my house,' Josephine sounds excited. 'Right opposite my house.'

'I spent five years in St Finian's College. I was happy afterwards, but not at the time.'

'It was a wonderful education. But it was very harsh. I don't know if was harsher on boys than on girls.'

'It was the 1960s. We weren't allowed out. We were confined. Happily, I had friendly day boys smuggle in magazines. But we didn't have much access to the outside world. We weren't allowed even a radio.'

'That's what it was like in Carrickmacross. To go out to the town you had to have special permission. I think I went out to the town in a crocodile [escorted schoolchildren walking in a line in pairs].

But to go out to the town to buy sweets and things like that was completely unheard of. It was incredibly protected. Maybe you would have resented that much more than … I think boys resent these restrictions more than girls. Maybe I'm wrong. I don't know. I also think that from what I've heard, boys' boarding schools were much, much harsher than the girls'. I've heard that from a number of boys who went to Irish boarding schools. You were not happy? Do you think it had a bad effect on you?'

'I suspect it probably did.'

I realise the conversation has taken a curious twist. Usually, I'd be wary of wasting valuable time divulging personal details to an interviewee. As interviewer, I'm the one hoping to discover something unusual. In this case, I can tell Josephine is relaxing into the exchanges. I could change the subject, but I decide to roll with it to see what unfolds. It's tricky territory but my hunch is that we could arrive at something insightful.

Looking concerned, like an older sister might, Josephine asks, 'Did they beat you?'

'Yes. I was terrified every morning for the first couple of years. Because I knew there were some men there who were just going to beat me.'

'That was just awful. What age were you then?'

'Thirteen, fourteen.'

'For your young adolescence to be terrorised like that is really terrible. That is brutality.'

'On the other hand, there were some teachers who were kind, enthusiastic and quite upbeat.'

'That's sadistic. That doesn't happen in girls' schools. Of course, there was … I was very susceptible to the idea that I was letting the school down. I used to race everywhere. I was notorious for running everywhere. And running was forbidden within the school. That used to make an impression. They weren't cruel though.'

'My next-door neighbour went to St Louis'. Una Skelly.'

'The Skellys from Kells?' It's Josephine's turn to be astonished. Una was a classmate and remains a close friend. They continue to correspond by letter, Josephine thankful for the long, detailed, newsy sheets from Una, often detailing how many of their classmates are and what they are currently doing.

'She's adorable,' enthuses Josephine of my old neighbour. 'My father adored her. She was just lovely. She used to wear her hair in a long ponytail. Lovely.'

It seems that quite often at the end of term or on half-term breaks, Josephine would travel in Una's father's VW Beetle to Kells, where she'd sometimes stay overnight before being collected by her father. Josephine Hart used sometimes to stay in the house next door to where I lived.

Although they were older than my very young teenage self, I distinctly remember Una and her attractive friend, smiling and laughing, buoyant on the glorious possibilities of life ahead. Carefree pretty schoolgirls. A young boy's dream. But this coincidence, this synchronicity, is too great, too unsettling. It's time to wrap up and say goodbye.

And, yes, we were in touch again.

SHEILA MOONEY – March 1990

It was the idea of the knocking sound coming from inside the coffin that did it for me. Captain John Lovatt Frazer was a genial man who had an interest in spiritualism and the paranormal. The story of his funeral caught my attention.

A surgeon in a hospital in China, Frazer lived in style with his wife and eight children until forced to flee the slaughter of the Boxer uprising at the turn of the last century. Back in Ireland, the Ascendancy family settled in a large Tudor house in County Roscommon, where they were attended to by the Chinese servants they brought with them.

In her memoir, *A Strange Kind of Loving*, his granddaughter, Sheila Mooney, recalls how, as his remains were being lowered into the grave, mourners heard a 'violent knocking from inside the coffin'. Insisting it was a manifestation of the deceased's interest in spiritualism, and believing the dead man's spirit was attempting to communicate with the living, the family continued with the burial.

When I meet Sheila, who was five when her grandfather died, I ask the obvious question. 'Did they not open the coffin to check?'

When Sheila had posed the same question to her mother, the eldest of the surgeon's four daughters, she replied indignantly, 'How could we? The funeral was all arranged.'

In her spacious coastal apartment in south Dublin in the spring of 1990, Sheila ponders the incident and remarks wistfully, 'Most of the eccentrics in the family have gone.'

When her Frazer grandparents separated, the four sons kept the name Frazer and were brought up Protestant. The four daughters changed the spelling to Fraser and were reared as Catholics before later becoming Christian Scientists. The only daughter to marry was Sheila's mother. At eighteen, and with a drink problem, she married

Charles O'Sullivan, a lieutenant in the Connaught Rangers, son of a wealthy Cork merchant and ten years her elder.

By the time Sheila was born, her mother was a confirmed alcoholic who had suffered a series of nervous breakdowns. 'She told me that I was steeped in John Jameson,' Sheila recalls. 'I once asked mother what her childhood was like and all she could say was, "I was a sad child." I have thought to myself ever since, *I wonder why she drank?*'

While Sheila craved her father's affection, he ignored her and, from childhood, kept reminding her, 'You're a flop at everything you do.'

'I loved my mother,' says Sheila, insisting her book was about love not hate. 'I was trying to explain that she was a lovely person but that she was controlled by this outside force called alcohol. When my father died, she outlived him by thirty years and never drank again.'

Bright-eyed and alert, the sixty-nine-year-old woman I meet has clear skin and the features of a film star. She's seen the Hollywood star system in action but didn't have the drive necessary to make it work for her – unlike her older sister, Maureen O'Sullivan, who at eighteen had been given a part in *Song o' My Heart*, a 1930 film starring John McCormack. When she signed with MGM, she became a bona fide box-office film star, featuring as Jane alongside Johnny Weissmuller in a series of *Tarzan* movies.

'When my father heard that his favourite child wanted to be a star, he didn't tell her that he didn't want her to go, he didn't stand in her way. He just said, "Just remember this, keep your head and keep your religion and you'll do alright."

'She came through hell and high water and she remained as unspoilt as the day she went out there.'

Mesmerised by her sister's fame, Sheila took a year's drama training and, with her mother in tow, booked her passage to Hollywood. On seeing her younger sister again, Maureen's advice was to lose weight and grow her hair.

In the late 1930s, the Hollywood studios were all-powerful, making and breaking global film stars. An innocent convent girl, Sheila hadn't quite grasped the concept of directors taking advantage of would-be stars and starlets. Having heard of MGM boss Louis B. Mayer's stable, and not realising that the expression referred to a harem of casting-couch showgirls, Sheila asked the mogul if she could go look at his horses.

'I really thought that in the studio he had these beautiful white horses,' she says. According to Sheila, Mayer, who 'was never without an expensive cigar in his mouth', was fit to be tied. 'Isn't it incredible that a girl of eighteen could have been so stupid.'

Maureen was married to producer–director John Farrow, and Sheila kept shtum on her fraught encounters with lecherous agents and directors. 'I never told her. She did tell me that a lot of the stars, names people wouldn't remember now, were all producers' "couch ladies". And one out of three made it because they could act.

'When I went to Hollywood, I hadn't a blind ghost of a notion what was going on. In those days the star system was in place. So, to a gullible eighteen-year-old, I thought they were all gods and goddesses and knew nothing of the heartbreaks and scandals. My mother kept saying, "They're the most miserable crowd of neurotics I've ever met in my life." She was right. Having lived as long as I have, I definitely think that money corrupts. I've seen people change. They don't get nicer. They get more selfish.'

Despite having had an image makeover before her screen test, Sheila didn't land a studio contract. Bitterly upset, she left

Tinseltown. While sailing home on the *Queen Mary*, she heard British Prime Minister Neville Chamberlain announce on a live radio broadcast, 'We are now at war with Nazi Germany.'

Back in Ireland, Sheila joined the Abbey School of Acting, where Wilfrid Brambell was in her class. Soon she threw herself into the social swirl and, some years later, met and married Jimmy Mooney, an accomplished yachtsman and Irish Olympian. Mooney, a dentist, was Protestant. 'His family were direct descendants of Charles Stewart Parnell. There were no Catholics ever.'

As Sheila states, 'In the 1940s mixed marriages were very difficult.' Quite how difficult, she had no idea. Both her father and the Catholic Church were unhappy at the prospect. Both parties expected children of the marriage to be reared as Catholics.

'It's like *The Barretts of Wimpole Street*. I had a choice of, "That man or me." It's a ridiculous thing to say to a young girl that's in love with a fella. "Are you going to chose him or your dad?"

'It's obvious she's going to choose the fella. It's only natural. And then I had my mother on the other side saying that I was pushing it and that it was time I got off.'

When her husband refused to promise to raise their children as Catholics, she was excommunicated and spurned by her father. The attitude of the Church and her excommunication had a dreadful effect on Sheila Mooney's fragile disposition.

'I found it hard when I was expecting my children. This monk used to visit me and he'd say, "All you can do is get down on your knees and say, 'Oh, my Jesus, mercy' in case you die having the baby." It wasn't much of a consolation.

'Were you excommunicated at this stage?'

'Yes, and in the Church's eyes my children were bastards. I was in a state of, I suppose you'd say, double mortal sin.

'It seems to me a terrible thing to say to a woman carrying a child. Because to me a pregnant woman is almost a sacred thing. She is going to give birth to a human being and I think it's marvellous.

'They made me very frightened. I was told that if I died, I'd go straight to hell. My first child was born and I was very ill. To my horror I looked around and there was a priest sitting beside me. He said, "You're in danger of death and I've come to give you the Last Sacraments." This was in 1951. I was received back into the Church and given the Last Sacraments. But I got better so I was excommunicated again, all within twenty minutes.

'It's ridiculous really. Had I died I'd have gone to Heaven, but had I gone out and got knocked down by a car I'd have gone down below.

'This priest was always putting forward my case and when [Archbishop] John Charles McQuaid confirmed my little girl, he said, "I think the time has come to be good to your mother. Tell her to go to confession."

'But my husband still wouldn't sign any papers. So the priest said if I signed the papers and promised to bring my children up Catholic they would recognise my marriage as valid.

'I went to confession and didn't know what to say. They arranged the confessions before ten o'clock Mass. He [the priest] came out robed for Mass with the altar boys. He came down the aisle and into the box and I went in, and every head turned round. It was as near to a public confession as you could have seen.

'"It's seven years. I haven't done anything," I said. So then the priest politely reminded me: "You lived with this man for seven years."

'I came out with a decade of the Rosary [as penance].'

As we sit in Sandycove, with afternoon sunlight brightening the room, it is difficult to imagine that these events took place just forty years earlier. Sheila has survived, but it is clear the stress has taken a toll on a sensitive woman who, after her father's death, learned from a newspaper report that she had been cut out of his will.

She is sanguine. Her three children, successful young adults, visit regularly. And she has a friendly collie and a garrulous parrot called Charlie ('from Newry, originally from the Cameroons') for company. The reaction to her book has been positive.

'It's funny. At the end of the day the sun comes out. It's a bit sad though, isn't it? The thing that's stopping me enjoying it is that certain sections of the family weren't happy about it. Not Maureen, of course. But my conscience is clear.'

When I ask Sheila if she is considering writing another book, she speaks candidly about her battle with depression. After her husband's death in 1972, Sheila suffered five years of a depressive illness, which resulted in hospitalisation and shock treatment.

'I was wondering whether I should write about my five years of mental illness. It could be too depressing for people, but again you have the funny side too.

'I remember when I was in with my first bad nervous breakdown, there was this chap who always wore a green and yellow paper hat with Kerry on it and he never spoke to anybody. I only had depression and he was a real nutter. [Laughs]

'I'd had a great friend who died and I was very upset. He came up to me and said, "You've had a bereavement, Sheila." And he took off his hat and put it on my head.

'I didn't dare take it off because it was his most prized possession. There I was with the hat on feeling like a real nutter.

'At the end of three days he came back and took it off and said, "You're over the worst now." And he put it back on his own head again. Here he was reaching out to me. He never spoke to the nurses or anyone, but he gave me the greatest gift he had.'

Had Sheila's illness led to her having to endure discrimination?

'Oh yes, there's still a great stigma attached to it. But it only makes me laugh.

'I didn't know what depression was until I got it. We all get down, but clinical depression is a much worse thing. It's a feeling of apathy and despair.'

Sheila has endured anxiety and trauma since she was a young girl.

'All these things happened and hadn't been spoken about and mounted up. I lost my father. I lost my mother. I married Jimmy Mooney and was very fond of his dad. His stepmother got cancer and we looked after her till she died.'

It feels as if there are areas that are out of bounds. Privacy needs to be respected. But there is one further topic that intrigues me: her sister's daughter, Mia Farrow.

I notice a copy of a Frank Sinatra biography in the room. The singer, who had been married to Farrow, had performed in Dublin the previous year. His show, billed as *The Ultimate Event*, was staged at the Lansdowne Road stadium for two nights. Did Sheila meet him while he was in town?

'I didn't. I could have, but I wouldn't quite know what way he feels about Mia now. He might be nasty. But I do know that I never heard her say one bad word about him.

'I asked Maureen what he is really like. She said, "A great host. He runs a wonderful house." But she said he can be a bit of a bastard.

'She'd make you laugh because there was a little silver cigarette box that held ten cigarettes and I opened it and inside was written, "To Maureen Love Frank."

'I said, "Is that Sinatra?"

'She said, "Would you know by the size of it?"

'He's supposed to be very mean and I can understand that because he came from a poor background.'

In 1968 Roman Polanski's film *Rosemary's Baby* created a wave of controversy as it depicted Rosemary, played by Mia Farrow, being raped by Satan. One of the greatest horror films of all time, it was banned by the film censor in Ireland. As a member of the Film Society in Trinity College, I was lucky to have seen the only screening in Ireland at the time.

'I went to a lot of charismatic prayer meetings because I wanted to write about them,' recalled Sheila. 'Mia's name came up at a prayer meeting. They said that Mia Farrow and The Beatles were the first to start all the drugs and meditation and evil. I stood up and said, "You call yourselves Christians?" I reminded them that she had nine children. Five adopted. The priest apologised then. These religious people are very quick to condemn.'

When her book was published, Sheila visited her mother's grave in Dean's Grange. 'We had a beautiful garden and people would always stop to look at the flowers. But my mum would say, "I love plastic flowers." Every Christmas, she would arrive with cut-glass tumblers, a bottle of whiskey and a big bunch of plastic roses for us. Dreadful-looking yokes.

'I went up to her grave and left a big bunch of plastic roses in the rain. The gravedigger said, "They all have their own taste." I told him, "That was her choice, not mine."'

Chapter Eight

Through the Mill

MANY OF THOSE WHOSE INTERVIEWS are revisited here are gone now.

Listening to old, taped interviews again has occasionally proved disconcerting. At times I come adrift. These aren't ghost voices. They are voices from another era, a lifetime ago. Suddenly, in an instant, the past is now and some exchanges take on an added weight. I hear thoughts expressed that sound like wisdom, useful advice. Did I miss the implied life lesson first time around, I wonder? But then, as I begin to chide myself, I realise that I missed nothing. Or, at least, very little.

One of the reasons I'm revisiting these tapes is because I had assimilated every nuance and filed away each insight. I realise I would have taken on board each precedent, parable or personal case history.

Sometimes it might seem we forget too readily. But do we ever really forget? I'm not so sure. Memories often lie dormant, waiting to be triggered.

Anthropologists create convincing case studies around the

discarded flotsam of centuries past. Archaeologists cultivate remote sensing in their study of the remnants of ancient societies. Every shard of ceramic, every weathered impression in stone is there to be deciphered. Similarly, each nugget recovered here speaks of experience tested in the furnace of full and eventful lives.

Each individual interviewee has their own preoccupations. The issues of the day may appear less significant in hindsight, but concerns are always anchored in a pertinent reality, however distant it may seem from our vantage point of knowing how things played out and what subsequently transpired for the interviewee.

I'm conscious of how, Tardis-like, we're bridging time. Even if it's just a span of thirty-five years. Saying that, I'm mindful of how thirty-five years is more than a lifetime for many, including my friend and colleague, the talented journalist and broadcaster Jonathan Philbin Bowman, who was just thirty-one when he died following an accidental fall in 2000.

Another journalist and wit, George Byrne, was older when he checked out. We'd been close friends for decades and had heard the chimes at midnight. Our adventures together are too many to recount here, but I envied George's great sense of recall as, from time to time, he would regale me with joyous details of a press conference we both attended in the exotic roof garden of the building in Kensington that had once housed the fashionable Biba. I'd last been there in the 1970s with the American-based writer who had since changed his name to Brixton Key. George could remember, word for word, the hilarious exchanges between David Coverdale of heavy rock band Whitesnake and some female journalists from Japan. His detailed observations are lost in time.

My mother is another who was thirty-one when she died, succumbing to breast cancer. The world changes. While still a child, my grief-stricken imperative was simply to change my world, my circumstances, my life.

Years later, I was appreciative of how those I interviewed for this series had contributed to change. We all do our bit, I suppose, to greater or lesser degrees. Looking back, it seems slightly silly that the only better world I could imagine for myself was a world that would have rock'n'roll as a soundtrack. Medicine, law, engineering didn't figure. I was already hiding in my imagination and connecting strands that might lead to a mythical new residence, not one constructed from gingerbread but built from blue lights and the boogie. Even if it was situated at the far end of a place called Lonely Street that was okay too. I knew the topography better than most.

In the Ireland of the 1950s, rock'n'roll was rare, except for what you might hear on Radio Luxembourg in the evening or, if you were lucky enough to be living on the east coast, catch on the weekend TV transmissions of the Jack Good-produced *Six-Five Special* and *Boy Meets Girls*. The Devil's music played second fiddle to a diet of schmaltz, come-all-ye's and the glorious stampede of céilí music. In the same way I believed Association Football didn't pose a threat to the integrity of Gaelic games, I convinced myself that beat group music could co-exist happily with 'The Rights of Man', 'King of the Fairies' and other traditional tunes my grandfather Johnny Carr played with his award-winning céilí band, The Silver Star. At least that's what I told myself. And so music, and music as a storytelling vehicle for incorporating in song my love of the Beat Generation writers, ancient Greek dramatists and the Irish poetic tradition, became my primary focus.

Entrepreneurs and athletes strive to create more efficient, more successful versions of themselves in pursuit of their goals. In a less defined arena, daydreamers work their way through variations and combinations of ideas, styles and forms searching for the best way of expressing the tantalising glimpses of truth that taunt them. Whichever medium or formula they settle on, their act of bearing witness can be described as art. Many of those whose interviews appear here are, in fact, artists.

Hearing their voices again on tape and noting their willingness to converse has a disquieting effect. I'm grateful for the short time we spent together. And I feel a sense of obligation to remind people of how they were and what they said.

WILLY RUSSELL – January 1990

The Beatles played their last gig in the basement Cavern Club on Mathew Street in August 1963. As a schoolboy, I yearned to breathe that stale air believing it might have mystical properties.

While my peers opted to become teachers, engineers or veterinary surgeons, or else familiarised themselves with 'Michael, Row the Boat Ashore' before joining a religious order, I packed a sleeping bag and walked up the gangplank of a cattle boat bound for Liverpool. It was the mid-1960s. I wouldn't be disappointed.

I made friends in the grimy old seaport: poets, musicians and painters who all had something to say and proclaimed it with varying degrees of impatience, humour and pathos.

I got to know the topography of the old town intimately. The aptly named Hope Street and the stretch between the city's two cathedrals became the fulcrum of my odyssey. The posters and flyers for the Everyman Theatre were alluring but, finance being problematic, I never got to check out the action.

I did, however, venture to read some excruciatingly juvenile poetry at the sessions in O'Connor's Tavern on Hardman Street. It was the encouragement and friendship of some of the Liverpool Scene poets that propelled me to set up a poetry reading group in Ireland which, when I met with the fastidious Peter Fallon, morphed into our joint venture Tara Telephone, publishers of *Capella*, the *Book of Invasions* broadsheet and some early collections under a Gallery Books imprint.

Since I'd seen photos of The Beatles in the music paper *Mersey Beat*, when they released their debut single 'Love Me Do', I was a fan. Later, I was intrigued by the stage play *John Paul George Ringo ... & Bert*, which opened in the Lyric on Shaftesbury Avenue in London in August 1974. By then I was based in London with Horslips and got to see the show. Willy Russell's play was clever and poignant. I saw it again a few years later in Dublin with Barry McGovern, John Olohan and Bryan Murray in the cast. I knew the play had been first staged in the Everyman in Liverpool and I wondered if maybe I'd crossed paths with the playwright.

In January 1990 I get the opportunity to interview Willy Russell, who's a household name thanks largely to the enormous crossover success of *Educating Rita*, *Shirley Valentine* and the musical *Blood Brothers*.

I immediately home in on the Liverpool 8 arts environment that I'd been familiar with.

'The whole late-'60s, early-'70s cultural scene in Liverpool was interesting. Did you frequent O'Connor's Tavern where they had poetry readings?'

'I did but only as a guest. I was never that literate. For me the heart had gone out of that after The Beatles left. But it was a terrific movement. The idea of poetry and rock'n'roll was sensational. Adrian [Henri, poet and painter] is a very dear friend. I was talking to him just yesterday.'

This is great news. Adrian was a supportive friend of mine and I'd often stayed at his place. We digress and chat about mutual acquaintances, the Liverpool Scene group and various local poets. I learn that John Peel's favourite singer-songwriter Mike Hart ('Harty') is currently living in Edinburgh and creatively active.

'You were playing guitar around then?' I ask.

'Yes, I was. I was part of a folky movement. I was playing the contemporary singer-songwriter clubs.'

'Had you gone back to college at that stage?'

'I went back in about 1969. I did O Levels and A Levels and started a teacher-training course. So I started playing in social clubs, working-men's clubs, that sort of thing, and then got more pure and went into more traditional folk clubs. I did that from about '72, I think.'

'So you would have spent about five years working prior to that. Did you have a variety of jobs?'

'Yeah. I was a ladies' hairdresser for six years.'

'Six years? You would have graduated as a hairdresser?'

'Oh yeah, I had my own shop. I hated it. I loathed it.' When Willy laughs, I detect a sense of relief. 'I spent all my time putting a Closed sign on the door and retiring to the back room to write songs and trying to write a novel and all that kind of thing. I couldn't wait to get out.'

'What was the transition from songs to drama? What was it about playwriting that attracted you to the form?'

'Well, I'd been fumbling to be a writer for so long. I got into writing songs, which I thought everybody did anyway. I never thought it was anything serious. And then, when I was hairdressing, I started to want to write stuff in a more serious form. Less ephemeral. A song it seemed to me was something you wrote on Tuesday, went out and sang it Tuesday night, and maybe at a couple of other gigs, and never used it again.

'And so, because I'd always been an avid reader, I thought I'd try and write a book. They were called novels in those days. I had a go at it, but it didn't really develop. I tried to write a couple of sketches for a thing called *The Northern Drift*, a great [radio] programme run by Alf Bradley that had lots of northern writers. I got a few rejection slips.

'I never thought I'd be in the lucky position of being able to do it for a living. During this time I began mixing with people who did write, who did go to the theatre. All these influences were coming in.

'By this time I was back at college and I remember when I was doing O Levels and A Levels, we used to do drama as an option for a couple of hours on a Thursday morning. We had an avant-garde teacher then who said, "We won't do a play. We'll write one." All these fifteen-year-olds went, "Ah yeah, great" and then pissed off, and I was the one left holding the pen and the paper. So I just wrote it. Again, I didn't think of it as anything serious, y'know. We put this play on.

'Then I went to teacher training college and whilst I was there I wrote a tele-play, which didn't work. I sent it to Barry Hanson, who was a producer at Pebble Mill. He wrote back an encouraging letter. He said, "These are the reasons it doesn't work. But there's something good in it so let me see anything you write in the future."

Which was very encouraging. But, again, I was only dipping my toe in it. Because really what I was doing was writing this novel, you see. I knew nothing about novels. Why in the name of God did I think I could write one?

'Then I was on a teacher-training course, doing drama as the main course, and halfway through the second year we would do a production of *Peer Gynt*. For some reason it fell through and we decided instead to do a compendium evening – one-acts, monologues and what have you. I must have been inspired by the effect of this rejection letter from Barry Hanson. I said, "Will you do a play of mine as part of the evening?" They said, "Sure. Bring it in. We can't guarantee we'll do it, but we'll read it."

'"Okay," I said. "I'll bring it in next week." I didn't tell them I hadn't written a play, so I went home, put some paper in the typewriter and went "Donk!" And wrote this play in five days.

'The second I began it I knew I'd discovered the voice in which I should be writing. The style. And that writing novels was a stupid thing to try and do, you know.

'I've since obviously rationalised that and come to understand it was the most natural thing in the world for me to be a dramatist rather than a novelist, because being brought up working class, the whole of your code is a spoken one. An oral means of communication. Not literary at all, you know. The middle classes do contain the whole of their culture by and large in the written form. Also, although my people had never been to a theatre, I lived in theatrical families. They were great storytellers in an unselfconscious way. If you ever told them they were a great storyteller, they'd drop dead.

'And they were great debaters. Saturday night in our house would be so loud on your eardrums as a little kid. They loved debating stuff. They were fighters. They were argumentative. And also, my dad was a musician. Not professional. A great mouth-organ player and a not-so-great accordion player. There was always music around, stories around and political debate around. So, although on the face of it I looked like a really unlikely candidate to end up writing for theatre, if you read between the lines, it was an obvious route to take really.'

In a busy Dublin hotel, I enquire if Willy would like a drink. He'll have a mineral water, so I order 'two Ballygowans'. As they're delivered, Willy brightens up. 'I thought you were ordering an esoteric whiskey,' he says with a smile. 'Cheers.'

'It just occurred to me,' I say, 'is there an Irish connection with your family?'

'I don't know. I think we had something to do with the Huguenots, according to my dad. But on my mother's side, yes, my maternal grandfather, I think he was born on the other side of the sheets, so I don't know how. My grandmother Annie – my wife is called Annie – would certainly have Irish connections. But I'm not a great one for going into family trees. These things are locked away in the cupboard with my family. It makes it a little bit exciting. I don't have that roots curiosity.'

The man who's chuckling now is wearing a smart suit, white shirt and tie with large wire-rimmed spectacles. He could be a company manager, local government official or ambitious school principal. It's winter. Although the hotel is warm, he doesn't bother removing the expensive scarf that drapes his shoulders.

'Did you knock around the Cavern Club in the early '60s?'

'Oh yes, but I wasn't part of that. When I went to the Cavern, I was fourteen. And you know at that age the difference between fourteen and eighteen was huge. I'd see people like John and Paul coming in as I was standing in the queue, but I couldn't speak to them. No way. It would be impossible.

'I started going there when I was fourteen. Up to that time in England the only rock music was polite. I remember Frank Ifield's "I Remember You" being top of the charts forever. Having become a guitar player and having seen The Shadows, and then walking into the Cavern and seeing all The Shadows lookalike bands, but then seeing these guys walk on who defied everything, it was just so visually shocking, apart from anything else, to see guys with their hair down there, wearing black, carrying black amplifiers, playing instruments that we'd never seen 'cos they came from Germany.

'Everything we had in England was a sort of polite version of things we knew in America. But these guys had brought something in from Europe. The hairstyles were European. We didn't know that. We never looked at Europe. All we'd ever looked at was America. And that was before they played. Once they started playing "Some Other Guy", all the rhythm'n'blues that you could hear on illicit radio and [Radio] Luxembourg was here in front of you.

'I became a bore. People on the school bus used to take the piss out of me talking about The Beatles. If you didn't know about it and were into things like Frank Ifield and The Shadows, the very name The Beatles was a shocking thing.

'Indeed, I remember writing an essay in my O Level English exam called "A Group Called The Beatles". Afterwards I wondered what the examiner must have thought. Six months later they were the biggest thing on the Earth. As I say, I was not part of it in terms of being one of the lads 'cos I was too young.'

'I caught your play *John Paul George Ringo ... & Bert* a couple of times. First in London and then later in Dublin. It's wonderfully evocative.'

'I still think it's the best bio-musical that there's been. I can take a distance from it and say that because it was so long ago. The major reason for that is with The Beatles there's a huge story to tell of ultimately slightly classic proportions.

'If you're talking about an unfortunate man who got on the wrong plane on the wrong day, that is not a tragedy. The poor bloke just got on the wrong plane. Whereas the emergence of the first people to do it, the first people to take America, from the most unlikely place in Britain, to conquer the world and then start to self-destruct is the very stuff of drama.'

'How did the individual Beatles react to it?'

'If you remember, I wrote it in '73 and it was on in '74. It was very acrimonious. John was in America and, without a green card, he couldn't get out because he wouldn't get back in. He sent a taped message of good luck to Bert. Paul saw some excerpts on an early Melvyn Bragg show and damned it.'

Willy had also worked on a screen treatment for *John Paul George Ringo ... & Bert*, which impresario Robert Stigwood planned to produce. Convoluted business deals scuppered the project.

'About three years after I wrote the script a journalist asked me why the film didn't get made and, idiotic and naive, I said, off the record, "Paul put the mockers on it and da-da-da-da-da." So the journalist's story was "Paul McCartney stamps on film." I was at home with an awful flu and the phone rang. I went downstairs and took the call.

'"This is Paul McCartney."

'I said, "It is like fuck." I thought it was a mate winding me up and I put the phone down. The phone rang again.

'An urgent voice said, "Don't put the phone down." He said, "I've just read what you have to say about me."

'I said, "It's not true. It wasn't intended for publication anyway. I've had many opportunities to say something about you but have never said anything. About any of you."

'He said, "Well come over and have a cup of tea and talk about it."

'So I went over, took the script, had a cup of tea and said, "If you read the script, Paul, you'll see there's no slur on you." In fact, you'll see there's a scene which specifically demonstrates it's Lennon who broke up the band.' But we got on well. [Macca affectionately dubbed Russell 'Woolly Rissole'.]

'Paul subsequently asked you to write a *Band on the Run* film treatment. Or did he?'

'That's right. He did. Yes, which has never been filmed. A few years after writing [the 1973 album] *Band on the Run*, Paul decided he'd like to get into films. He was writing scripts himself. That was called *Give My Regards to Broad Street*. Thank you very much. We'll say no more about that. I did not write *Give My Regards to Broad Street*.

'I knew Brian Brolly fairly well. He was head of MPL [McCartney Productions Limited] in those days and then moved over to Andrew Lloyd Webber's company. Brian [preferred] theatre to the rock'n'roll business. I think Paul had said, "We want to make a film now." And Brian probably said, "What about William?"

'And Paul said, "Well I want to make a film now."

'I said, "What's it about?"

'"It's about Wings. I'm going up to Scotland. I'm recording [*Back to the Egg* in 1978]. Do you want to spend a week up there?"

'No way could I turn down the opportunity of sitting around in the recording studio with one of the most gifted songwriters and best musicians of the twentieth century. So I went up there. It was very difficult, really, because I had to write a film which had parts for all his current band members. And it was a new band, a new Wings line-up. Linda and Denny Laine were still in it. I was sat around for a week and, you know, film is a very exacting, demanding medium. You can't do it on a whim.

'Paul had done *Magical Mystery Tour* and there was still a bit of the "happening", art student thing about Paul. He's into avant garde. I'm not. Making a film [involves] a lot of forward climbing. You have tears before bedtime. So I eventually said in Scotland, "I'm going to have to take this away." I can't be thinking, recording sessions at seven o'clock in the morning and all that. So I came back and I thought of the song "Band on the Run" and what it's always meant for me.

'Remember when Wings went on the road playing clubs. So when I had that genesis, I outlined the film and Paul said, "Terrific."

'I then sat down and wrote it and spent some time on it, given the restrictions. And yet, again, "We're really going to do it. We'll start next week." The whole thing was "next week".

'It was great fun. Then I went to see Paul at a gig just before he went to Tokyo [in 1980]. "Listen, you're never going to do the fucking thing." [Laughs]

'"Fuck off. You did a great job. You've no problem."

'"You'll never make this."

'And with that he went to Tokyo and the rest is history. [McCartney was arrested and jailed for the possession of marijuana before being deported. After a period of reflection, Paul changed the course of his musical career.]

'Occasionally still Linda will call and say, "We should have made that. Can we still do it?" It was a lovely time, actually. You don't make films that way.'

Willy is being really generous with his time and his recollections. As a Beatles fan, I feel privileged that he is taking the time to go back over what must be familiar old ground for my benefit. I'm conscious of not wanting to push my luck.

'Did you feel under pressure to repeat the heavy-duty success of *John Paul George Ringo ... & Bert*?'

'Quite the opposite. I'd written a play very much in the Everyman house style – lewd, Brechtian, Joan Littlewoodian, Everyman house style y'know – I had a performer's instinct going back to the early days so I knew it would be … or I hoped I knew, because I'd been taken on early by Peggy Ramsay, the doyen of dramatic agents. So I had the great support of Peggy at a very difficult phase. That happened to me when I was twenty-six. If I'd been eighteen when all the attention had happened, I wouldn't be alive today. My son had just been born so I had the security of family. I was a bit older and had been through the mill in a certain way. Then I knew that to try to write anything else in a similar vein would be an invitation to disaster.

'I did what I felt I should do and I wrote what I thought was a proper play. A play that would observe the unity of the time and place. I wrote a play called *Breezeblock Park*. When I'd been in London with the Beatles play, I'd started to become aware of Alan Ayckbourn's work and whatever. And I'd seen very conventionally, beautifully crafted plays but exclusively about the middle classes. Back at the Everyman, being really fucking radical, it was real dedicated lefties presenting the working classes as people who were plotting revolutions in the kitchens of England. Unlike most people in theatre, I was of that class, and I knew that most of them were not plotting revolutions. If they were doing anything, they were plotting where the next valium was coming from.

'So all those things were coming in on me. I wrote *Breezeblock Park* as a sort of working-class comedy of manners *à la* an Ayckbourn, knowing that the sort of working-class audience we were getting in the theatre would completely identify with having their clothes taken off them in public. Which is what middle-class audiences were having. They love it. Well, of course, in Liverpool it caused uproar. The theatre was terrified of doing it because it was sneering at the working class and all that. You know, the middle class can be very protective in a romantic way, which didn't bother me. Because I was of them. The audience just adored it, wet themselves.

'At the same time, it was my first attempt at writing a very crafted … I suppose I wanted to say, "Yeah, look, I'm known for writing that play about The Beatles but I want to show you that I can write a play that observes all the traditional unities about play-making." Structure has always been something that has intrigued me greatly. I'm not complaining when I say this, but it's something in my work that's often overlooked. The craft that goes into. I'm glad about that because I don't like plays which demonstrate their craft – look how clever I am, deh-deh-deh-deh-deh.

'But it seems to me that plays which last and which really engage have to be more than just their content. Let's just say that content has to be orchestrated in such a manner. And there are very very deep, profound rules in relation to theatre, which you'd better know. You break them, fine. You can break them positively to your advantage. But you'll find it hard to break them positively unless you know what they are.

'They're not rules that anybody lays down. They're rules that evolved out of the hearts and souls of men and storytelling.'

'So you find it a very different discipline crafting for stage as opposed to cinema?'

'The one common thing is that you're telling a story, and you have to keep that in mind constantly. But you're just using different means to tell the story, y'know. Theatre … crudely put, your problem is always how to contrive to bring the action before the eye of the audience. Cinema is always taking the eye of the audience to where the action is because the camera is the eye of the audience.

'The other really interesting element from a technical point of view is – in the theatre, as a play has a beginning, a middle and an end, so a scene has a beginning, a middle and an end. It's not true in the cinema. You go into a scene in cinema at the latest possible moment. You don't need to have a beginning, a middle and an end.

'But I don't actually like all these mystiques about the differences between them. I think it's important to bear in mind that you're telling a story. In a medium. Be honest with the medium. Be honest with the story.'

Russell's plays had struck a nerve with the general public. I wonder how he arrived at them. 'With any of your plays have there been specific incidents that inspired you to think, *That's a great story. I'll tell that story about [Educating] Rita or Blood Brothers or Shirley [Valentine]?*'

'No. Never. Sometimes one gets a story in advance. As with *Blood Brothers*. One moment I didn't have the story in my head and then the next minute it just came down from the sky. "Thank you, God." I was nervous of it for eight years. It took me eight years to get around to writing it. Because I knew it was a musical story. I wasn't known for composing music in the theatre. All those prejudices would be brought to bear. So, for eight years, I thought I'd have to get someone to compose the music or I'd have to use existing music or whatever. So I kept dithering.

'Something like [*Educating*] *Rita* and *Shirley Valentine* were written facing deadlines and weeks and weeks and weeks of getting it wrong. Not even knowing what you're going to write. Trying plays you thought you might write and finding you don't want to write them any longer. All that sort of stuff. The bin getting ever fuller.

'In both cases, with Rita and Shirley, they walked onto the page. And thank Christ. From that moment on I know I've got a play. It might be agony and hell, but I've got the rock-bottom solidity of the facts that I know there's a play there because they come out in the character.

'With Rita, a character started talking. I wrote the first fourteen pages of scene one, but I didn't know where she was going. And I didn't ask any questions. She was the one who started talking.

'That's when I know I've got it. When I start writing things that I did not know I knew. It's almost like, and I don't want to make it sound mystical, but it's almost like being possessed. In a situation like Rita, and certainly Shirley, the character takes you over totally. I see it happen. It's funny.

'It's like when Barry Humphries became Edna. He's incapable of some of the wit that Dame Edna has. It's only when he becomes her that he can see things in a certain light. [Laughs] It's the same with me. I have to totally allow the character to take me over but retain an objective bit at the back that's the playwright. But I don't argue with her. I let them have their way.

'It tends to be after the first few days that I get to a point where I know that if I don't start mapping it out then it will go badly wrong. So I'll start to take stock and find out what it's telling me. 'Cos often a play is not what you want to write. You need to allow … it's this bizarre hybrid sort of unconscious imaginative/conscious structuring thing, y'know.'

'Have you got your work finished on *Dancin' Thru the Dark*, the film version of your play *Stags and Hens*?'

'I thought I had until nine o'clock last night. I'd just delivered the final music, but there are some technical problems with it. I finished in the studio at the beginning of the week. It's been a long job, you know what I mean. And I said to the fellas, "Right, there's the DATs [Digital Audio Tapes]. Deliver them." I feel so knackered with it. Just the idea of going in to do a remix ...'

He lets the idea hang, while no doubt contemplating the dread of further long hours of engineering and the concentration required for extra mixing sessions in a sterile control-room environment. Nevertheless, I'm intrigued by his engagement with music.

'Do you have special intro theme music for the film?'

'There's a song called "Once in a Lifetime", which I've used as the theme. It's not a picture that you could use a theme in that way. I feel quite frustrated because of that. Because there's so much music in the picture, all sorts of music, there's no room for a symphonic, orchestral thing. When you're writing songs that's the really tasty stuff.'

Although I hadn't seen it on the night, I'd heard that Terry Wogan had recently introduced a real-life Shirley Valentine on his television show. Was Willy aware of this development beforehand?

'That's right. What happened was, when I was writing the play, I called the character Shirley. It got to the point where I was at home one evening doing a bit of work on it and I knew that I needed to reveal what her second name was. I called her Shirley Smith. I was reading it back to my wife, Annie, and she said, "Is that the level of your imagination? Shirley Smith?" We'd already discussed that Shirley might be the title.

'She said, "Think of it on the title."

'I thought back to when I was at school. There were three girls who used to sit together, Shirley Smith, Shirley Valentine and Barbara Browne, so I said, "I'll call her Shirley Valentine." I made the assumption that the Shirley Valentine I went to school with all those years ago would no longer be Shirley Valentine 'cos she'd have married. She had a child, but she never married.

'So the play opens in Liverpool and my sister Dawn, who was working in the box-office at the time, got a call. "Can I book twelve tickets for tonight?"

'"What name?"

'"Shirley Valentine."

'Dawn phoned me and said, "Do you know somebody called Shirley Valentine?"

'I said, "Yeah."

'She said, "I think she's coming to the show tonight."

'I said, "I'll get down there."

'And she was great. The twelve tickets were for, would you believe, twelve women, all married or in relationships, in their forties who, every year, go on holiday abroad and arrange postcards from Devon and Hull and places like that. Their husbands don't know they're out of the bloody country.

'I haven't seen her for a couple of years. She's a smashing girl. She's very interesting and not remotely like the character. But I didn't know that was coming up on *Wogan*.'

'Do you think that sense of escapism, the dream of Shirley Valentine to escape or re-create herself, is as great today as it was ten or fifteen years ago among people in your environment in Liverpool?'

Willy pauses before replying. 'I think it's ever-present in all of us wherever we are. I'm reminded of the Paul Simon song on *Hearts and Bones* ["Train in the Distance"]:

> The thought that life could be better
> Is woven indelibly
> Into our hearts and our brains.

'It's that which probably best summarises all of my work to date. The thought that life could be better. It's often a blessing and a curse.'

When I arrived to meet Willy Russell, I certainly wasn't expecting our conversation to get down to the nitty-gritty of artistic endeavour. But here he is, sitting in a spacious hotel lounge, surrounded by shoppers coming from the January sales, with a pianist working his way through a repertoire of rococo variations of popular middle-of-the-road hits, sipping mineral water and giving serious thought to his creative process.

'I never sit down to write about that theme. It just, inevitably, happens. I suppose it's because it's so close to me. I went through a particular re-direction in life and found out how hard it was to go against the tide and often how seductive it would be to just say, "Aw, I give in."

'But if you've got something beating away inside of you, you've got to follow it. Even if you break your fucking neck, it's better to have followed it. I meet too many bitter people.'

This seems like a good time to switch gears. So I begin a ramble about living in interesting times. 'With all the stuff going on in Europe at the moment ... you've got [Václav] Havel being appointed president of Czechoslovakia ...'

'Isn't that amazing.'

'Do you think it's possible that something like that could ever happen in Britain? Who would your candidate be in the UK? Someone to take over from Mrs Thatcher.'

Willy explodes with laughter. 'No. Revolution in Britain? No. Christ Almighty, I hope they never make an English playwright the head of the country in Britain. The first thing they'll do is close the theatres. Knows how dangerous they are.'

He's still laughing when I add, 'I think it's brilliant.'

'I do too, but I temper that with a great caution.'

'It seems to me that theatre isn't being taken as seriously by the general public in Britain.'

'The degree of esteem in which theatre is held is always a mark of the level of freedom of a country. In economic terms, not only in physical terms. It's always there, ready to shout loudly again. When did we last shut down theatres in England? Cromwell, wasn't it? The Reformation. "Shut the theatres down."

'To go back to an earlier question, I can't see that happening. The more you oppress a people then the more these expressions, all of them – not just theatres, pages of books, things that hang on walls – the more people need them for their sustenance. We need it in Britain in a different way because you can't compare.

'I've always found it a ridiculous thing comparing Thatcherite England with the 1930s. You cannot compare it. It's a much more complex form of spiritual deprivation in which, because of the particular nature of capitalism, we have all colluded and it's therefore far more difficult for us to turn around and say, "They are the baddies. It's their fault. They did it to us." Which you could say in the 1930s: "A massive labour force crushed under the heel of a kind of capitalist force."

'It's not like that now because we've been encouraged to have our own houses, our own mortgages, our own shares, our own foreign holidays.'

If I've ever doubted that Willy Russell is acutely aware of social and cultural norms and a man of steadfast political ideals, then I am being set right.

'The anti-revolution, the Thatcher revolution began a long time before in that movement towards the erosion of the street, the erosion of the community. The idea of "my private plot of land, my private house, my car", which everybody wanted – my dad desperately wanted – "I want a house" – it was a terribly important mark of honour and a very noble impulse. It's what's done with that impulse that is the big question mark. So it makes the addressing of politics a much more subtle pastime. Addressing what is happening now. It's going to be probably far more interesting, in a sense, to look at what will be happening in Czechoslovakia after ten fucking years of Coca-Cola. That's what saddens me.'

He's in the zone now and fully focused on those social anomalies that prick his conscience daily. His anger remains controlled but there's no mistaking his frustration and his zeal.

'There's a scene in *Educating Rita*, which is my favourite piece in the play, where she says, "They think they've got choice because they can choose between Stork and butter, because they can choose between Everton and Liverpool, because they can choose between one fucking lousy party and the next, because they can choose between BBC and ITV. That's no choice."

'Now, what's happening with Czechoslovakia is they go, "We'll have that. We want Coca-Cola." It's broken. You can't tell them that because people have got to have the freedom to gorge themselves and to crucify themselves and maybe come back from the abyss. But you can't tell them.

'We can't tell them they're going from one very obvious form of oppression to a far more sophisticated and subtle form of multi-corporate global sort of oppression.

'If I had to choose between the brutality of East Germany as it was six months ago and the brutality of New York, I'd say, "Well, we're better taking our chances probably in New York."'

He laughs at the irony.

'You've decided to continue to live in Britain. But it would appear that the people of Liverpool are getting hammered as is anywhere north of Watford.'

'The population has dwindled enormously. But mostly by political design because they want to break down those post-industrial revolution complexes because they're not needed any more. That's another thing. One cannot be left wing, sentimental and romantic. It's because we were sentimental and romantic and thought we'd achieved some version of Jerusalem that Thatcherism came to power. We were all patting ourselves on the back because we were a bit radical, because we got creative writing in the school, y'know. We thought we'd made the world a better place. We never thought we could go backwards. We were that arrogant because we didn't understand the scope of history.'

'How do you see things developing in the '90s?'

'I'm always optimistic. I'm optimistic that man will survive, and if he doesn't, he goes down the drain. So what? If he's not had the fucking wit to survive, he'd better go.'

TONY WARREN – November 1991

The name Tony Warren first became familiar in the 1960s at a time when I was living with my grandmother and TV was still in black-and-white. His name appeared on the credits of a TV soap opera called *Coronation Street*, which depicted the working classes of Manchester. The characters who orbited a pub called the Rovers Return were vivid personalities: strong women, flawed men.

A staunch Irish republican, whose husband had fought and suffered in the War of Independence, my grandmother wasn't a fan of *Coronation Street*. The entire culture of the British working class – accents and lifestyles included – had blighted the lives of my grandparents' generation decades earlier. It's what they had struggled to escape from. The emotional wounds were still raw. I only got to see the soap when I was alone in the house.

The arrival of television in the 1950s ushered in a new, more entertaining, colonisation. From the Television Toppers to the Busby Babes, *Six-Five Special* to *Dixon of Dock Green*, Oliver Cromwell was having his revenge as far as the BBC and ITV transmissions extended, although admittedly in ways that would most likely have appalled him.

The opportunity to interview Tony Warren when he is in Dublin promoting his debut novel raises what seem like a lifetime of memories for me – reminders from an era that has long since slipped into a distant shadowland, a foggy terrain explored by a different, long-lost explorer – another version of myself.

Tony is dressed in a stylish Fair Isle jumper and slacks and loafers when we meet in the Shelbourne Hotel. Sporting a neatly cropped crew cut, his look is a mix of preppy and astronaut. He looks healthy and proves to be a natural conversationalist, happy to shoot the breeze and easy to like.

'How does it feel, having been a boy wonder, to be having another spell in the limelight at fifty-five?'

Tony laughs. 'An *enfant terrible*. Mmm ... I had to write this book [*The Lights of Manchester*] to prove that I wasn't a flash in the pan. But now, of course, when I finished the book, the day they read it they took up the option on the next one. Now I have to prove I'm not a flash in the pan twice. Great things are happening. Yesterday they announced they're reprinting before the actual publication date. It's amazing.

'We start it off in Manchester on Monday with a launch in the town hall in the lord mayor's parlour. I'm going to have on one side of me the original landlady of the Rover's Return. Doris Speed is coming out of retirement; she's now ninety-two. And my mate Hughie on the other side of me. So that's going to be one for the memory album.'

'Have the film rights been sold yet?'

'A lot of people are sniffing round in every way. What fascinates me is my agent called to say there was huge interest from all the Scandinavian countries for the translation rights. That really thrilled me. Because now I do feel that I'm standing on my own two legs because they've never seen *Coronation Street* there. Although of course the foundations of *Coronation Street* were built on my own two legs. There are no two ways about that. The people tend to see me as Mr *Coronation Street* and I want to be Mr *Lights of Manchester*.'

He chuckles at his pretensions before adding, 'It's not just a book about Manchester. It's a book about belonging. I have a huge Irish family in it. The Dolans. You can't have a book about Manchester without having the Irish. Like everybody in Manchester, I have an Irish great-grandmother.'

He laughs again, like someone who worries he's sounding cliched.

'That might qualify you to play for the Irish football team.'

'Well, the guy I live with, even though he grew up in England, had a trial for Ireland, but he didn't make it.'

Warren began acting when he was twelve. The initial idea for a street drama, one he called Florizel Street, occurred to him when he was nineteen, and four years later he successfully pitched the concept to Granada Television as *Coronation Street*. The initial run of thirteen programmes was extended indefinitely, with Warren writing episodes throughout the 1960s.

'*Coronation Street* was such a wonderful idea and a wonderful concept ...'

'It wasn't just an idea. Originally, I was instructed to write twelve episodes.'

'It has been such a classic, I wonder how you didn't progress into film screenwriting.'

'Oh, people tend to forget that I did some screenwriting in the '60s. By the time I was twenty-three I was under exclusive contract to Granada. And then Brian Epstein commissioned me to write a film and I came up with the title *Ferry Cross the Mersey*. Gerry Marsden wrote the song with the title. I created that film. I did a trilogy of television plays, *The War of Darkie Pilbeam*, which was the inspiration for *A Family at War*.

'Then, at the end of the '60s, I wrote an autobiography called *I Was Ena Sharples' Father*, and then I vanished. As a matter of fact, I went to California. Everybody was going to California at the end of the '60s. I'd not had a childhood, so I decided to have a childhood. The trouble is along the way I discovered rather adult toys. I discovered drink and hard drugs. So I played around with those on two continents for a long time.

'Everybody says, "Why did you do it?" I think addicts are born and not made. And I think I had it to do. I was one of the lucky ones. I came out the other side. It's ten years since all that went out the window. It took me a long time to get my head together after that. At the end of those ten years, I was barely capable of writing a postcard.

'I would write a postcard and, because people expect good words from a writer, I wouldn't have the confidence to post it. It took a long time to come back.

'Then I had to do a debate on soap opera at the Edinburgh Festival with Melvyn Bragg. On the way back – it was a bank holiday – I shared a train compartment with Cate Haste, his wife, and as you do on long bank holiday journeys, we talked about love, life, death, God, war, sex, ourselves, ourselves, ourselves, and Cate said to me, "God gave you great talent. Why did you never use it?"

'I said, "Well, I did, but then it all went wrong." … And I said, "I don't know if I can put the words together in the same way any more."

'What I said was, "I'm too afraid of failure to get started."

'She said, "I heard you speak today, and you can put the words together and you should start. What would you like to do?"

'I said, "I'd really like to write a great, provincial novel. I'd like to write a novel about Manchester because I know Manchester very well. I'd like to write it so anyone who knows Manchester will identify with it and also anybody who's fed up with being told that the only place to live is London or New York will empathise with it. I want to say, 'It's alright to come from wherever you feel comfortable. It's alright to come from where you were born.' As simple as that."

'Then my agent said to me, "Have you got any ideas?"

'And I said, "I'd like to write a novel."

'She said, "You should write a novel. Do it in your own good time."

'Those are very comfortable words. It was also a challenge because it meant, "Now or never."

'She said, "Do a hundred pages."

'She took them away from me and then rang me up sounding as though she had strong drink taken. She said, "Guess what. One of the best publishers in London is mad about it. They don't want you for a one-novel contract. They want you for one with an option for a second." And that option has now been taken up.'

'A happy scenario.'

'It's amazing.'

Tony Warren's history has the air of a fiction novel written by someone for whom fantasy was their stock-in-trade. I'm captivated, intrigued and curious to dip into parts of it. The topic I need to visit is Tony's fight back from addiction to both drugs and drink, which was clearly a major achievement.

'Do you now advise people not to take drugs or alcohol, or did you gain anything positive from the experience?'

Having been through the mill and survived to tell the tale, Tony is happy to look back into the darkness. 'Yeah. It brought me to who I am today. And what's more, I seem to live much more vividly than people who don't have those missing years, probably because I've got shadow to contrast light against. When I'm happy now I consciously think *I am happy*. And I don't know many people who can say that. Because I spent too many years …'

He pauses momentarily, as if searching for the most effective analogy. 'I was the type of drunk who likes to be on his own. I like a bar where the music is dreamy and sad. A bar with a jukebox. What I liked was Edith Piaf singing she had no regrets in a voice that sounded like she was going to cut her throat any second. Then I'd drink one for my baby and ninety-eight more for the road.'

'What were your drugs of choice?'

'The drug of my choice was morphine.'

'That's serious.'

'It's a heavy drug, but I used a lot of others. "Drug of my choice" is very much a recovered addict's phrase. I also say that the other drug of my choice was alcohol, because alcohol is a drug.'

'Did you have a Road to Damascus moment of enlightenment and conversion? What brought you to the decision to change?'

Tony lowers his voice and speaks softly. His tone is one of affection. 'A miracle. No two ways about it. A real, genuine miracle. I'd totally dried myself out and I'd been lying in bed for a week terrified to get out of bed. I got rid of the drink first of all.'

I worry that I might be crossing a line, or that I'm being too intrusive, but Tony seems relaxed and confident. I press on. 'What was it that made you say, "No, I'm not going to have a drink?"'

'Nature stepped in. My body could no longer tolerate anything. I couldn't keep anything down. So I was totally dried out and had been for a week. I was scared to get out of bed because the road leads two ways, to the pub and the off-licence.

'And I said, "God, I'm beaten." Suddenly I wasn't alone in the room. There was a figure there who was the cleanest person I've ever seen. It was a guy and he was all white and he had his own light. I think he was my holy guardian angel. I really do.

'He wasn't a sissy angel like in bad church art. This man was made of energy and vigour. I'm flying on it to this day. All he did was look at me. He knew and he understood. And I wasn't alone any more. It's a tremendously solitary occupation, using drink and drugs. All I knew was, I wasn't alone. And I said, "Help me. I'm beaten." And somebody had come to help …

'So I went downstairs and I said to my father, "I've just seen an angel. There should be a rainbow." And he said, "You can't see the rainbow from your side of the house." And there was a most extraordinary rainbow coming north. An extraordinary rainbow right over the house with another rainbow inside it.

'I then told the story. My mother thought I was barmy. She was convinced I had gone barmy, or barmier. But my father said in a rather holy voice, "Something very remarkable has happened in this house." I said, "It's my angel." I claimed it. Which was probably very wrong of me.'

He chuckles at the incongruity of the scenario before continuing. 'Then a week later I decided that I should try just one more drink. I had one and then I was going for a second when something picked me up, threw me across the room. I don't know what it was. I hit the floor and came to surrounded by ambulance men who said, "Do you have fits?" I said, "No, not that I know of."

'All I knew was that something had stepped in and stopped me. That's the very last drink I ever had. I remember it clearly. Then I knew that I could tackle the other stuff as well. The other stuff didn't want to let me go. It hung around for some time. But that had to go and it went. Praise God. God's done it all.'

'Had you been a spiritual person prior to that?'

'I love God, but I'm not very keen on Holy Mother Church. I'm an Anglican. A High Anglican. I used to go to Mass. But I don't go to church. Not out of lack of gratitude. Only because the Church of Rome and the Church of England are both highly judgemental.'

'But what of your figure of light?'

'He's as real as anything. Believe you me. He beats speed. I'm still flying.' He chuckles again at the drug reference. 'My energy levels are not like a fifty-five-year-old. And that's over ten years ago.'

During the year (1991), actor Bill Roache, who played the character Ken Barlow, sued *The Sun* for branding him boring and unpopular with his colleagues. He won his case, but the sum he received in damages was less than his legal costs. Given that Tony was living in Manchester and acting as a consultant to *Coronation Street*, I wonder whether he had become involved in what was dubbed the 'Boring Ken' saga.

'No,' he states emphatically. 'My one fear in the middle of launching a book was that the tipstaff was going to arrive and tap me on the shoulder and say, "You're needed in the High Court." Because, of course, I created the character, and they seem to have asked everybody. Do you want to know what I think of Bill Roache?'

'Yes, please. I find him an intriguing individual.'

'He is a quiet charmer. He's a man who's been on a lifelong spiritual trail. He's not boring. He's polite. He's intelligent. He's quietly entertaining, but he's not boring. My father used to say, "To call a man a bore is the meanest thing you can do." Because it's very difficult to disprove and the label sticks. You can look for boredom in anybody and, with that label, you can find it. But I've known a lot of bores and Bill isn't one.'

'Of course he is a Druid.'

'He's been into all sorts of things. He's a very skilled astrologer.'

Clever response, I think.

Given that he's so vibrant, I assume Tony already has an idea mapped out for the second novel of the option?

'Oh yes, I've already started plotting it. I'm having to turn my whole career around because I'm seen as so much a part of

Coronation Street that I have to remind them that I can stand on my own two feet and that I'm holding in my hands a copy of a book called *The Lights of Manchester*.'

I had worked on the television production of Graham Reid's play *The Hidden Curriculum* (supplying the soundtrack with my musical partner Johnny Fean) with Stephen Butcher, who had directed many episodes of *Coronation Street*, and I learned from Stephen of how directors would frame certain camera angles and establish shots as an homage to earlier episodes. I mention this to Tony.

'We've got one of the best producers we've ever had in the whole run of the show, Mervyn Watson, and I went in the other day and I was congratulating him on a show and he said, "Well I'll tell you something. That episode had the right blend of comedy and drama, the right balance of baddies and goodies. In short, it was a 1990s version of the show you wrote in 1960. And when the show's right, exactly the same show, the episode's right."'

'What of the Street dealing with the major social issues, be it addiction, AIDS and so on?'

'If they were to naturally arise within the plot, I don't see why not. However, the Street is not a platform. The Street is entertainment. Many people have tried to turn it into a platform, and they would have stopped it in its tracks. It's been running for thirty years, so we're on the right lines.'

At this point we digress and discuss all sorts. It occurs to me that Tony is such a busy man, I wonder how he finds time to read. His boyish enthusiasm is raised another level.

'Oh, I read the same books over and over again. I like one Irish writer very much – Myles na gCopaleen.' He begins to laugh at the idea of Myles (aka Flann O'Brien, aka Brian O'Nolan).

'I love reading about *The Brother*. I've been looking for *The Brother* in Dublin.' He laughs joyously.

'And do you know who I love? Somerville and Ross. One of theirs that hasn't been published for years is coming out. Virago are bringing it out in England. I read Evelyn Waugh, like everybody else. End of century. Great days of writing. Like E.F. Benson. A young American writer, Armistead Maupin, makes me laugh a great deal. His *Tales of the City* books are absolutely wonderful. I read sports books if I have nothing else to read.'

I could sit and enjoy Tony Warren's company all day, but I remind myself that I'm here on business. So, before I leave, I should finish on the topic that's central to his being.

'Your *Coronation Street* characters ...'

'My secret monsters!' exclaims Tony, happy to consider his favourite subject.

'Do you see any comparable characters in other television dramas today?'

'I don't know. But in real life we're going to see them, because we've been going through very difficult times in the north of England and adversity breeds backbone. Backbone produces characters like Ena Sharples, Elsie Tanner and Annie Walker. There'll be a new generation. The next copywriters will have plenty to write about.'

'Surely the popularity of the Street is underlined by the likes of *Brookside* and the shock value of social realism in ...'

Alive to the subject, Tony heads me off. '*EastEnders* is the one that absolutely fascinates me. Friends say I ought to have my own screen credit on that – "Based on an idea by Tony Warren" – because it really is a Cockney translation of the same idea.

'At my funeral, as the coffin rolls away, I'm not having the *Coronation Street* theme music. I'm having the *EastEnders* theme music, because they pinched quite a lot from me during my lifetime and I'm having a bit back at the end.'

He laughs heartily at the idea. And he would no doubt be pleased to know that his name continues to appear on the credits of every episode of *Coronation Street*.

Epilogue

MOST COLUMNISTS WILL TELL YOU how, like athletes, they find a rhythm in their practice that helps them achieve their aims. But sometimes the goalposts are moved. In my case, editorial changes resulted in a questing new features editor deciding to shake up the 'Face to Face' format. In this instance, the weekly interview would now be sponsored by an affordable wine brand. My job would be to persuade someone to be interviewed over dinner – and photographed with the wine label in a prominent position. To me, this was a rum do. The shadow of advertorial was in danger of falling across the page.

Over the past few years I'd interviewed famous people (including a sitting taoiseach and two future taoisigh) in a wide variety of locations, from theatre rehearsal rooms, a science laboratory, a library and an animation studio to the corner of sports grounds or someone's kitchen. The demands of the new protocols would undoubtedly narrow my prospective client list drastically. It seemed like an ill-judged concept conceived by an ambitious corporate individual with an eye on the bottom line and with scant experience of the nitty-gritty realities of journalism.

But I thought I'd better show willing. And so I called in a favour and prevailed upon Oscar-winning film director Jim Sheridan to have dinner in a smart restaurant of his choice. I was reassured by the new features editor that there was nothing to worry about and that the maître d' would have the correct wine to serve. I was determined to have a positive experience. In vino veritas.

Somewhat distracted after a long day's rehearsal for an upcoming stage production, Jim arrived. Ushered to a table in the corner, we perused the menu and agreed that neither of us fancied eating. It was early in the evening and the restaurant was empty. We'd press on with the interview though.

Jim is fascinating, and there was so much I wanted to know, beginning with how he first got involved in theatre. I wasn't prepared for his response. 'My brother Frankie died when I was seventeen,' he began. 'He had a tumour on the brain. Certainly, my father never recovered from it ...'

We were heading deep into painful personal reminiscence when the ominous clack-clack-clack of approaching stiletto heels on the hardwood floor signalled impending disaster.

'Good evening,' announced a PR woman brightly. She was on a mission, in control, and was someone I'd never seen before. 'I hope you haven't ordered yet. The wine is on the way.'

Jim looked startled. This was now her show. 'I'll have the waiter open a bottle and then we can discuss the photographs. I'll just wait at the other table until our photographer arrives.'

I was freaked. Our intimate confessional had been ram-raided and derailed.

I can't remember exactly what I said, but it was something along the lines of, 'Would you mind clearing off. We're conducting an interview. We don't need to have photos taken. And we're not drinking. Speak to your contacts at the newspaper.'

'What's going on?' asked Jim.

'Fucked if I know,' says I. 'Never mind that, tell me again why an Oscar-winning movie director is getting stuck into a testing piece of agit-prop theatre?'

As you'd expect, Jim was brilliant. Meeting him was always a buzz. I remember describing him as 'a rogue intellectual who hijacks philosophies and belief systems and appropriates whatever might be useful to his cause'.

I filed the interview copy in the usual style and then informed the features editor that I'd had enough. It had been a good run. While I'd initially hoped the column might run for three months, calendars had come and gone, and the seasons had rolled by. I had found myself conducting weekly high-profile interviews for a few years rather than a few months. It had been an exhilarating adventure. Sometimes it had been thrilling. It was always demanding and intense. Crucially, the feedback from readers had been overwhelmingly positive. But I couldn't cope with this new format foisted on me by middle-management. It was time to move on.

Of course, the new format suggestion may well have been a ploy designed to encourage me to step away from the column. Who knows? Most journalists will agree that the behind-the-scenes workings of the newspaper business can often be as Machiavellian as the convoluted plot lines of the Godfather trilogy.

Many of the interviews I'd done then were condensed to fit the newspaper format. So I'm glad of this opportunity to finally present this selection in full. Revisiting those exciting years, I'm humbled by the generosity of spirit I find in the conversations. There's great humanity on display here. At times, there's anger, frustration or sadness. But there's also wisdom, humour and resilience. Insights into the creative process. Flashes of illumination and hints of regret. All the stuff that makes up life.

'You know something,' said a Dublin taxi driver en route to the airport on hearing I was flying to Munich to interview a global star. 'You must have an amazing collection of autographs.'

ACKNOWLEDGEMENTS

IN ADDITION TO THE WELCOME support I received from Síne Quinn, who encouraged and guided this book from when she first heard an anecdote or two over brunch with poet Catherine Ann Cullen, I am indebted to a vast number of people who either helped set up interviews, proofed original transcripts, or offered a novice interviewer sage journalistic advice.

As well as Michael Denieffe, who set the whole project in motion, in alphabetical order they are: Jim Aiken, Michael Brophy, Declan Cahill, Áine Carmody, Mary Carr, Alan Corr, Tadhg Coughlan, Linda Cullen, Andy Cummins, Declan Cummins, Lorraine Curran, Margaret Daly, Kieron Ellis, Professor Kamal Fadalla, Mannix Flynn, Robbie Foy, Paddy Goodwin, Justin Green, Maurice Haugh, Paul Hyland, Darim Jeong (Voici), Kieran Kelly, Declan Lynch, Ferdia MacAnna, Colm MacGinty, John McHugh, Régine Moylett, Dr Trevor Nicholson, Philip Nolan, Dee O'Keeffe, Dave Robbins, Helen Rogers, Niall Stokes, Paul Verner, John Waters and Sharon Wheeler.

I am grateful to Wendy Logue for the level of sophistication she brought to the manuscript. Heidi Houlihan's eagle-eyed attention to detail is also hugely appreciated.

I extend thanks to the staff of the National Library of Ireland who, I realised recently, have been facilitating my research with great courtesy for over fifty years, since I first investigated the papers of W.B. Yeats for clues when retelling The Táin saga in album form in the early 1970s.